BEING
CATHOLIC

Believing, Living, Praying

Mary Petrowski

BEING CATHOLIC
Believing, Living, Praying

Michael Pennock

FRIENDSHIP
in the Lord
Series

AVE MARIA PRESS
NOTRE DAME, INDIANA 46556

Excerpts from THE DOCUMENTS OF VATICAN II, Abbott-Gallagher edition, reprinted with permission of America Press, Inc., 106 West 56th Street, New York, NY 10019. © 1966 All Rights Reserved.

Unless otherwise noted excerpts are from THE NEW JERUSALEM BIBLE, copyright © 1985 by Darton, Longman & Todd, Ltd. and Doubleday & Company, Inc. Reprinted by permission of the publisher.

International Standard Book Number: 0-87793-527-0

Library of Congress Catalog Card Number: 93-73883

Cover and text design by Katherine Robinson Coleman

Cover photograph by Jim West

Photography: CNS/Joe Rimkus 254; SEF/Art Resource, NY, 40; Cleo Freelance Photo 18, 23, 24, 78-79, 125, 130, 146, 162, 168, 192, 230, 248-249, 264-265; Gail Denham 139, 169, 253; Rohn Engh 183, 184; Robert Finken 32; Art by Elizabeth French 72; Luke Golobitsh 58, 148; John Howard Griffin 109; Art by Lavrans Nielsen 43, 51; Marilyn Nolt 44, 123, 185, 187, 198, 261; Richard T. Nowitz 267; Painet 174; Rev. Gene Plaisted 29, 31, 48, 50, 60, 66, 68, 85, 86, 96-97, 105, 106-107, 114-115, 120, 136, 210, 211, 213, 214, 215, 219, 221, 225, 234, 242, 245, 247, 258, 263, 269; James L. Shaffer 243; Florence Sharp 46; Vernon Sigl 22, 76, 131; Steve & Mary Skjold 28, 92, 118, 124, 151, 157, 159, 163, 165, 176, 222, 223, 233, 236; Vada Snider 88; Justin A. Soleta 74-75, 90, 132-133; Steinbrück, German, 1802-1882, *Adoration of the Magi* (detail), 1838 courtesy of the Snite Museum of Art, University of Notre Dame 34; Sunrise/Trinity 84; Renaud Thomas 122, 127, 204; UNICEF/David Robinson 154-155; Jim West cover, 55, 178, 181, 188, 189, 191, 194, 197.

Printed and bound in the United States of America.

I dedicate this book with profound thanks
to my friends in the theology department
at St. Ignatius High School in Cleveland, Ohio:
Tom Healey, Jim Brennan, Mike McLaughlin,
Jim Hogan, Gayle Scaravilli, Ray Guiao, SJ, Rich Clark,
Dan Galla, Marty Dybicz, Paul Prokop, and Jim Skerl.

Their support, encouragement, and love make this their book, too.

Acknowledgments

I wish to thank the Jesuit community at St. Ignatius High School in Cleveland, Ohio for the privilege of teaching with them and for their support and prayers over the years.

I wish to thank all the wonderful people at Ave Maria Press for helping me in my writing ministry, especially Frank Cunningham who assisted me in planning, executing, and completing this *Friendship in the Lord* series; Charlie Jones; Fr. Dave Schlaver, CSC, publisher; Mike Amodei, the editor of this book; and all the unseen, but great people, who made this and all my books a reality.

I wish to express my gratitude to all my current and past students. Their acceptance of me as their teacher is truly a wondrous gift of God's love. They inspire and sustain me.

In a special way, I wish to thank my loving wife of 25 years, Carol, and our four children — Amy, Christopher, Jennifer, and Scott. The Lord has blessed me with a wonderful family whom I love dearly.

Finally, I wish to thank and praise the Lord himself for using such a vehicle as me to spread his word. I pray that he may become known more clearly so that he can be loved and served more dearly — day by day.

Contents

Introduction

Faith is the realization of what is hoped for and evidence of things not seen.

— Hebrews 11:1 (*NAB*)

An Academy Award winning film, *Chariots of Fire*, recounted the true story of the actual events leading up to the 1924 Olympic Games by contrasting the personal experiences of British track stars Eric Liddell and Harold Abrahams. Liddell's challenge was to find a way to balance his desire to run track with his desire to become a Christian missionary. Abrahams, a Jew, had to cope with the ever-present anti-Semitism of his fellow citizens.

Harold dealt with the pervasive anti-Semitism by taking on his bigots one by one and "running them off their feet." Along the way, he developed a rivalry with Eric, a man whose running accomplishments he greatly admired. Harold's dream was to defeat his teammate in their specialty—the 100 meter race—at the 1924 Olympic Games.

But a problem developed. Eric Liddell, a deeply religious young man, refused to race on Sunday, the day the 100 meter preliminaries were scheduled. Despite enormous pressure, including newspaper charges that he was a traitor, Liddell refused to go against his convictions. He dropped out of the competition, switching to the 400 meter event instead. It was a race he had never tried before.

Harold won the gold medal in the 100 meter event. His fierce determination and hard work helped dispel prejudice against Jews. He was a hero to the British people.

When it came time for Eric to run his race, an American runner, Jackson Scholz, passed a note to him. The note read, "It says in the old book 'He that honors me, I will honor.' Good luck." Eric ran the race with this note clutched in his hand. Amazingly, he won. His sincere conviction had been rewarded. He became a hero to those with similar religious convictions.

■ *discuss* ■

1. Share examples of people you know who do not give in to pressure to go against their beliefs.
2. What would you have done if you were in Eric Liddell's position? Explain.

■ *journal* ■

Write about three of your most strongly held beliefs. Under what circumstances, if any, would you compromise them?

8

The Importance of Beliefs

Chariots of Fire illustrates the power of personal beliefs. For example, the anti-Semites believed that Jews were inferior. Their deeply held, but misguided convictions made life miserable for Harold Abrahams. Anti-Semitism, in fact, has been one of the cancers of Western civilization. Its worst manifestation took place in the 1930s and 1940s when the Nazis killed millions of Jews. This unspeakable crime, known as the Holocaust, was the result of seriously misguided beliefs.

The movie, however, also shows the power of good beliefs. Harold's faith in his abilities led to his victory. It drove him to discipline his body and will as he strived for excellence. Eric's deeply held convictions about what God's law permits on Sunday showed the entire world what it meant to follow one's conscience. Later, his beliefs would lead him to a life of service as a missionary in China.

The stories of Harold and Eric illustrate three truths about the importance of beliefs. They are:

1. Beliefs affect attitudes.
2. Beliefs affect actions.
3. Beliefs affect relationships with others.

Beliefs are powerful and can affect both human history and your own personal history. A key question for you to ask yourself is "What set of beliefs is worth my full commitment?" In a pluralistic society many competing systems of beliefs—systems sometimes known as *isms*—are tolerated. There are many "isms" vying for your allegiance. For example, note the following ideas and beliefs that are preached in today's world:

Secularism preaches . . . self-reliance apart from God.

Materialism preaches . . . self-indulgence and personal enjoyment.

Consumerism preaches . . . acquisitiveness and self-gratification.

Humanism preaches. . . self-adulation and trusting only in oneself.

Communism preaches. . . collectivism and self-surrender to the group.

Athleticism preaches. . . self-mastery and physical discipline.

Do any of these belief systems seem attractive to you? Are any worthy of your full life commitment? Do any help to answer the question "What do I believe?"

■ *activity* ■

Locate three magazine advertisements that illustrate a particular *ism* or belief system. Share the ad with your classmates. Explain how the ads are representative of the *ism*.

■ *discuss* ■

What do you feel is the most dangerous *ism* in today's world? Why?

The Catholic Faith

Catholicism, too, is a system of beliefs. It also seeks your allegiance. But unlike secularism and humanism which preach reliance on self, Catholicism holds to a reliance on God as communicated through the person and teachings of Jesus Christ. Likewise, Catholicism also stresses the importance of others. At baptism, Catholics become members of a church, a community of believers. Whereas consumerism and materialism view people as easy to exploit and manipulate, Catholicism stresses God's gift of freedom and the person's ability to say "yes" or "no" to Christ's invitation to accept him and his gospel. Communism, Nazism, Fascism and the like are built on lies and evil that are designed to deceive. Catholicism has its roots in Jesus Christ who is "the Way, the Truth, and the Life" (see Jn 14:6).

This book is about the beliefs of the Christian community known as the Catholic church (Catholicism). It has been written in light of *The Catechism of the Catholic Church*. The Catholic church has both a divine and human dimension. The history of the church is filled with stories of both successes and failures. Yet, Catholics in every generation have held fast to the belief that Christ guides the church and will never let it stray from his way, truth, or life.

Literally millions of people have found the key to their own personal happiness by believing in, living, and celebrating their Christian and Catholic faith. Church teachings have helped them to answer life's important questions: Why am I here? What is the meaning of life? of death? Where am I going? Is there a God? And if so, who is God? What difference does God make? And a host of other related questions.

It is likely that you are already a member of the Catholic community. Through your baptism and your participation in the life of the church over the course of your life, you may have a good sense about what it means to be Catholic. But, have you answered the question "Is this set of Catholic beliefs worth my full commitment?" This book will help you examine what it means **to be** Catholic by examining the Catholic faith as it is professed in the traditional Nicene Creed, as it is lived out in the personal and social lives of its members, and as it is celebrated in prayer and worship. The text is divided into three parts:

Part 1 focuses on the *creed*—a statement of beliefs—that includes Catholic teaching about God the Father (Chapter 1), Jesus (Chapter 2), the Holy Spirit and the doctrine of the Trinity (Chapter 3), the church (Chapter 4), and human destiny (Chapter 5).

Part 2 reviews the Catholic moral *code*, that is, how Catholics should live moral life both personally (Chapter 6) and socially (Chapter 7).

Part 3 explains Catholic *cult*, the Catholic way of sacramental worship (Chapter 8) and of praying and growing in holiness (Chapter 9).

A concluding chapter suggests what it means to live as a Catholic Christian today.

Making a commitment to any belief system is a difficult process. Commitment to the Catholic faith is no different. As Harold Abrahams and Eric Liddell from *Chariots of Fire* discovered, commitment to a good belief brings good rewards. It is only through understanding your Catholic faith that you are able to be open to the possibility of living it fully.

■ *journal* ■

Develop the following open-ended sentences into short one-paragraph reflections.

"As a Catholic, I believe..."

"To me, being Catholic means..."

"A fully committed Catholic is someone who..."

▪ *focus questions* ▪

1. List two *isms* that are influential in today's world.
2. What is something that you are committed to? Why do you hold this commitment?
3. List and discuss at least five positive qualities of the Catholic faith.

▪ *activities* ▪

1. View the *Chariots of Fire* on video. Write a detailed profile of Harold or Eric.
2. Interview three Catholic adults. Ask them to share a definition of their Catholic faith and why it is important to them.
3. Prepare a short report on an *ism* that has been influential in the twentieth century.

▬▬▬▬▬▬▬ ▪ ▬▬▬▬▬▬▬

Prayer Reflection

Faith, hope, and charity (love) are known as the theological virtues. A virtue is an ability or power to accomplish something good. Three traditional prayers are associated with these virtues. The Act of Faith empowers Catholics to truth as revealed by God. The Act of Hope helps Catholics to proclaim trust in God's promises. The Act of Love proclaims a person's love of God above everything and of love for neighbors and his or her self.

Use these prayers in times of devotion. Commit them to memory.

▪ *vocabulary* ▪

Look up the meaning of the following words in the dictionary. Transcribe their definitions into your journal:

adulation   humanism
collectivism   materialism
consumerism   pluralistic
Holocaust   secularism

Act of Faith

O my God, I firmly believe that you are one God in three divine Persons, Father, Son, and Holy Spirit. I believe that your divine Son became man and died for our sins, and that he will come to judge the living and the dead. I believe these and all the truths which the

Holy Catholic Church teaches, because you have revealed them, who can neither deceive nor be deceived. Amen.

Act of Hope

O my God, relying on your infinite goodness and promises, I hope to obtain pardon of my sins, the help of your grace, and life everlasting, through the merits of Jesus Christ, my Lord and Redeemer. Amen.

Act of Love

O my God, I love you above all things, with my whole heart and soul, because you are all good and worthy of all my love. I love my neighbor as myself for the love of you. I forgive all who have injured me, and I ask pardon of all whom I have injured. Amen.

▪ *reflection* ▪

How do you express the virtues of faith, hope, and love in your daily actions?

▪ *resolution* ▪

Perform some "act of love" for a family member. Keep your act a secret. Expect nothing in return.

PART 1

CREED

The Nicene Creed

We believe in one God,
the Father, the Almighty,
maker of heaven and earth,
of all that is seen and unseen.

We believe in one Lord, Jesus Christ,
the only Son of God,
eternally begotten of the Father,
God from God, Light from Light,
true God from true God,
begotten, not made, one in Being with the Father.
Through him all things were made.
For us and for our salvation
he came down from heaven:
by the power of the Holy Spirit
he was born of the Virgin Mary,
and became man.

For our sake he was crucified under Pontius Pilate;
he suffered, died, and was buried.
On the third day he rose again
in fulfillment of the scriptures;
he ascended into heaven
and is seated at the right hand of the Father.
He will come again in glory
to judge the living and the dead,
and his kingdom will have no end.

We believe in the Holy Spirit,
the Lord, the giver of life,
who proceeds from the Father and the Son.
With the Father and the Son
he is worshipped and glorified.
He has spoken through the Prophets.

We believe in one holy catholic and apostolic Church.
We acknowledge one baptism for the forgiveness
    of sins.
We look for the resurrection of the dead,
and the life of the world to come. Amen.

The Nicene Creed summarizes Christian beliefs about God the Father, Son, and Holy Spirit, the church, salvation, and human destiny. The word creed comes from the Latin *credo* which means "I believe." But what Christians really proclaim is "we believe." A creed is not something one invents on his or her own; in this case, the Christian beliefs were formulated at a church council at Nicea in 325. By reciting the Nicene Creed, a person is bound not only to those beliefs, but to the Christian community of faith as well.

The Nicene Creed was the result of decades of controversy in the church. Arius, a popular preacher in Egypt, could not understand how Jesus had always existed with God the Father. In effect, Arius denied Jesus' divinity. The resulting Arian controversy caused the emperor Constantine to call for a general or ecumenical council or meeting of church leaders. It was the first of 21 such councils in the church's history. A major achievement of the council of Nicea was to declare clearly the divinity of Jesus by issuing the Nicene Creed. The second ecumenical council, the Council of Constantinople (381), endorsed and expanded this creed. Recited at liturgy, it has served well as a short summary of Catholic faith ever since.

Part 1 of the text will examine the articles of this profession of faith, the Nicene Creed.

chapter 1

Our Loving God

Bless Yahweh, my soul,
Yahweh, my God, how great you are!
Clothed in majesty and splendor,
wearing light as a robe!

How countless are your works, Yahweh,
all of them made so wisely!
The earth is full of your creatures.

— Psalm 104:1, 24

In This Chapter

You will examine:

■ belief in one God

■ belief in God the Father, the almighty

■ belief in God, the maker of heaven and earth

■ belief in all that is seen and unseen

A famous French king, Louis XIV, was an arrogant monarch who once said of himself, "I am the state!" His court was the most magnificent in all Europe. When he died, his funeral was mind-boggling. His body lay in state in a casket made of gold. To accentuate the dead king's greatness, the cathedral was dimly lit. Only one special candle burnt above his coffin. Thousands of the king's subjects stood by in hushed silence. Then the Bishop Massillon began his funeral oration. Slowly, dramatically, he reached down and snuffed out the candle! He proclaimed, "Only God is great!"

The consideration of death forces most humans to ask basic questions: "Why was I born? What is the purpose of life? What is happiness and how do I attain it? What is the meaning of suffering and death? What, if anything, comes after this life is over?"

Questions like these often lead to still other questions: "Is there a God? If so, who is God? And what is God like?" Most people who believe in God agree with Bishop Massillon—"Only God is great." Whoever pretends to be great, like King Louis XIV, is not. Death touches all people, the so-called high and mighty as well as the most humble. Christians accept this truth and also acknowledge their dependence on a God who is indeed great, loving, creative, healing, and desirous of eternal salvation for all.

Who Is God?

The question of God's existence remains an intriguing one. Listed below are some statements made about God by both believers and non-believers. Circle the number that best describes your feelings about each.

1—strongly disagree
2—disagree
3—unsure
4—agree
5—strongly agree

1. If God exists, I don't see how God could possibly   1   2   3   4   5
   be interested in me. I am like a grain of sand in the
   immense universe. God is all-powerful, infinite, and
   much greater than I.

2. God is simply an idea humans have dreamed up to cope   1   2   3   4   5
   with the nothingness beyond death. It would be nice if
   God existed, but God is just wishful thinking.

3. There is a God, and God does indeed make a difference. 1   2   3   4   5
   God made and cares for everything, including me.

4. If God exists, then how could there be suffering: 1   2   3   4   5
   innocent children born with the AIDS virus, countless
   victims of senseless wars, helpless fatalities of natural
   disasters like hurricanes? The best argument against
   God is the existence of so much evil in the world.

5. If God exists, so what? What difference does God make? 1   2   3   4   5

6. Jesus Christ is God!   1   2   3   4   5

7. God is just an excuse for things that can't be explained. 1   2   3   4   5
   As scientists better explain the "mysteries" of the
   universe, then we will discover that we simply do not
   "need" the idea of a God.

8. God is dead.   1   2   3   4   5

▪ *discuss* ▪

Explain your choices. Share three proof statements that support any one of your responses.

■ *journal* ■

Imagine you are God. What would you do to make people aware of your identity?

━━━━━━━━━━━━━━━━━━━ ■ ■ ━━━━━━━━━━━━━━━━━

We Believe in One God

Most people acknowledge the existence of some type of *deity*. Even people with little or no religious experience tend to express a belief in God. In addition, a study of human history shows that most cultures have professed belief in a higher being who transcends the people and the society. For example, the ancient Greeks worshipped a supreme god called Zeus. Likewise, Jupiter was the name of the supreme god of the Romans. Some Native Americans believe in supernatural beings and a Great Spirit.

The major world religions of today also hold that some invisible, all-embracing reality (God) exists. For Hindus, this reality is Brahman. Buddhism does not recognize a *personal* deity, but it acknowledges an Ultimate Reality in the universe. Another eastern religion, Sikhism, affirms the existence of one God who spoke through prophets.

Jews, of course, believe the one, true God is Yahweh ("I Am, Who Am") who is revealed throughout the history of the Jewish people, beginning with the patriarch Abraham. Christians and Moslems also trace their origins to Judaism through Abraham. Both Christianity and Islam define a belief in one God. Moslems refer to this one God as Allah. They hold that Mohammed was Allah's greatest prophet. Further, Christians understand the one God as having three distinct Persons—Father, Son, and Holy Spirit. For Christians, Jesus Christ is God's only Son who came to save and redeem humanity.

There are also many differences among the world religions and their understandings of God. Popular Hinduism, for example, has many gods. Some religions have imaged a vengeful, spiteful god. Others see good and evil in the world and postulate the existence of both benevolent and malevolent gods. Another idea is of a god who is like watchmaker

For what can be known about God is perfectly plain to them, since God has made it plain to them: ever since the creation of the world, the invisible existence of God and his everlasting power have been clearly seen by the mind's understanding of created things.

— Romans 1:19–20

who constructs a masterpiece but then is content to allow it to run itself. (This religion, Deism, was favored by men like Thomas Jefferson and Benjamin Franklin.) Still others imagine capricious gods who show love for their creatures one day, only to tease and torment them the next.

These differences do not disprove God's existence. Rather, they show that though human intellect knows something of a supreme being, God's complete identity remains a mystery. Christians believe that God's direct help is needed in order to reveal the true nature of the divine.

Over time, humans have developed "proofs" of God's existence—ways to explain a Supreme Being, one, true, God—operating in the universe. Here are three of the most popular proofs:

1. **God the Uncaused Cause.**   A basic universal principle is that there is a cause for everything that exists. In other words, everything in the universe was caused by something else. Logically, then, there must be a source which is a first cause— an Uncaused Cause, if you will— which always had existence. This Uncaused Cause is a philosophical name for God. Even those who propose that the universe resulted from a "big bang" of matter cannot explain the source of the primeval matter which started everything off. By asking where this matter came from, one is really arguing for God's existence.

2. **God the Intelligent Designer.**   Have you ever looked at the inside mechanisms of an old-fashioned pocket watch? If so, you would have noticed the intricate workings that make its various parts tick off the seconds, minutes, and hours. Does such a watch presuppose an intelligent being who made it?

   How much more complex is a human person or the entire universe itself? There is a beauty, immensity, symmetry, and power in creation that forces one to conclude that an Intelligent Designer made it all. A simple spider spinning its web, a beaver building its dam, the earth rotating around the sun, the chemical mix that produces life, the awesome process of human reproduction—all these and countless other realities suggest a Supreme Being who implanted natural laws in the universe. A famous convert to Catholicism, G.K. Chesterton, once said, "Show me a watch without a watchmaker, then I'll take a universe without a Universe-Maker."

3. **Human Existence.** The simple fact of human existence and human history argue for the existence of God. First, scientists have yet to explain how life could have "evolved" from matter. Second, statisticians say it is virtually impossible for intelligent, human life to appear by mere chance. (A famous illustration holds that it would be more likely for a monkey in a jungle to sit down at a typewriter and compose Shakespeare's *Hamlet* than for human life to appear by chance.) Third, the very fact that life does evolve—from the primitive ways of the first humans to the super technological world of the late twentieth century—hints strongly at a powerfully present Intelligence that leads and guides the human journey.

It is also possible to discover God in your own personal experiences. St. Augustine once wrote, "You are great, Lord, and infinitely worthy of praise. . . . You have made us for yourself, and our hearts are restless until they rest in you."

Augustine recognized that God has implanted in all people a yearning for their true source—the one, true, Creator God. When you look at a starlit sky and ponder your smallness in the enormity of the cosmic scheme, you may experience God, the Creator. When a song lyric speaks to a particular emotion, you may find a God who understands you. When you feel cared for by a family member or friend, you may come to know a God who likewise personally loves and cares for you.

The experiences of beauty, joy, love, the inspiration of a new idea, the profound touch of goodness—all these have moved people to recognize God who is at work in our lives. Here are three other common experiences that help "demonstrate" God's existence:

1. **An unquenchable thirst for happiness.** Everyone wants to be happy. People spend a lot of time and energy on things that they think will make them happy. Yet, that happiness soon fades. It isn't long after that they find themselves desiring something else. Are human beings

doomed to be ultimately frustrated? People want happiness, but the more it is pursued, the more it seems to slip away.

Can it be that a Creator made human beings with a hunger for happiness which nothing in this world can completely satisfy? Recall St. Augustine's words. Might it be that the restless hearts that desire happiness can only find **total** happiness by discovering the God who made them?

2. **Sense of justice.** Have you ever felt that the people who do evil will someday pay for their crimes? It seems unfair that those who cheat, lie, and even murder are able to prosper in this life while some good people suffer and are taken advantage of. There seems to be a fundamental feeling built in to each person that says that things will be reversed someday, that there is a Power that will right all wrongs, if not in this life, then in the next.

3. **Love.** Is there any way to explain the greatest reality of all, the sense of being cared for and loved? Love is a spiritual reality that the material universe cannot define. Love must have an origin. Spiritual realities come from Spirit. The origin of love is Love itself, the spiritual being called God. (The same argument holds for intelligence; it must ultimately come from Intelligence itself, God.)

What Is Your Image of God?

Everyone imagines God in a slightly different way. However, there are two major perceptions. Some people stress God's being **beyond** this world. This is known as God's *transcendence*. Others focus on God's being **in** the world, or God's closeness to all people. This is known as God's *immanence*. In the chart below, mark the descriptions of God "T" or "I" to show whether they reflect a transcendent or immanent view.

_____ 1. God is all-powerful, all-knowing, almighty.

_____ 2. To know Jesus Christ is to know God.

_____ 3. God is a stern judge.

_____ 4. God is a friend, a constant companion who walks beside me.

_____ 5. God is *Abba*, "Daddy."

_____ 6. God gets "angry" when people sin.

_____ 7. You can know God by experiencing true love.

_____ 8. God forgives and rarely shows anger with people.

_____ 9. God is the omnipotent creator of heaven and earth.

_____ 10. God is like a kind and loving mother who is willing to sacrifice all for her children.

We Believe in God the Father, the Almighty

To prove God's existence is one thing; to know what God is like is quite another. Trying to understand God through human reason is like trying to experience a kiss from its definition: "a caress with the lips, gentle touch or contact." This definition is sterile. It does not adequately capture the reality of a mother kissing her newborn infant, or a young couple kissing each other good night, or a faithful husband and wife kissing on their fiftieth wedding anniversary. One attribute of God is that God is *mystery*. Although natural human intellects can discover God's existence and even conclude that the maker of the universe must be intelligent, omnipotent, powerful, and the like, limited human minds cannot begin to fathom the truth about God. In fact, people cannot really "know" God unless God shares the divine nature and divine life with them.

Divine Revelation. The free gift of God's self-communication is known as supernatural or *divine revelation*. In Latin, revelation means "unveiling." Christians believe that God

▪ *discuss* ▪

1. Which description is closest to your own image of God? Why?

2. What are your two main reasons for believing or not believing in God? Share these with a partner. How are they different?

3. What kind of God (immanent or transcendent) do you experience when you are happy? suffering? anxious?

▪ *journal* ▪

Choose a favorite piece of instrumental music (classical or otherwise) that represents for you beauty, truth, or goodness. Listen to the piece. Be aware of the images the music creates for you. Write a short paragraph explaining how this music speaks to you of God or other spiritual realities.

chose to be unveiled in human history, to seek friendship with humankind, and to invite all people into fellowship with the Blessed Trinity. This revelation is called supernatural because, as God's creatures, people do not have a natural right to this intimate friendship with God. God's self-disclosure and invitation to a deeper life of love is purely a divine gift.

God's divine revelation is accomplished within, not outside of, human history. Beginning with creation itself and continuing through the forming of a Chosen People, the Israelites, humanity was gradually prepared in stages to accept God's self-revelation that led ultimately to the person and mission of Jesus Christ. *Salvation history* is the term used to describe God's loving participation in the lives of humans.

What did people learn about God through these events? The Hebrew scriptures dramatically show how God created human beings and offered them a plan for salvation, even after they had sinned. For example, God made a *covenant* with Noah (and all living things) to sustain the human race despite its sins. A covenant is an open-ended contract, a commitment of both parties to remain faithful to one another and their promise. This covenant was a divine pledge to reach out to a scattered humanity and make known the divine plan of salvation for all nations. Hebrew scriptures also record how God established a covenant with Abraham, promising to create from him a special people.

Salvation history demonstrates how God kept the divine promises. For their part of the covenant, God's People were to worship God alone and live loving and just lives according to the Law summarized in the Ten Commandments. However, the Chosen People often fell short of returning God's love. Although God often had to reprimand the People the way a parent must punish children to help them learn, God remained faithful to the covenant. Here is a summary of God's actions as revealed in Hebrew scriptures:

1. **God chooses the Hebrews and makes them a people** (see Gn 12:1–2).

2. **God frees the Jews from Egypt** (see Ex 3:8).

3. **God establishes a covenant with the Israelites by giving them the Law through Moses** (see Ex 19:5–6).

4. **God gives the Israelites a land** (see Jos 1:11).

5. **God establishes the kingdom of David** (see 2 Sm 7:8–16).

6. **God sends prophets to guide the Chosen People** (see 2 Kgs 17:13–14).

7. **God sustains the Chosen People in captivity and restores them to Israel** (see Is 40:1–2).

The portion of salvation history told in the Hebrew scriptures reveals much of God's nature, yet much else about God remains hidden. Even Yahweh, the name God reveals to Moses in the Hebrew scriptures, is as mysterious as God is mysterious.

Word of God

God's action in human history lives on in God's word, the Bible, and in the tradition of the church. The Bible is the written record of revelation. God *inspired* the biblical authors, who wrote over a span of many centuries, to record the theological truths that God wanted recorded for our spiritual benefit.

The Bible is actually a library of many books which include many literary types: prose, poetry, history, myth, prayers, songs, fact, and fiction.

Christians divide the Bible into two sections: the Hebrew scriptures (Old Testament) and the Christian scriptures (New Testament). The Hebrew scriptures serve as the foundation for God's self-revelation in Christ. It contains the inspired writings of prophets and other writers who recorded God's teaching to the Chosen People and God's interaction in their history. The New Testament chronicles the life and teachings of Jesus Christ and announces the good news of God's plan of salvation for all people everywhere.

▪ *journal* ▪

Read the following passage from Psalm 23. Then write your answer to **one** of the questions that follow.

> Yahweh is my shepherd, I lack nothing.
> In grassy meadows he lets me lie.

By tranquil streams he leads me
   to restore my spirit.
He guides me in paths of saving justice
   as befits his name.

Even were I to walk in a ravine as dark as death
I should fear no danger, for you are at my side.
Your staff and your crook are there to soothe me.

You prepare a table for me
   under the eyes of my enemies;
you anoint my head with oil;
   my cup brims over.

Kindness and faithful love pursue me
   every day of my life.
I make my home in the house of Yahweh
   for all time to come.

1. What is a contemporary image that would be a good substitute for "shepherd?" Explain.
2. This psalm also images God as a host who sets a table and serves a meal. What symbolic meaning might be behind this image?

Almighty God.   The name Yahweh both reveals and conceals, hinting at a God who is the perfect Being, the Being who is revealed as perfect Truth and Love. This infinite God—the basis of all that is—is beyond total human comprehension. The Catholic creedal belief in a God having unlimited power, of a God who is almighty, and of a God who cannot be completely understood, is rooted in the events of salvation history. The suffering Job understood this well:

I [Job] was the man who misrepresented your
   intentions with my ignorant words.
You have told me about great works that I cannot
   understand,
about marvels which are beyond me, of which I know
   nothing (Jb 42:3).

Job learned that God's almighty power clarified itself. The

Canon of the Bible

The word *canon* means official list. The Catholic canon of the Bible contains 46 Old Testament books and 27 New Testament books.

revelation of God's almighty power is really revelation of the divine mercy which is extended to all. Salvation history is the story of an almighty God turning humans from sin and restoring them to divine friendship.

God's almighty power can be described by way of analogy. First, God's *perfection* is affirmed in some qualities found in creatures, for example, intelligence. Second, God's intelligence is not understood to be the same as human intelligence, which is limited. Third, it can be stated that God *transcends*, that is, goes infinitely beyond anything human beings can understand. God is perfect. God is intelligence. God is all-knowing.

Though human language is lacking, several basic attributes can be assigned to God based on God's revelation in history. St. Thomas Aquinas listed nine attributes that seem to make up God's nature. Passages from the Hebrew scriptures help to support these descriptions:

Saint Thomas Aquinas

1. **God is eternal.**   God always was and always will be. God is the one being who *cannot* not be. God is. (See Is 40:28.)

2. **God is unique.**   There is no God like Yahweh. (See Is 45:18.)

3. **God is infinite and omnipotent.**   God has no limits, is everywhere, unlimited, and all-powerful. God can do everything. (See Ps 135:5–6.)

4. **God is immense.**   God is not limited to space. (See 1 Kgs 8:27.)

5. **God contains all things.**   (See Wis 8:1.)

6. **God is immutable.**   God does not change—ever. (See Ps 102:26–28.)

7. **God is utterly simple—a pure Spirit.**   The opposite of simple is complex, which means divisible into parts. In God there are no parts, no divisions. God is not material and God's image cannot be made. (See Ex 20:4.)

8. **God is personal.**   God is alive (the source of all life), knows all things, and loves and cares beyond limit. The saving God manifested personal love through the compassionate acts in the history of the Israelites and most

supremely by sending the Son, Jesus Christ, to all people. (See Jer 31:3.)

9. **God is supremely holy.**   Holiness is a quality of being absolutely other than creation. God's goodness and love are unlimited. In Jesus, it is revealed that God is love. God cannot be praised by creation enough. (See Is 55:8.)

What Is Tradition?

One of the ways that Catholics believe that God is revealed is through *tradition*. Derived from the Latin word "to hand on," tradition refers to the *content* of revelation (teachings and practices of the faith) and the *process* of handing on the faith through oral tradition and the written scriptures. *Tradition is the living communication of the word, brought about by the Holy Spirit.*

■ *exercise* ■

Read the following scripture passages. Review the list of God's attributes. Write which attribute of God is being described in each passage.

Lamentations 5:19–20: _____

Jeremiah 10:10–12: _____

Psalm 139:1–6: _____

Isaiah 55: _____

God as Father.   The good news of Christianity is that God—who is primarily a mystery and thus beyond the total comprehension of human beings—has indeed been revealed in the personhood of Jesus Christ. Recall Jesus' words to Thomas at the Last Supper:

"If you know me, you will know my Father too. From this moment you know him and have seen him" (Jn 14:7). Jesus' coming to earth in flesh is the most complete and perfect source of God's revelation. Jesus' revelation of God as Father was a new and more complete understanding of who God is.

Chapter 3 will discuss in more detail God the Father who "begets" the Son from all eternity. For now, simply note that God is love within the Trinity and that this love spills forth into creation. God "fathers" creation, creating people out of love and inviting all into the divine family. As God's children, people can address God as "our Father." This marvelous truth transforms each person's identity, making all people brothers and sisters to each other.

However, God is certainly beyond the biological distinction of male and female. In fact, since both men and women are made "in the image and likeness of God," both masculine and feminine traits can be used to describe God.

Yet Christians cannot abandon their addressing God as a loving Father because Jesus used this image many times. He taught his disciples to pray to God as *Abba* ("Daddy"). This title implies that God's love is infinitely great, beyond that of any human parent. It also implies that God is very close to each person and seeks an intimate relationship with all people. God must be addressed in human language. Divine revelation, highlighted in the person and teaching of Jesus, holds that God should be called Father.

We Believe in God, the Creator of Heaven and Earth

Many of life's deep questions pertain to the origins of the universe. Also, many people wonder about their own beginnings. You may have asked yourself "Why am I alive at this time in history, at this particular place?" The two creation accounts in the Book of Genesis (1:1–2:4; 2:5–25) teach that God created the entire universe "out of nothing." One message of both stories is that everything in the world, including human beings, is entirely dependent on God.

These Genesis stories are interested in the *why* of creation; they do not describe *how* the world began. In taking the role of Creator, God's love for human beings is revealed. The Book of Genesis teaches that God is the source of all that is. In studying God's creation, you can also come to a clear understanding of who the Creator is. St. Paul wrote that intelligent people can discover God's existence by reflecting on God's creation:

> Ever since the creation of the world the invisible existence of God and his everlasting power have been clearly seen by the mind's understanding of created things (Rom 1:20).

What are some things you can learn about God from the creation stories? Here are some examples:

The goodness of God.   From creation, it is easy to conclude that the Creator God is most generous, simply because God

did not *have* to create. God did so because God is love. God wished to show forth and communicate the divine goodness.

God made an ordered universe. Every created thing reflects God's goodness. Unlike other creation stories told in various ancient cultures, the Book of Genesis presents a picture of a God of supreme goodness, power, freedom, and generosity. Many other religious explanations of the origins of the world hold that an evil god existed alongside a good god, and that human existence is the result of evil.

Though infinitely greater than all creation, the Creator God remains intimately present to all created things, especially to people, because God is goodness. According to the Acts of the Apostles: "In God . . . we live, and move, and exist. We are God's children" (Acts 17:28).

Humans in the divine image.   The most important truth of the creation stories for human beings is summed up in the following:

> God created man in the image of himself,
>   in the image of God he created him,
>   male and female he created them.
> . . .God saw all he had made, and indeed it was
>   very good (Gn 1:27, 31).

These passages show that people are not accidents. They are not freaks of nature. They are not made fundamentally evil.

Because people are made in God's image, each human possesses incalculable dignity. All of creation is intended to be used by people who, in return, must serve and love God and show gratitude by wisely using the gifts God has provided. Gratitude is shown when people live as brothers and sisters—for indeed they are that, made in God's image.

Human beings have a material and spiritual dimension (body and soul).   Of all God's creations, only human beings possess a knowledge of God and are able to enter into a relationship with God. Humans possess both a physical body and a spiritual nature. It is the spiritual nature which images God; it enables people to think, to choose between right and wrong, to love. God also bestowed immortality on humans; though you have a beginning, you will never cease or go out of existence. The church teaches that God creates each human soul at the moment of conception; it is not produced by human parents.

Humans are given the role of co-creators.   God created a world in a state of "becoming." It is moving toward a final perfection that has yet to be attained.

The creation stories tell how God wants people to be responsible co-creators. First, God made people as male or female, sexual beings (the word *sex* comes from the word *se-care* which means "split into two"). Within each person, God implanted a craving for human love and companionship. God separated human beings into two sexes so that each person might recognize his or her *social* nature. God made man and woman *together* and willed each *for* the other. God created man and woman to be *procreators*, that is to share in the divine activity of bringing new life into the world.

Also, since humans are the summit of God's creative work, God also gave them the role of stewardship for the rest of the world and all creation. A steward is someone who "administers," or is "in charge." God said:

> "Be fruitful, multiply, fill the earth and subdue it. Be masters of the fish of the sea, the birds of heaven, and all living creatures that move on earth" (Gn 1:28).

The meaning of this passage is that humans are to take dominion of the world, renew the earth, and responsibly and obediently cooperate with God who has given them this priceless gift of existence. *Divine providence*—God's active interest in guiding creation to perfection—is always present to help the world develop according to God's plan. From divine providence God wills the interdependence of all creatures. Thus, God's gift of creation carries with it an awesome responsibility. You must ask yourself "How can I act responsibly? How can I protect and steward the gifts of creation?"

■ *research* ■

Read the two creation accounts in the Book of Genesis (1:1–24 and 2:5–25). List several differences in the two stories. Check a bible commentary (for example, *The New Jerome Biblical Commentary*) and write a short paragraph explaining what the scripture writers were trying to teach in either the first or second creation account. Share what you discovered with your classmates.

God's Faithfulness to Humanity

The first people, Adam and Eve, committed a personal sin that affected human nature. This sin of Adam and Eve—

the original sin—resulted in the loss of God's friendship. The Book of Genesis reveals that Adam and Eve did not initiate their disobedience; rather, they gave into the outside temptation of Satan in the disguise of a serpent. Because of this sin, humans are easily corrupted with evil. Humans needed to be saved from this condition of sinfulness.

The story told in salvation history is of God's willingness to save people from sin. God's covenant with Abraham and his descendants promised God's incredible fidelity despite their sinfulness. In time, God would send Jesus Christ, the Savior, as the one who would bring salvation and offer a renewal of a relationship between God and all people.

We Believe in God, Maker of All that Is Seen and Unseen

The creedal statement that God is the "maker of all that is seen and unseen" expresses the Christian belief in more than meets the eye. This belief is most easily understood in describing the church's belief in good and bad angels.

Angels. Scripture reveals the existence of *angels*. Angels (a word meaning "messenger") are spiritual created beings, immortal like humans and capable of thinking and loving. Also, like humans, angels have an opportunity to love and accept God or reject God out of prideful self-interest.

Scripture describes the main functions of angels as being God's servants and messengers. They are also mediators between God and humans. There are many examples in the gospels of how angels are active during critical times of salvation history: the angel Gabriel is at the annunciation to Mary and angels are present at the birth of Jesus. Angels are also with Jesus in his trials in the desert and the garden of Gethsemane, and at his resurrection and ascension. On September 29 the church celebrates the feast of Sts. Michael, Raphael, and Gabriel, the only angels named in the Bible.

Traditionally, Catholics and other Christians have believed that each person has a guardian angel. A guardian angel watches over and protects people from danger and temptation. Church tradition strongly supports belief in and devotion to guardian angels and asks for their spiritual help, especially in times of temptation. The feast of guardian angels is on October 2.

Devils and Satan. The church also teaches the existence of fallen angels known as demons or devils (from a word meaning "slanderer"), and Satan (the "deceiver"). The Book of Genesis tells of the serpent tempting Adam and Eve and the Book of Revelation reports a symbolic heavenly battle between good and evil angels. Created good by God, Satan and the other demons became evil by their free choice.

In Jesus' ministry, evil spirits appear frequently. He exorcised demons in many of his healings. At the end of his forty day fast in the desert, Satan appears as a tempter, trying to entice Jesus to stray from doing God's will (see Lk 4:1–13).

Based on this scriptural testimony, Jesus' own belief in demons, and the teaching of the early church, the church today continues to teach the existence of devils and Satan. God allows devils to tempt people, but God will not permit them to do permanent harm.

There are several ways for you to protect yourself from temptations; for example, praying to your guardian angel, reading scripture, and appealing to the Blessed Mother are all valuable ways to resist temptations and grow in a grace-filled life. The church cautions people to be aware of the subtle thoughts, lies, and tricks that can reduce personal freedom and turn them away from God's love.

Finally, Christians believe in the power of Jesus Christ who has conquered Satan. Those people who stay close to Jesus need not fear Satan's influence. Evil is a great mystery. But the greater reality is the victory of Jesus who has triumphed over evil and death.

From the Documents

The church teaches that the battle against evil and the power of Satan is ongoing; it can only be overcome by remaining in union with Christ and the church:

For a monumental struggle against the powers of darkness pervades the whole history of man. The battle was joined from the very origins of the world and will continue until the last day, as the Lord has attested. Caught in this conflict, man is obliged to wrestle constantly if he is to cling to what is good. Nor can he achieve his own integrity without valiant efforts and the help of God's grace...Hence if anyone wants to know how this unhappy situation can be overcome, Christians will tell him that all human activity, constantly imperiled by man's pride and deranged self-love, must be purified and perfected by the power of Christ's cross and resurrection. For, redeemed by Christ and made a new creature in the Holy Spirit, man is able to love the things themselves created by God, and ought to do so. He can receive them from God, and respect and reverence them as flowing constantly from the hand of God.

—*Gaudium et Spes*, #37

Conclusion

If God exists, then our universe is not absurd. It must have a purpose to it. If God exists, then life has tremendous meaning.

This Creator God described in Hebrew scriptures is almighty and full of power. Yet, this tremendously powerful God also wants to enter into a *personal* relationship with you. Jesus described the intimacy of this relationship by referring to God as "Abba" or "Daddy."

People are made from God's goodness. An old catechism says, God made people for a purpose: "to know, to love, and to serve God in this world and *to be happy with God forever* in the next." God wants you to enjoy and celebrate the marvelous gift of life. God promises to remain loyal to you always, even when you sin. God's promises should prompt you, in the words of St. Richard of Chichester,

> To know God more clearly,
> Love God more dearly,
> And follow God more nearly,
> Day by day.

■ *focus questions* ■

1. What is one of life's deep, basic questions?
2. What do three of the major world religions believe about God?
3. Share an example that illustrates the meaning of Deism.
4. Summarize one of the three so-called proofs for God's existence.
5. What do we mean by God's *transcendence*? by God's *immanence*? Give two examples of each.
6. Define the terms *divine revelation* and *salvation history*.
7. What was the Israelite's response in following the terms of the covenant?
8. What is the meaning of *tradition*?
9. What is the meaning of *Yahweh*?
10. Define covenant.
11. Why do Christians call God "our Father"?
12. List and explain four attributes of the almighty God.
13. Discuss two things you can learn about God from creation.
14. What is the Catholic belief about angels? What is the main function of guardian angels?
15. What is the meaning of the word *devil*? *Satan*? What is Catholic belief on the existence of devils?

■ *exercises* ■

1. Research the meaning of the following terms: *atheist*, *agnostic*, and *practical atheist*. What are the characteristics of people in each of these groups?
2. Research and report on the understanding of the deity in the following religions: Islam, Hinduism, Buddhism, and Sikhism.
3. Prepare a brief report on diabolical possession or obsession.
4. Read the *Dogmatic Constitution on Divine Revelation*. Copy into your journal twenty of the most significant quotes.

5. Write a compare and contrast paper detailing the theories of evolution and creationism.

■ *vocabulary* ■

Look up the meaning of the following words in the dictionary. Transcribe the definitions into your journal:

arrogant	immutable
agnostic	malevolent
capricious	postulate

Prayer Reflection

The Apostles' Creed is a short formula of Christian belief. Its twelve articles of faith contain the basic doctrines of Christianity. Tradition credits the substance of these articles to the apostles.

Slowly reflect and pray this Christian creed.

The Apostles' Creed

I believe in God,
the Father almighty,
creator of heaven and earth.

I believe in Jesus Christ, his only Son, our Lord.
He was conceived by the power of the Holy Spirit,
and born of the Virgin Mary.
He suffered under Pontius Pilate,
was crucified, died, and was buried.
He descended to the dead.
On the third day he rose again.
He ascended into heaven,
and is seated at the right hand of the Father.
He will come again to judge the living and the dead.

I believe in the Holy Spirit,
the holy catholic Church,
the communion of saints,
the forgiveness of sins,
the resurrection of the body,
and life everlasting. Amen.

▪ *reflection* ▪

How do you know that God exists?

▪ *resolution* ▪

Memorize the Apostles' Creed. Recite it at least once each day during the coming week.

━━━━━━━━━━━━━━━ ▪ ━━━━━━━━━━━━━━━

chapter 2

Jesus Christ

He is the image of the unseen God.
the first-born of all creation,
for in him were created all things
in heaven and on earth. . . .

He exists before all things
and in him all things hold together,
and he is the Head of the Body,
that is, the Church.

He is the Beginning,
the first-born from the dead,
so that he should be supreme in every way;
because God wanted all fullness to be found in him,
everything in heaven and everything on earth,
by making peace through his death on the cross.

—Colossians 1:15–20

In This Chapter

You will explore:

■ belief in Jesus as Lord, Christ, and Son of God

■ belief in Jesus as God from God, Light from Light, begotten not made

■ belief in the incarnation

■ belief in Jesus' giving of himself to bring salvation to all

■ belief in Jesus' resurrection

The artist Holman Hunt painted a thought-provoking picture entitled "The Light of the World." In it the figure of a gentle, compassionate-looking Jesus stands before a closed, ivy-covered door. He is wearing an armor breastplate and holds a lamp in one hand. He is at the door.

In the picture no one is there to answer. Yet, Jesus still knocks. His eyes emote love; his face beams welcome.

If you study the painting you will soon notice there is no knob or latch on the outside of the door. It can only be opened from within.

This chapter will examine major beliefs Christians hold about Jesus Christ, as stated in the Nicene Creed. Beliefs about Jesus are central to the Christian faith. One key belief is the truth that Jesus continues to reach out to people today. Jesus calls out to you too. He patiently waits and knocks at the door leading to your heart. He wants you to respond to his friendship, but he respects your freedom. Jesus understands that it is your choice whether or not you will unlatch the lock and invite him into your life.

As you study this chapter, you might spend some time listening to how Jesus speaks personally to you. Ask yourself these questions: "How does Jesus speak to me? What does it mean to be a friend of Jesus? What can I do to show my love for Jesus?"

━━━━━━━━━━━━━ ▪ ━━━━━━━━━━━━

What Do You Believe About Jesus?

Here are some basic beliefs many Christians hold about Jesus. Explore your own faith in Jesus by rating each according to this scale:

1—strongly agree
2—agree
3—disagree
?—not sure

——— 1. Jesus is the Messiah, Son of the living God.

——— 2. Jesus is the Way, the Truth, and the Life.

——— 3. Jesus is the Lord God.

——— 4. Jesus is the Word of God, the Second Person of the Trinity.

——— 5. Jesus is *the* "person for others."

——— 6. Jesus lives!

——— 7. Jesus is truly present in the eucharist.

——— 8. Jesus is my Savior who loves me beyond compare.

——— 9. Jesus is my best friend.

——— 10. Jesus forgives me when I am sorry for my sins.

——— 11. Jesus will come again to judge the world at the end of time.

——— 12. _____

_____

[Write your own belief.]

▪ *discuss* ▪

1. What is your own belief about Jesus? Share your response to item 12.

2. Who is someone you know who believes in Jesus Christ? What is one sign of his or her faith?

3. How is Jesus present in the world today? Give two examples.

▪ *journal* ▪

Compose a short reflection discussing each of the following:

- your relationship with Jesus when you were in the second grade
- your relationship with Jesus right now
- what you hope your relationship with Jesus will be like fifteen years from now

---

We Believe in One Lord, Jesus Christ

The very first verse of Mark's gospel reads, "The beginning of the gospel about Jesus Christ, the Son of God" (Mk 1:1). This is privileged information, given only to the reader. As the reader, you are provided insight into Jesus' identity that even his first disciples did not have. Each of these words—Jesus, Christ, and Son of God, as well as the title *Lord*—reveal unique truths about the identity of a man who lived in Nazareth 2,000 years ago. What can be learned from each of these titles?

Jesus. The name Jesus comes from the Hebrew word *Yehoshua* (Joshua) which means "God saves" or "God is salvation." This name was revealed to Mary by an angel (see Lk 1:31), thus pointing to his identity and his mission. From his conception, God had destined that Jesus would save the world from sin and death. Matthew's and Luke's gospels place Jesus' birth at Bethlehem. Each of the four gospels cite Nazareth as Jesus' hometown.

Who was this Jesus of Nazareth? What is known about his historical identity? What records are there that confirm that he actually lived? Although most of what is known about the historical Jesus appears in the four gospels written by believers, there are other objective sources that confirm Jesus' existence.

For example, the Roman historian Tacitus placed the blame for the great fire in Rome in AD 64 on Christians. He derived their name from "Christus," taken from the man who was put to death by the Roman governor Pontius Pilate. Also, Pliny the Younger, the Roman governor of Bithnyia, wrote to the emperor Trajan (c. AD 112) telling him about

Christians who worshiped Christ as a god. Neither he nor the emperor in his return letter ever questioned Jesus' actual existence.

Josephus, a famous Jewish first century historian, mentioned Jesus in two of his writings. The Jewish rabbinical collection of writings known as the Talmud likewise has a record of Jesus. Had Jesus never lived, then it is likely that the Jewish leaders would have tried to disprove the Christian belief in Jesus' existence. But to the contrary, they take for granted in their writings that he indeed was once alive.

Answering the question: "What did Christians have to gain by inventing the historical Jesus?" is another convincing proof of Jesus' existence. Certainly there were no political, social, or economic advantages to being a Christian. Christianity was illegal in the Roman empire. Many early Christians—including all of the apostles, except John—were martyred because of their faith.

Perhaps the best argument *for* the existence of Jesus comes from the gospels themselves. The words attributed to Jesus bear the stamp of someone who taught with unique insight and ability. For example, Jesus' parables utilize an original style. More importantly, their content and message describe a novel understanding of God, people, and reality. Also, Jesus taught that God is "Abba-Daddy" and that people can address God with this intimate term. He taught that God's reign had been initiated by his coming. He taught love for enemies and he reached out to those on the edge of society— women, the poor, and the sick.

Gospel Formation

The gospels resulted from the following three-stage process of formation spanning perhaps seventy years:

- First was the period of the *historical Jesus*, the time of his life on earth. This period may have spanned from his birth in approximately 4 to 6 BC to his death in about AD 30.

- Second was the time of *oral preaching* when the first

disciples proclaimed orally the good news that "Jesus is risen!" Preaching was the normal way of passing on information in the ancient world, so writing a systematic account of the Jesus story was not a top priority. Besides, many early Christians believed that the Second Coming, or return to earth by Jesus, was immanent.

■ Third came the period of the *written gospels*. Mark's gospel was likely the first written, in AD 65–70. Because Jesus did not return when expected and the eyewitnesses to his life and teaching were dying or being martyred, it became necessary to have a permanent written record of the good news to counteract any false teachings or beliefs about Jesus and to instruct new converts to the faith.

All twenty-seven books of the New Testament proclaim the doctrine of the *incarnation*, that God took on human flesh in the person of Jesus of Nazareth. The New Testament announces the fulfillment of God's promises to the Chosen People and to all humanity. The gospels especially give dramatic testimony to Jesus' historical ministry.

Here is a short summary of the key points of Jesus' teaching. Read each point, its accompanying gospel passage, and the follow-up question. Make the proper notations in your journal.

The reign of God is here.   The term *reign (or kingdom) of God* refers to God's active participation in life, both in heaven and on earth. God's presence can be detected in the actions of justice, peace, and love. It is Jesus who ushers in God's reign. Jesus' healings of people's physical, emotional, and spiritual hurts were signs of the kingdom. Jesus taught that although the reign of God starts small and will meet resistance, it will inevitably grow and powerfully transform all humanity.

■ *Read Mark 4:30–32. How is the mustard seed an appropriate image for the reign of God?*

God is a loving Father.   Jesus' use of "Abba" to describe God awakened an understanding of a God who loves all people as a parent loves a child. Jesus taught that God can be approached confidently and that Abba will answer each and every need.

- *Read Luke 11:1–13. What is your image of the Father described in the prayer?*

God is merciful. The parable of the lost son shows the depths of God's mercy. In the parable, the father accepts his wayward son back into his household even though the son has squandered his inheritance in a sinful, wasteful life. Because God is so forgiving, Jesus taught that people should be the same way, imitating the father by forgiving others and showing mercy.

- *Read Luke 15:11–32. How can you translate the father's actions into a similarly merciful response to others in your own actions?*

God's love is for everyone. Jesus' first mission was to the Jews, God's Chosen People. But gradually, his followers realized he had come to minister to all. Jesus told a parable in which **all** people were invited to the heavenly banquet. He also taught that the love of God and neighbor are one.

- *Read Luke 10:29–37. According to the story, who is your neighbor?*

Serving others is essential. To be a follower of Jesus means to serve others. In this way, God's love is expressed through the work of his followers. In addition, Jesus taught that service done to those most in need—the hungry, naked, imprisoned—is, in fact, service done to God.

- *Read Matthew 25:31–46. When have you seen the Lord in the forms that Jesus describes? How did you respond?*

Jesus is present in his church. Jesus promised that he would remain with his disciples until the end of time. One way he does this is through his church, which he established through the apostles. He entrusted special authority to Peter and his successors (the popes). The bishops and their helpers forgive sins in Jesus' name, teach in matters of doctrine, and guide in matters of church discipline. Jesus is also active in the communal life of the church, participating in the lives of all its people. A name for the church is the *Body of Christ*.

■ *Read John 21:15–19. What do you think Jesus expects from you in service to his church?*

Jesus is present through the Holy Spirit. Until Jesus returns to earth in glory, he has sent the Holy Spirit to unite his people in love with one another and with the Father and the Son. The Spirit—the third person of the Trinity—guides, strengthens, and sanctifies the followers of Jesus.

■ *Read John 14:15–31. What is the Holy Spirit's task as the church awaits Jesus' return?*

To accept Jesus is to accept the cross. Jesus' disciples were shocked to hear him predict that he would suffer, be rejected, and killed. Jesus' acceptance of his cross was a necessary element of his achieving salvation for humankind. Likewise, he told his disciples "Whoever wishes to come after me must deny himself, take up his cross, and follow me" (Mt 16:24). Doing God's will requires self-denial and sacrifice. Jesus also promised that he would make the burden "light and easy" and that all who are faithful will share in the joy of his resurrection. A life of service means dying to selfishness, but it leads to an eternal life of happiness.

■ *Read Mark 8:31–33. How does your reaction to Jesus' call to discipleship compare with Peter's reaction?*

■ *journal* ■

Check the teachings of Jesus on the following themes. Read and transcribe the following quotes into your journal.

Possessions (Lk 12:15)	*Faith* (Lk 17:6)
Forgiveness (Mt 18:21–22)	*Sincerity* (Mt 6:1)
Discipleship (Lk 9:23)	*Judgment* (Mt 7:1)
How to Live (Mt 7:12)	*True Happiness* (Lk 11:28)
Enemies (Mt 5:44)	*Prayer* (Mt 7:7)
Humility (Mk 10:31)	*Worry* (Mt 6:33–34)
Love (Jn 15:17)	

Christ. Jesus accepted the title Christ for himself, albeit reluctantly. "Who do you say I am?" he asked his disciples. Peter spoke up and said, "You are the Christ." Jesus then gave them strict orders not to tell anyone about him. The title Christ—a Greek word for the Hebrew "Messiah"—was

a politically charged word in Jesus' time. The meaning of Christ is "the anointed one."

In the first century, the Jews had great expectations that the Messiah would restore Israel to its rightful position of glory by overthrowing the oppressive Romans. Although Jesus accepted the title (see Mt 16:13–17) from his apostles, he was cautious about using it around his contemporaries because so many of them expected the Messiah to be a military leader with specific political intentions. Jesus rejected this interpretation. In contrast, he saw the Messiah's role as one who undergoes suffering for the purpose of ushering in God's reign.

After his resurrection, the disciples came to a clearer understanding of the title Christ, as it related to the Risen Jesus. They recognized how the Father anointed Jesus in power and in the fullness of the Holy Spirit. As God's anointed one, the Church assigned him other titles. Among those are:

- **Great Prophet.** Jesus is the one who spoke for his Father and shared the full message of salvation.
- **High Priest.** Jesus offered his life for all humanity on the altar of the cross. He continues to fulfill the role of High Priest at each celebration of the eucharist.
- **True King.** Jesus is the rightful ruler of the universe. His rule is one of gentleness and compassion. He uses the power of love and service to attract followers to his way.

The title Christ became so revered that members of the church began to call themselves *Christians*, "anointed ones of the Anointed One." By taking the name Christian at baptism, the followers of Christ assume Jesus' roles of prophet, priest, and king. As prophets, Christians speak Christ's truth. As priests, Christians worship God and bring Christ's love to others. As kings, Christians lead others to the kingdom through loving service.

Lord. The term Lord has various meanings. A ruler or someone with great power is often called "lord." The term can also be used as a polite and respectful form of address, much like "sir."

However, when used to describe Jesus the title *Lord*

means much more than any of those definitions. Rather, Lord refers to its Greek translation, *Kyrios*, which in turn renders the Hebrew *Adonai*. Adonai was the word spoken aloud by Jews whenever the most sacred name Yahweh would appear in the Hebrew scriptures. Thus, to call Jesus Lord (*Kyrios*) is to state that *he is God*. Christians claim that Jesus has the same sovereignity as God and that his death and resurrection have won eternal life for humanity, a gift only God can grant. His sacrifice conquered suffering, evil, and death.

For Christians, Jesus alone is the "one" Lord, the only one deserving of total allegiance. Because he became the Lord of all,

> . . . God raised him high.
> and gave him the name
> which is above all names;
> so that *all beings*
> in the heavens, on earth and in the underworld,
> *should bend the knee* at the name of Jesus
> and that *every tongue should acknowledge*
> Jesus Christ as Lord,
> to the glory of God the Father (Phil 2:9–11).

Jesus Christ is worshipped as Lord because he is the God through whom everything was made and kept in existence. Christians thank him for his greatness because of his gift of salvation and eternal life.

We Believe in the Only Son of God

Jesus was brought to trial and eventually killed because he revealed himself as the unique Son of God the Father. By doing so, he had made himself God's equal. He said: "The Father and I are one" (Jn 10:30).

At his trial, the members of the Jewish court asked Jesus, "So are you the Son of God then?" Jesus answered: "It is you who say I am" (Luke 22:70–71).

After Jesus' resurrection, the early Christian community used the term "Son of God" to describe Jesus' unique relationship and identity with God, the Father. This term expressed a one-of-a-kind relationship Jesus had with God

from the very beginning of his life. For example, as the story of Jesus' annunciation was recounted, it was the "Son of God" the angel told Mary she would conceive (see Lk 1:35).

The term "Son of God" came to express the early Christian's belief in Jesus' divinity. As the church spread throughout the Roman Empire, however, some people began to misinterpret the title. *Heresies*, usually centering on a false belief about Jesus' humanity or divinity, arose. In general, two extreme beliefs resulted—one that denied Jesus' humanity, the other which denied his divinity. Here is a summary of two of the major heresies of the time:

> **Docetism** (from the Greek word "to seem") taught that Jesus only "seemed" to be a man. Docetists could not accept that the almighty God would really be demeaned by taking the form of a human. Hence, they taught that Jesus only took on the *appearance* of a man. Under this belief, this meant that Jesus only appeared to suffer, die, and rise. Docetism undercut the firm Christian belief that God became human in order to win salvation for all of humankind.

> Oppositely, the **Arianism** heresy claimed that though Jesus was God's greatest creature, he was **not** God. The Arians held that as a human son comes after his father in time, so too the Son of God must have come after his Heavenly Father. In other words, there must have been a time when Jesus did not exist. Since under Arianism Jesus was not considered divine, salvation for humankind was not guaranteed.

Because of these controversies, Christian belief about Jesus became confused. As a result, the church leaders met in a series of *ecumenical* or worldwide councils in the fourth and fifth centuries to define clear teachings about Christ and God. These decisions of the Council of Nicea helped to clearly state the classic beliefs about Jesus Christ in the articles of the creed.

Only Son of God.   Although Jesus Christ had a natural human mother, Mary, he had no natural *human* father. Rather, Jesus' father is the first person of the Trinity, God the Father.

All humans are the adopted children of God; only Jesus is the natural son. Jesus shares in the very nature of God.

God from God, Light from Light.   The Son, like the Father, has a divine nature. The Son proceeding from the Father is of one substance with the Father. Jesus Christ is true God just as light is identical to the light from which it comes.

Begotten, not made, one in Being with the Father.   The Council of Nicea distinguished between *begotten* and *created*. It stated that the Father begets his Son and creates the world. Christian faith holds that the Son is not *made* by the Father because the Son is not a created being. Rather, the Father "begets" the Son who is one in being with the Father. The Son always existed in relationship to the Father from whom he proceeds. If Jesus is truly the only Son of God, then he must always have been so. As John's gospel states:

> In the beginning was the Word [the Son]:
> the Word was with God
> and the Word was God (Jn 1:1).

Through whom all things were made.   Since the Son is one in being with the Father, he also shares in the creation of the world. According to John's gospel:

> Through whom all things came into being,
> not one thing came into being except
>   through him.
> What has come into being in him was life,
> life that was the light of men (Jn 1:2–4).

Human history originates with God and moves back toward God. Through Jesus, God's Son, humans are able to come to a close, deep relationship with the Father. Since Jesus is the author of the universe he is likewise entitled to human praise and thanksgiving.

Other Conciliar Teachings about Jesus

After Nicea, later councils—Ephesus (431), Chalcedon (451), Constantinople II (553), and Constantinople III (680)— took up issues that dealt with the relationship of Jesus' human nature to his divine nature. Here is a summary of the teachings from those councils:

- There is only one person in Christ, the divine person, the Word of God, the second Person of the Blessed Trinity. Thus, everything in Christ's human nature is to be attributed to his divine person, for example, his miracles and even his suffering and death.

- Mary, by conceiving God's Son, is truly the Mother of God.

- There are two distinct natures in the one person of Christ. Jesus has a divine nature and a human nature. He is perfect in divinity and perfect in humanity. Jesus Christ is true God and true man.

- As a true human being, body and soul, Jesus embodies the divine ways of God in a human way.

- As true God and true human, Jesus has a human intellect and a human will. Both are perfectly attuned and subject to his divine intellect and will, which he has in common with the Father and the Holy Spirit.

- The union of the human and divine natures in the one person of Jesus is so perfect that it is said that in Jesus God truly shared humanity, truly suffered, truly underwent death, and truly rose victorious over death.

- Jesus, God-made-man, is the Savior. Those who unite themselves to his death and resurrection through faith will share in the eternal life he has promised.

Son of Man

"Son of man" was a term used in the Hebrew scriptures (especially in the Books of Ezekiel and Daniel). It included two realities—the human and divine. Jesus used "Son of Man" in two ways. One way referred to Jesus as the Suffering Servant. The other described his role as judge and savior who had been given glory by God.

Note below how Jesus uses the title "Son of Man." Is it used to describe his suffering or his glory? Check the following passages in Mark's gospel. Write the appropriate word.

1. Mk 8:31: *suffering*   4. Mk 10:33: _____

2. Mk 8:38: _____   5. Mk 14:21: _____

3. Mk 9:12: _____   6. Mk 14:62: _____

He Came Down from Heaven

Can you imagine your reaction if you came to your sixth period government class one day and found the President of the United States seated among you as one of the students? Or, if you discovered that a high-flying, shoe-selling, pro-basketball star had become a member of your high school team? Those scenarios are unlikely—if not impossible—because those with important positions just don't humble themselves to take on a lesser role. However, the salvation of humankind was won by a similar—though much greater—occurrence, that of God taking on human flesh.

In Jesus, God became human so that all might participate in the divine life, so that all might become God's children. Belief in the doctrine of the *incarnation*, that God's own Son became human, is the distinctive sign of the faith of Christians.

For us and for our salvation.   It is most appropriate that the name Jesus means "God saves." Christians acknowledge Jesus Christ as the Savior who has brought the world salvation. From a theological sense, salvation means "a spiritual rescue from the state of sin." Jesus came to rescue people from those evil forces present in the world since the first people—Adam and Eve—disobeyed God and committed the first sin. The result of the *original sin* was that death became a part of the human condition. God becoming flesh in the person of Jesus was the way for humans to reconcile their relationship to God. It was the way for all creation to be renewed. One of the titles for Jesus is the *New Adam*. Can you understand why he would be called this?

When the church speaks of salvation it means the good and happiness that God intends for all: the healing of hurts and the attainment of God's peace. Salvation also means:

- the mending of broken relationships which have caused alienation from God and other people,
- the full restoration of God's grace on humanity,
- adoption into God's family,
- the forgiveness of sins and redemption from the power of evil and death.

Born of the Virgin Mary. Jesus' virginal conception by the power of the Holy Spirit affirms his true identity—he is God's Son, the pre-existing Word, the promised Redeemer, the second person of the Blessed Trinity. By being born of the Virgin Mary, Jesus also became a human being, like all other people in everything but sin.

In Jesus, God embraced human nature in all its fragility. The New Testament paints a portrait of Jesus reaching out to those most in need. He did this on their terms and experienced all the same difficulties that they did. He was tired. He cried. He felt real pain when he was slapped and scourged. He also shared the joy of being human. He ate and drank with friends. He loved his friends with the deepest of emotion.

Jesus' whole life revealed the Father; everything he said and did was pleasing to God. Likewise, when people choose to live like the human Jesus, they become like the Christ who is God. This is the meaning of discipleship ("one who learns"). Disciples of Christ learn from the Master, imitating him in word and in action. His spoken words teach people how to live. His healings and exorcisms exemplify compassion. His death and resurrection show the way to eternal life.

No one was more like Christ than his mother Mary. Her response of "Yes" to the angel who told her she was to conceive God's Son was the first act of discipleship. Her "Yes" made her the Mother of God. She is a model for others who have desired to be Christ's disciples. What are some characteristics of a disciple of Christ? Those who best live this calling are those who are able to best imitate the

From the Documents

For Jesus Christ was sent into the world as a real Mediator between God and men. Since he is God, all divine fullness dwells bodily in Him.... He is the new Adam, made head of a renewed humanity, and full of grace and truth (Jn 1:14). Therefore the Son of God walked the ways of a true Incarnation that He might make men sharers in the divine nature. He became poor for our sakes, though He had been rich, in order that His poverty might enrich us (2 Cor 8:9). The Son of Man came not that He might be served, but that He might be a servant, and give His life as a ransom for the many— that is, for all...(*Decree on the Missionary Activity of the Church*, No. 3).

life Jesus lived while on earth. Jesus' human characteristics included the following:

Jesus was honest with his emotions. For example, when the moneychangers violated the sanctity of the Temple Jesus was angry. Read Mark 11:15–19 to see what he did. Jesus expressed his impatience at the apostles' slowness to understand him (see Mt 16:5–12). Jesus also cried. When he witnessed the sadness surrounding the death of his friend Lazarus he was moved deeply (see Jn 11: 1–44).

Jesus was humble. He came from Nazareth, a poor, out-of-the-way place that was ridiculed even by his disciples (see Jn 1:46). As a child, he obeyed his mother and foster father (see Lk 2:51). At the Last Supper, Jesus left his disciples a sign of the humility they were to imitate when he washed their feet (see Jn 13).

Jesus was a healer. Jesus never explained to his disciples the meaning of suffering, but he did heal any suffering he encountered. He cured not only friends—like Peter's mother-in-law—but also perfect strangers, people who were lepers, the blind, the deaf, epileptics, the crippled, the demon-possessed, and many others with various afflictions. He also brought the dead back to life (see Lk 7:11–17). Jesus' healings showed people that God's love has the power to overcome evil.

Jesus was forgiving. Jesus' mission was to sinners (see Lk 5:32). He called others to examine their own lives before they inflicted judgment on others. When a mob of people brought him a woman accused of adultery he told them, "Let the one among you who is without sin be the first to throw a stone at her" (Jn 8:7–8). Jesus gave people what they really needed: the healing touch of God's forgiveness and the good news that they were loved.

Jesus was courageous. He stood up to the false religious leaders of his day; he called them blind guides and hypocrites (see Lk 13:10–17). Jesus boldly preached

God's will, knowing that the jealousy it caused among the religious leaders would lead to his death. But he did not back down, though he feared death as any normal person would:

> "*Abba*, Father!" he said, "For you everything is possible. Take this cup away from me. But let it be as you, not I, would have it" (Mk 14:36).

Jesus was self-giving. Jesus was an innocent man who was falsely arrested and sentenced to die. He freely gave his life for all people everywhere. As he told his disciples:

> No one can have greater love
> than to lay down his life
>   for his friends (Jn 15:13).

Jesus had given all that he had for the salvation of the world.

Birth Narratives

Although the infancy narratives from the gospels of Matthew and Luke come from different traditions, they agree on the following points. Read Matthew 1:18–2:23 and Luke 1:1–2:52. Then, complete the following chart.

1. The key characters in both accounts are _____, _____ and _____.

2. These events took place during the reign of this king: _____

3. Mary was a virgin, _____ to Joseph.

4. Joseph was descended from _____.

5. Jesus was conceived of a virgin by the power of the _____.

6. Mary gave birth to Jesus in this town: _____

7. Jesus was given this name before birth: _____

8. A famous Old Testament king, _____, was an ancestor of Jesus.

9. The Holy Family eventually settled in _____.

■ *research* ■

Note some of the differences in the birth narratives. Read some information in a biblical commentary to explain your findings. Write a summary and share the information in class.

Miracles of Jesus

Jesus' miracles were wondrous events that helped to clearly show God's saving plan of reconciling all to himself. Jesus' miracles can be divided into four categories: healings, exorcisms, nature miracles, and resurrections. Read one of each kind of miracle story from the gospels. Report on the following for each: (1) the problem; (2) how Jesus solved it; (3) the meaning (what the miracle meant for the person involved or those who witnessed it).

Healing miracles:
    Cure of the leper (Mt 8:1–4)
    Blind man of Jericho (Mk 10:46–52)

Exorcisms:
    Cure of demoniac (Lk 4:33–37)
    Expulsion of demons in Gadara
    (Mt 8:28–34)

Nature miracles:
    Calming of the storm (Mk 4:35–41)
    Feeding of the 5000 (Lk 9:10–17

Raising from the dead:
    Lazarus (Jn 11:1–54)
    Jairus' daughter (Lk 8:41–42,
    49–56)

For Our Sake He Was Crucified

Someone once remarked that the way a person dies is to their life as a punctuation mark is to a sentence. If so, Jesus' death is an exclamation point of profound love—both for the Father who sent him and for humanity for whom he won salvation. Jesus' earthly life—his actions and his words—reach their dramatic completion on the cross. He came to bring the very life of God to the world and he accomplished this by *freely* surrendering his life. Jesus said:

> "I am the good shepherd
> the good shepherd lays down his life for his sheep.
>
> No one takes [my life] from me;
> I lay it down of my own free will,
> and as I have power to lay it down,
> so I have power to take it up again" (Jn 10:11, 18).

Why did Jesus have to die? Jesus, himself, explained that he came "to give his life as a ransom for many" (Mk 10:45). A sinless man, Jesus Christ took on the guilt of others, dying a death others deserved in order to buy their freedom with his very personal and eternal love. The depth of this love was explained by St. Paul in his letter to the Romans:

> " . . . You could hardly find anyone ready to die even for someone upright. . . . So it is proof of God's own love for us, that Christ died for us while we were still sinners" (Rom 5:7–8).

Jesus Christ died for all human beings. Jesus took the sins of humanity with him to the cross. In his suffering and death, Jesus' humanity became the free and perfect gift of love to be given to God on behalf of all. Jesus' death restored the gift of eternal life that was lost at the time of the original sin.

The Nicene Creed speaks of Jesus' death by listing four verbs: Jesus was *crucified, suffered, died,* and *buried.* Each of these verbs has special significance.

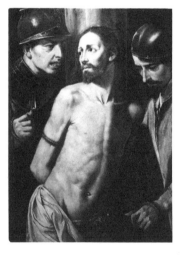

Jesus was crucified under Pontius Pilate. Jesus was accused of religious blasphemy, that is of making himself God's equal. Under Jewish law, blasphemy was punishable by death. However, only the Romans, the ruling government, could exercise the death penalty. Thus, some of the Jewish authorities turned Jesus over to Pilate for execution. They had convinced the Roman procurator that Jesus was a threat to Caesar, the emperor.

Who Killed Jesus?

Jesus' death **cannot** be attributed to the Jews as often has been done in the past. The gospel record clearly shows that Jesus' trial was very complex. He had a number of supporters among the Pharisees (for example, Nicodemus) and at least one ally among the Sanhedrin (Joseph of Arimathea). Furthermore, all of Jesus' apostles, disciples, and early converts were Jews. Jesus even forgave his executioners on the cross, acknowledging that they did not know what they were doing. **All humanity** actually shares in the blame for Jesus' death. It was for the collective and individual sins of humanity that Jesus died.

Besides Jesus and Mary, only Pontius Pilate is mentioned by name in the Creed. This significant detail roots Jesus' death in history, specifically during Pilate's reign as the fifth Roman procurator of Judea, Samaria, and Idumea from AD 26–36. First-century Jewish historians Josephus and Philo also attest to his existence. Pilate's behavior at Jesus' trial displayed a man who refused to embrace the truth (see Jn 18:28–38). Knowing Jesus was innocent, Pilate violated his conscience and condemned God's Son to death.

However, it is important to remember that Jesus freely accepted crucifixion. In the ancient world, crucifixion was the most severe, painful, and humiliating form of capital punishment. It was devised to torment a criminal to the point of insanity and to prolong the agony of death for hours and even days. Romans reserved crucifixion for slaves; thus, Jews viewed it as an especially loathsome and degrading form of punishment. Jesus accepted crucifixion to prove beyond doubt his immense love for humanity.

From the Documents

The Fathers of the Second Vatican Council clearly denounce the thesis that Jews were collectively guilty of the death of Jesus. For generations this mistaken notion has contributed to prejudices and discriminations against the Jewish people. According to the Council:

True, authorities of the Jews and those who followed their lead pressed for the death of Christ (cf. Jn 19:6), still what happened in his passion cannot be blamed upon all the Jews then living, without distinction, nor upon the Jews of today. Although the church is the new people of God, the Jews should not be presented as repudiated or cursed by God, as if such views followed from the holy scriptures. All should take pains, then, lest in catechetical instruction and in the preaching of God's Word they teach anything out of harmony with the truth of the gospel and the spirit of Christ . . . The church repudiates all persecutions against any man. Moreover, mindful of her common patrimony with the Jews, and motivated by the gospel's spiritual love and by no political considerations, she deplores the hatred, persecutions, and displays of anti-Semitism directed against the Jews at any time and from any source.

—*Nostra Aetate*, #4

Jesus suffered.   The Creed clearly states that Jesus suffered. By doing so, it underscores the fact that Jesus was *truly human* (and not some ghostly apparition as the Docetists held) and that he experienced suffering in a human way.

Jesus endured the *physical* pains of scourging, the crowning with thorns, and the crucifixion. He also suffered the *psychological* pains of being rejected. Jesus did not want to suffer. In the garden of Gethsemane he anticipated the torture he would endure and asked God to "take this cup away from me." He then added, "Nevertheless, let your will be done, not mine" (Lk 22:42–43).

To the end Jesus was obedient to his Father's will, even if it meant accepting something that is naturally abhorrent to all people.

Jesus died and was buried.   Death is the separation of a person's soul from his or her body. Jesus experienced this condition between the time of his death on the cross and his resurrection. The Apostles' Creed states that during this time Christ "descended to the dead." This means that he went to the abode of the dead (*Sheol* in Hebrew, *Hades* in Greek) and there proclaimed the gospel to the just souls who had died before he came to earth.

All four gospels agree that Joseph of Arimathea, a member of the Sanhedrin, buried Jesus and that others witnessed his burial, including Nicodemus, his mother Mary, and Mary Magdalene. Matthew's gospel mentions that Pilate posted guards at the tomb to assure that his corpse would not be stolen (see Mt 27:62–66). However, because Jesus' human soul and body were still linked to the second person of the Trinity, the Son, Jesus' mortal corpse was preserved from corruption.

Because of original sin, death touches all humans. By accepting death, Jesus in effect conquered death, the most severe result of sin. According to St. Paul:

> His purpose in dying for all humanity was that those who live should live not anymore for themselves, but for him who died and was raised to new life (2 Cor 5:15).

■ *journal* ■

Read Matthew 26:36–27:66, the passion narrative. Outline the key events in chronological order.

On the Third Day He Rose Again

Jesus' resurrection from the dead is the central belief of the Christian faith. It is the heart of the good news about Jesus: "If Christ has not been raised, then our preaching is without substance, and so is your faith" (1 Cor 15:14). The Easter event took the apostles and disciples by surprise. Hiding and frightened in Jerusalem after the crucifixion, the apostles did not immediately believe the women when they reported finding an empty tomb. The empty tomb, however, was an essential sign of Jesus' resurrection—a first step in acknowledging God's work in bringing the Son back to life.

The second step was the appearance of the Risen Lord himself to Mary Magdalene, to Peter, to the travelers on the road to Emmaus, to the apostles in Galilee, to Saul, the persecutor of Christians, to more than 500 disciples at one time (1 Cor 15:5–8). Along with the coming of the

Holy Spirit, these appearances transformed frightened, confused, and disappointed followers of Jesus of Nazareth into bold, courageous witnesses who willingly died proclaiming, "Jesus Christ is Lord!"

Christ's resurrection to a glorious body, not limited by space or time, confirms the following:

- the Old Testament promises concerning the resurrection (for example, see Is 53),
- Jesus' divinity,
- new life, including a share in the resurrection, for all of Christ's followers. Jesus' resurrection is the promise of eternal life with God.

The ascension. The ascension of Jesus refers to the time when Jesus stopped appearing to the disciples in visible form and his glorified body took its rightful place in heaven as equal to the Father (by the Father's right hand). In heaven, Jesus continues to intercede for the needs of the world through prayer and action.

The church celebrates Jesus' ascension to heaven forty days after Easter Sunday. The Acts of the Apostles reports how Jesus appeared to his disciples over forty days before "he was lifted up, and a cloud took him from their sight" (Acts 1:9). In his glorified state, Jesus—true God and true man—is not limited to time and space. He lives and reigns forever.

He will come again. The Creed proclaims that Jesus will return in glory at the end of time. This Second Coming of Christ, known by its Greek name, the *Parousia*, will mark the end of the world. At that time, all creatures in the universe will acknowledge the Lordship of Jesus Christ and God's full reign of justice, love, and peace will be established. No one knows when this day will occur. Jesus himself said this knowledge was hidden: "But as for that day or hour, nobody knows it, neither the angels in heaven, nor the Son; no one but the Father" (Mk 13:32). The important message of this teaching is that people should live each day as if it were their last.

The Paschal Mystery

Collectively, the passion, death, resurrection, and glorification (ascension) of Jesus Christ are known as the Paschal Mystery (or Easter Mystery). Through these events, Jesus "passes over" from this world into the Father's glory. These salvation events bring redemption to the world. Catholics celebrate this mystery of faith in the sacraments, especially in the eucharist.

He will judge the living and the dead. The Son has been assigned the role of judge of all people and nations. Matthew 25 lists the criteria of judgment: deeds of mercy done for the **least** of Jesus' brothers and sisters. According to the story, Jesus will ask questions like: "Did you give food to the hungry and drink to the thirsty? Did you extend hospitality to strangers? clothe the naked? visit the sick and imprisoned?" In brief, how well did you respond to Jesus through others, especially those most in need?

Chapter 5 will cover more about the issue of human destiny. For now, suffice it to say that faith in Jesus has profound meaning. God will reward those who have lived as other Christs: loving, forgiving, healing, and reconciling. This was Jesus' mission. It is the mission of all his followers.

Conclusion

Jesus asked the apostles on the road to Caesarea Philippi what people were saying of him. Some others were saying that Jesus was a great prophet—maybe Elijah or John the Baptist come back to life. These answers were intriguing, but Jesus wanted to know more:

> "But you...who do you say I am?" Then Simon Peter spoke up and said, "You are the Christ, the Son of the living God" (Mt 16:15–16).

Jesus continues to ask this question today. Who do you say Jesus is? Do you...

- recognize him as the Savior of the world, God's Son who gave you life and won for you eternal salvation?

- accept him as the one who forgives your sins and calls you to live joyfully in love and service of others?

- see him as your friend who is always there to help, to guide, to encourage, and to challenge you?

- model your life on him as God's Word who is the Way, the Truth, and the Life?

Who is Jesus for you?

■ *journal* ■

Read Matthew 28:1–10, Luke 24:1–53, and John 20:1–29. Note the differences in these three separate accounts of resurrection appearances by Jesus.

▪ *focus questions* ▪

1. What does the name *Jesus* mean?

2. Name two non-biblical sources that confirmed Jesus' historical existence.

3. What is the *incarnation*?

4. What is the meaning of the term *reign of God*? What did Jesus teach about it?

5. Discuss two key themes in the teaching of Jesus.

6. What do the titles *Christ* and *Lord* mean when used to describe Jesus?

7. How do Christians take on the prophetic, priestly, and kingly roles of Jesus?

8. Discuss the church's answers to the heresies of Docetism and Arianism.

9. What does it mean to say that Jesus was "begotten, not made?"

10. How many persons, natures, and wills are there in Christ? Explain.

11. What is the significance of the title *Son of Man* when used to describe Jesus?

12. What is one meaning of salvation?

13. What do we affirm when we say Jesus was born of the virgin Mary?

14. List and describe two qualities of the human Jesus.

15. List four categories of Jesus' miracles and give an example of each.

16. What was accomplished by Jesus' death?

17. Why does the Nicene Creed mention Pontius Pilate?

18. Why is the resurrection of Jesus the central belief of the Christian faith?

19. What is the meaning of the term *Paschal Mystery*?

20. What is the meaning of the ascension of Jesus?

21. In light of the Second Coming of Christ, how should people live their lives?

22. Define the following terms:

gospel   apostle   Arianism
evangelist   heresy   ecumenical council
Docetism   Parousia   disciple

■ *exercises* ■

1. Write a one-page prayer reflection to answer Jesus' question: "Who do you say I am?"

2. Look up information on one of the following. Write a three paragraph summary of what you discovered.

   ■ Pontius Pilate

   ■ crucifixion in the Roman world

   ■ the symbolism of the cross

3. Read Isaiah 52:13—53:12. Share insights on the meaning of service to others.

■ *vocabulary* ■

Look up the meaning of the following words in the dictionary. Transcribe the definitions into your journal:

   ecumenical   squander

Prayer Reflection

The Stations of the Cross are a meditative prayer based on the passion of Jesus. This devotion grew out of the custom of Holy Land pilgrims who retraced the last steps of Jesus on his way to Calvary. Most Catholic churches have the stations depicted on their side walls.

Traditionally there have been fourteen stations, ending with the laying of Jesus in the sepulcher. In recent years a fifteenth station—depicting the resurrection—has been added to show the glorious conclusion to Jesus' sacrifice.

To pray the Stations, use the following procedure. First, *imagine* the gospel scene. Second, *converse* with the Lord, telling him what you think. Third, pause and *listen* to what the Lord might be telling you. Sample meditations are given for some of the stations. In your journal, write your own meditations for the others.

The Stations of the Cross

1. *Jesus is condemned to death.* [How unfairly they treat Jesus. The crowd turns on him and asks for his death. *Lord, how often have I been disloyal to you? Yet, you never abandoned me.*]

2. *Jesus takes up his cross.*

3. *Jesus falls for the first time.* [The weight of the cross appears to break Jesus physically. Yet, he is determined to go on, to do what he knows he must do. *Lord, do I, like you, "stick to it" in the midst of adversity? Or do I too easily give up? Give me your strength.*]

4. *Jesus meets his mother.*

5. *Simon of Cyrene helps Jesus carry his cross.*

6. *Veronica wipes the face of Jesus.* [A stranger comes from the crowd to help Jesus. She steps out of line to do right. *Lord, how often do I respond to those who need me? Give me the courage to stand out.*]

7. *Jesus falls for the second time.*

8. *Jesus consoles the women of Jerusalem.*

9. *Jesus falls the third time.*

10. *Jesus is stripped of his garments.*

11. *Jesus is nailed to the cross.* [*Lord, how much you must have suffered to endure such pain . . . for me. Give me the courage to bear with the small crosses that come into my life.*]

12. *Jesus dies on the cross.* [Jesus said the greatest love a person can have for his friends is to give up his life for them (Jn 15:13). Jesus not only spoke love, he put it into practice. *Lord, help me to be authentic like you, to do as I say.*]

13. *Jesus is taken down from the cross.* [*Lord, thank you for saving me.*]

14. *Jesus is laid in the tomb.*

15. *The resurrection of the Lord.*

▪ *reflection* ▪

Visit a church. Look at the images of the stations of the cross. Imagine the pain of Jesus' ordeal.

▪ *resolution* ▪

Pray the Stations of the Cross using the meditations you have developed on each of the next four Fridays.

chapter 3

The Holy Spirit

When the Paraclete comes,
whom I shall send to you from the Father,
the Spirit of truth who issues from the Father,
he will be my witness.

—John 15:26

In This Chapter

You will study:

■ the Holy Spirit traced through scriptures and the life of Jesus

■ the Holy Spirit as Lord and giver of life

■ the Holy Spirit who proceeds from the Father and the Son

■ the Holy Spirit who has spoken through the prophets

Five-year-old Miguel Garcia's father had cancer. The chemotherapy treatment caused the father to grow weak and to lose his hair. The sickness also left him feeling alone and depressed. This was natural enough.

However, Miguel did not understand what was happening to his father. He only knew that his father was sad and that he wanted to do something to help him.

One evening, Miguel called his dad to come to his bedroom. He had taken some scissors and cut off all his hair. He told his father, "I did it because I love you." (The story is from *Three Minutes a Day*, vol. 28, by Fr. John Catoir.)

This sharing of love between a son and a father represents in a dramatic way the meaning of the Holy Spirit, the third person of the Blessed Trinity. The Holy Spirit is the love connection between God the Father and God the Son. This love is a gift shared; it is the love of the Holy Spirit that creates and sustains the Christian community.

This chapter examines the Christian belief in the Holy Spirit. It will help you to understand what Catholics mean when they say,

> "We believe in the Holy Spirit, the Lord, the giver of life, who proceeds from the Father and the Son. With the Father and the Son he is worshipped and glorified. He has spoken through the prophets."

This chapter will help you to see how the Holy Spirit is active and present in your life.

Your Gifts

Miguel shared his greatest gift—love—with his father. In the sacrament of confirmation, the bishop prays that the Holy Spirit will share special gifts with those who are to be confirmed. He lays his hands over the candidate and says these words:

All powerful God, Father of our Lord Jesus Christ,
by water and the Holy Spirit
you freed your sons and daughters from sin
and gave them new life.
Send your Holy Spirit upon them
to be their Helper and Guide.
Give them the spirit of *wisdom* and *understanding*,
the spirit of *right judgment* and *courage*,
the spirit of *knowledge* and *reverence*.
Fill them with the spirit of *wonder and awe* in your
    presence.
We ask this through Christ our Lord.
Amen.

Below is a short description of some values each of the seven traditional gifts represent for Christians. Think about each gift. Then, use the scale to explain how often you feel these gifts are present in your life.

1—There is much evidence of this gift in my life.
2—There is some evidence of this gift in my life.
3—There is little evidence of this gift in my life.

_____ 1. **Wisdom**:   Looking on reality from God's point of view. Praying before deciding. Seeking guidance from those more experienced than I am.

_____ 2. **Understanding**:   Taking time to reflect on the deeper meaning of my faith. Working to my ability in academic pursuits as I try to understand the mysteries of God's magnificent creation. Seeking to understand why I act the way I do.

_____ 3. **Right Judgment**:   Forming my conscience in light of church teaching. Consulting knowledgeable people before making a decision on moral issues. Praying for the Spirit's help in judging right from wrong.

_____ 4. **Courage**:   Strength to follow my own convictions. Being my own person in the face of peer pressure. Being willing to suffer for my beliefs in Jesus.

_____ 5. **Knowledge:**   Taking note of how God is working in my life and in the world. Learning about the great moral and political issues of the day. Developing a lively curiosity that sees life as a banquet for me to enjoy.

_____ 6. **Reverence:**   Respecting the Lord through praise and worship. Respecting the dignity and worth of others. Appreciating the beautiful creation God gave me. Cherishing those whom society looks down on.

_____ 7. **Wonder and Awe:**   Being concerned about the reality of sin in my life. Avoiding anything that might alienate me from God and others. Loving God above everything and my neighbor as myself. Developing a personal relationship with God.

▪ *discuss* ▪

When was a time you shared one of the gifts of the Holy Spirit with someone else? Explain the actions that went along with your sharing.

▪ *journal* ▪

Select three of your most significant talents. Write a short reflection explaining how you are using and developing these through daily, mid-range, and long-range plans.

We Believe in the Holy Spirit

When Jesus addressed God as "Abba" he did much to reveal who God is. The God of the Hebrew scriptures, the Creator God known as Yahweh is Jesus' loving Abba-Father. Jesus says that God is also "our Father" and should be addressed that way in prayer by all people.

Jesus reveals that God is Father, but he also reveals that he and the Father are one. Jesus himself is God.

> Anyone who has seen me has seen the Father,
> so how can you say, "Show me the Father?" . . .
> You must believe me when I say
> that I am in the Father and the Father is in me
>   (Jn 14:9, 11).

If Jesus is God, then everything about him revealed the Father. Jesus' presence, his words of forgiveness, his healing touches, his death and resurrection show the real nature of God. The gospel of John explains that Jesus is the Word of God that became flesh:

> For this is how God loved the world:
> he gave his only Son,
> so that everyone who believes in him may not perish
> but may have eternal life (Jn 3:16).

Jesus also reveals there is a third person in the one true God: the Holy Spirit. The Holy Spirit is often the person of the Trinity that is neglected. You may have clear images for God the Father and God the Son, but how do you imagine God the Holy Spirit? Most people share a preference for addressing God in prayer as Father or Son. How often do you pray to the Holy Spirit? In fact, the Holy Spirit is God just as Father and Son are God. Jesus' very life reveals the Holy Spirit. When Jesus came as the incarnation of the invisible Father, it was the Holy Spirit who revealed him.

The Holy Spirit is the very presence of the risen, glorified Lord, the Spirit of love who *always* existed with the Father and Son. The Holy Spirit has been present in the world since the beginning. The life and actions of the Spirit are described in the scriptures and defined in the teachings of the church.

The Holy Spirit in the Hebrew scriptures.   The concept of the Holy Spirit develops gradually in the Hebrew scriptures. In the creation stories, the biblical authors use the Hebrew word *ruah* (wind or breath) to speak of God's mysterious, powerful, and life-giving presence. In the later writings, the notion of Yahweh's spirit is described in more personal terms as one who guides and instructs people.

Primarily, however, the Old Testament view of the Spirit is that of a divine power and presence. It lacks a clear idea of the Spirit as a separate person. It is only through Jesus' revelation—included in the New Testament—that the Spirit can be understood as a distinct person of the Blessed Trinity.

However, examining the Hebrew scriptures from a Christian perspective can provide valuable insights into the Spirit's activity. For example, the Spirit:

- is at work in creation (see Gn 1:1–2),
- gives the breath of life to Adam and Eve (see Gn 2:7),
- inspires and gives strength to judges and kings (see Jgs 6 and 1 Sm 16:13–14),
- anoints Israel's prophets (see 2 Kgs 2:9 and 2 Kgs 2:15).

The Chosen People often turned away from Yahweh and the covenant. Their history was filled with many struggles. At times they came under the rule of various foreign powers like the Assyrians, Babylonians, Persians, and Greeks. When they repented of their sins, the prophets promised the coming of a new king, a servant—the Messiah. On this person God's Spirit would rest in a special way. According to the prophet known as Second Isaiah:

> Here is my servant whom I uphold,
> my chosen one in whom my soul delights.
> I have sent my spirit upon him,
> he will bring fair judgment to the nations.
> He does not cry out or raise his voice,
> his voice is not heard in the street;
> he does not break the crushed reed
> or snuff the faltering wick.
> Faithfully he presents fair judgment;
> he will not grow faint, he will not be crushed
> until he has established fair judgment on earth
>   (Is 42:1–4).

Christians recognize this promised one to be Jesus.

The Holy Spirit in the life of Jesus. The gospels tell how the Holy Spirit is present in Jesus' entire life on earth from beginning to end. For example, the Holy Spirit's power enables Mary to conceive and give birth to Jesus (see Mt 1:18–20). The Holy Spirit descends on Jesus at his baptism (see Lk 3:22) and then leads him into the desert for prayer and fasting (see Lk 4:2). Jesus returns from the desert to Nazareth to begin his preaching in the Spirit's power (see Lk 4:14). Once there, Jesus' ministry begins. He testifies that the Spirit is upon him, anointing him to preach good news to the afflicted, proclaim liberty to the captives, give sight to the blind, and let the oppressed go free (see Lk 4:16–21).

■ *journal* ■

Read the following passages from the Hebrew scriptures. In your journal, summarize briefly the main point about God's Spirit described in each passage.
a. Genesis 1:1–2; 2:7
b. Isaiah 11:1–3
c. Isaiah 61:1–2
d. Ezekiel 36:26–28
e. Ezekiel 37:1–14
f. Joel 3:1–3

In his public ministry, Jesus reveals more of the mystery of the Holy Spirit. He speaks of the necessity of a new birth in the Spirit, of the Spirit who reveals truth (see Jn 4:23–24), of the Spirit who gives the gift of eternal life (see Jn 6:62–63).

The Spirit remains with Jesus to the hour of his death. When a soldier stabs him with a spear, blood and water gush out of Jesus' wound, symbolizing the life and waters of the Holy Spirit flowing out to the world (see Jn 19:34). Through the Spirit, God raises Jesus from the dead. When Jesus meets his disciples after the resurrection, he breaths on them and says, "Receive the Holy Spirit. If you forgive anyone's sins, they are forgiven; if you retain anyone's sins, they are retained" (Jn 20:22). Just as the breath of the Spirit had brought life to the first man and woman, it now brings the disciples new life in Jesus.

The Holy Spirit at Pentecost.   In his last days with the apostles, Jesus promised that the new age of the Holy Spirit would soon be coming:

> "I shall ask the Father,
> and he will give you another Paraclete
> to be with you forever,
> the Spirit of truth
> whom the world can never accept
> since it neither sees nor knows him;
> but you know him,
> because he is with you, he is in you.
> I shall not leave you orphans . . .
> the Paraclete, the Holy Spirit,
> whom the Father will send in my name,
> will teach you everything
> and remind you of all I have said to you"
>   (Jn 14:16–17, 26).

Christians believe that this age began on the feast of Pentecost. *Pentecost* means "fiftieth day." It was a Jewish harvest feast fifty days after Passover. Jews from all over the Roman empire came to celebrate in Jerusalem. At the time, some of the disciples, including Jesus' mother Mary, were in the Upper Room, the site of the Last Supper. Perhaps they were still frightened and confused over the meaning of Jesus' death and resurrection. The Acts of the Apostles describes the event:

When suddenly there came from heaven a sound as of a violent wind which filled the entire house in which they were sitting; and there appeared to them tongues as of fire; these separated and came to rest on the head of each of them. They were all filled with the Holy Spirit and began to speak different languages as the Spirit gave them power to express themselves (Acts 2:2–4).

The Jews from different places who spoke various languages nevertheless understood the apostles. About three thousand people were baptized that day. The Pentecost event was the fulfillment of the prophecy of Joel:

> "In the last days—the Lord declares—
> I shall pour out my Spirit on all humanity.
> Your sons and daughters shall prophesy,
> your young people shall see visions,
> your old people shall dream dreams. . . .
> And all who call on the name of the Lord
>   will be saved" (Acts 2:17, 21).

Through the coming of the Spirit, God completes all the covenants made with humanity. The Holy Spirit is a Spirit of love who unites the disciples into a community, or church. Jesus calls the Holy Spirit a *Paraclete*, a legal term meaning advocate or counselor. The Holy Spirit inaugurates a new age, the age of the church, uniting Jesus' followers into a family of love.

Images of the Holy Spirit

The Hebrew term *ruah* denotes breath, air, wind, or soul. It is used 379 times in the Old Testament to image the following activities of God:

- *Wind* (Ps 18:11). Wind connotes power and mystery. Thus, it is an apt image for God's Spirit. For example, wind (God's spirit) is present at creation. God also uses the wind as a messenger.

- *Breath* (Ez 37). Breath is the principle of life; its absence means death. People need God to live; it is God's breath that gives life.

Some other scriptural images of the Holy Spirit include:

- *Fire.*   God appeared to Moses in a burning bush and led the Israelites through the desert by pillars of fire. Fire purifies to make one holy. It punishes the wicked, as in Sodom (see Gn 19:23–25). In brief, fire represents the transforming energy of the Holy Spirit.

- *Oil.*   The New Testament associates the anointing of one with oil to being anointed with the Holy Spirit. Baptism and confirmation both use oil to represent the coming of the Holy Spirit.

- *Tongues of fire.*   The tongue empowers people to speak. Filled with the Spirit, Jesus spoke his Father's truth. He had the power to forgive sin, to cure, to control nature, and to bring the dead back to life.

   The Spirit which Jesus gives to his disciples enables them to reverse the prideful confusion of language that occurred at Babel (see Gn 11:1–9). The Spirit empowers followers of Jesus to proclaim Christ, to speak the truth, and to create community in the Lord's name.

- *Water.*   The rich symbol of water represents both death and life. For example, God punished humanity in the time of Noah by sending a flood (see Gn 7:4–10). But God also sustained the Hebrews in the desert by providing them with springs of fresh drinking water (see Ex 17:1–6).

   Jesus clearly associated water and the Spirit when he said to Nicodemus:

> "No one can enter the kingdom of God
> without being born through water
> and the Spirit" (Jn 3:5).

These words are reflected in the sacrament of baptism. The waters of baptism initiate people into Christ's body, the church, and bestow on them the gift of the Holy Spirit.

- *Dove.*   In the Hebrew scriptures, a dove released by Noah returned with an olive tree branch to show that the flood waters were receding. A dove is also frequently mentioned as a purification offering for the poor (see Lv 5:7). In fact, Mary and Joseph offered "two turtledoves" at the time of Jesus' presentation in the Temple.

▪ *journal* ▪

Read the following scripture passages. In your journal, note the passages. Highlight which symbol of God's Spirit or presence is depicted.

Ps 42:1–2 _____

Ex 19:18 _____

Lk 7:36–38 _____

Also, the gospels describe the Spirit's descent on Jesus at the time of his baptism as being "like a dove." The descending dove may suggest God's Spirit hovering over the waters at creation. The dove is also a symbol of gentleness, virtue, and peace—all gifts of union with the Holy Spirit.

▪ *discuss* ▪

What are some contemporary images that would capture the Holy Spirit's presence in the world today?

We Believe the Holy Spirit Is the Lord and Giver of Life

While the Council of Nicea (325) clearly taught the divinity of Jesus to counteract the Arian heresy, the Council of Constantinople (381) strongly affirmed the divinity of the third person of the Blessed Trinity—the Holy Spirit. It said that the Holy Spirit is **not** a creature like an angel who serves as God's messenger. Nor is the Holy Spirit some impersonal force. Rather, the Holy Spirit is *Lord*, God, whose important role is to give humanity a share in God's own divine life. The Holy Spirit does this by conforming people to Christ, by making people Christ-like. Thus, drawn to the Son, Christians have access to the Father as the church teaching clearly states: "To the Father through the Son in the Holy Spirit."

The Holy Spirit as Lord.   The New Testament gives many examples of how the Holy Spirit acts as Lord by drawing people to the life and teachings of Jesus. For example:

1. **The Spirit teaches.**   Jesus promised his apostles that the Spirit would teach them "everything and remind you of all I have said to you" (Jn 14:26). The Holy Spirit is the internal teacher, the one who makes it possible to recognize the truth about Jesus:

   "Nobody is able to say, 'Jesus is Lord' except in the Holy Spirit" (1 Cor 12:3).

   Thus, the Spirit provides the knowledge needed to have faith in the Lord. The Spirit continually enlightens the

minds and hearts of Christians to help them to live the Truth who is Jesus Christ.

2. **The Spirit directs.**   A good alternative name for the Acts of the Apostles is the "Gospel of the Holy Spirit." Acts tells the remarkable story of the spread of early Christianity under the inspiration and guidance of the Holy Spirit. For example, the Spirit guided Philip to preach to the Ethiopian eunuch (see Acts 8:27–35). And the Spirit was present at the Council of Jerusalem, guiding church leaders like Peter to accept Gentiles into the Christian community without their first having to submit to all the burdensome regulations of the Mosaic law (see Acts 15:28). The Spirit was inspirational to St. Paul, leading him on his missionary travels (see Acts 13:4).

Today, the Holy Spirit enlightens the intellects and inclines the affections of all Christians to act morally. In addition, the Spirit also directs and enlightens church leaders (especially the bishops and pope) to teach the church in a spirit of truth, compassion, and wisdom, especially in proclaiming God's commandments and Christ's charity (*The Splendor of Truth*, #25, 45, and 109.)

3. **The Spirit strengthens.**   As "school spirit" may empower a team, group, or club to give its all, so too the Holy Spirit emboldens Christians to live Christ's life. At Pentecost, the Holy Spirit transformed the frightened disciples into courageous witnesses of Christ. The Spirit also gave many saints like Stephen the "grace and power" (Acts 6:8) to work among the people and preach the good news of Jesus Christ. The Holy Spirit continues to inspire Christians to do as Christ did and provides the spiritual gifts to help them do so.

The Holy Spirit is giver of life.   The Spirit teaches, directs, and strengthens by providing countless gifts to all people. The Holy Spirit not only is a giver of gifts, but also the best gift of all. The Holy Spirit is God's gift of everlasting, divine life.

To state this another way: the Holy Spirit is the gift of God's *grace* to us. Grace is a traditional term meaning good will, benevolence, or a gift given. At baptism, the Spirit comes to Christians. The grace of the Holy Spirit *justifies* the baptized, that is, cleanses them of their sins and communicates to them God's righteousness through faith in Jesus. The Spirit initiates in the person the lifelong conversion and healing process that leads to eternal life, and elevates him or her to share in God's own life.

The most incredible effect of the Spirit's gift of life is, in fact, adoption into God's own family. By virtue of God's unmerited friendship and love, the Spirit changes a person's identity from that of slave and mere creature to that of son or daughter of a gracious, loving Father. The Spirit enables people to call God, "Abba." St. Paul wrote:

> "You received the spirit of adoption, enabling us to cry out, '*Abba*, Father!' The Spirit himself joins with our spirit to bear witness that we are children of God. And if we are children, then we are heirs, heirs of God and joint-heirs with Christ, provided that we share his suffering, so as to share his glory" (Rom 8:15–17).

The Holy Spirit and the Lord Jesus continue their divine mission in the church. The Holy Spirit builds, gives life to, and sanctifies the church. Through the church, the Spirit draws people to Christ, reveals the Lord to them, and makes present to them the Paschal Mystery of Christ, especially in the sacrament of the eucharist.

No description of the Spirit's gift of life would be complete without mention of the gift of love. Love is God's gift to the world through Jesus. Love is the central gift— bestowed freely and independently of personal talents or merits. A popular saying goes, "God does not love us because we are good. We are good because God loves us." Christians believe that when you allow the Spirit to reign in your heart, then love and all its many rich facets will shine forth in your life.

What Is Grace?

Grace is a term that has been ascribed many meanings. Among the types of grace are:

■ **Sanctifying grace.**   Traditionally, the church has spoken of sanctifying grace as the *gift of divine life* in those who have been made holy by rebirth in baptism and union with the Holy Spirit. A person's righteousness before God comes from God's grace. Sanctifying grace results from the gift of the Holy Spirit's presence in a person. Sanctifying grace introduces people to the intimacy of the Blessed Trinity. It affects their entire being. It enables them to become the "image and likeness" of God.

Only mortal sin, a radical rejection of God, can drive out God's life (sanctifying grace) in someone who has been gifted. But even then, through repentance and recourse to the sacrament of reconciliation (penance), a person can regain God's favor and allow the Holy Spirit to once again live in his or her life.

■ **Actual grace.**   Another benefit of sanctifying grace is the divine help it provides a person to live the Christian life through his or her daily actions. Actual grace is *God's help to do good and avoid evil* in the concrete circumstances of everyday life. The Holy Spirit calls all people to greatness—to live heroic, Christ-like lives as brothers and sisters of the Lord and children of a loving God. But the Spirit will never require anything of a person that is not possible to achieve with divine help. Actual grace is the divine assistance given to a person *to act* as a child of God, filled with faith, hope, and charity.

■ **Other graces.**   *Sacramental graces* are gifts specific to each of the sacraments. *Charisms* are special gifts—like virtues—which the Spirit gives to certain members of Christ's body for the common good in serving and building up the church.

Cardinal Virtues

A *virtue* is a general merit or good quality. Theologically, a virtue is a God-given power that enables you to live a

Christian life. *Cardinal virtues* are life's basic virtues. Traditionally, the cardinal virtues are prudence, justice, temperance, and fortitude. These virtues are among the helps the Holy Spirit gives to assist people in living a holy life.

Read the descriptions of each virtue. Rate yourself on how well and how often you are living out these virtues in various situations.

> 4—describes me well
> 3—describes me most of the time
> 2—describes me some of the time
> 1—does not describe me

Prudence is spiritual common sense. It is the ability to make a correct moral choice and decide the means to achieve it through proper behavior.

_____ I weigh the pros and cons of decisions before acting.

_____ I assess how my actions will affect others *before* acting.

_____ I consult people I respect before making decisions.

Justice is the quality of being faithful; of giving God and other people their due.

_____ I do not cheat.

_____ I treat others fairly; I give people the benefit of the doubt.

_____ I give an "honest day's work for an honest day's pay."

Temperance means self-restraint, the moderation of one's appetites for pleasure and the control of one's instincts and desires.

_____ I abstain from harmful substances like drugs, alcohol, and tobacco.

_____ I am modest in my language, dress, and behavior.

_____ I avoid inappropriate sexual behavior.

_____ I eat healthy food and get proper amounts of exercise and rest.

Fortitude is the courage to live the Christian life, especially when it is difficult to do so.

_____ I am willing to do what is right even if it is not popular with others.

_____ I stick to a task, even when it is boring or difficult.

_____ I speak out to defend those people unable to defend themselves.

▪ *journal* ▪

A potential employer has asked you for a succinct paragraph describing your best attributes. Write that paragraph in your journal.

▪ *activity* ▪

In Galatians 5:22–23, St. Paul lists nine "fruits of the Spirit." The fruits are the visible results of the Spirit living in individual lives. The fruits are *love, joy, peace, patience, kindness, goodness, faithfulness, gentleness,* and *self-control.* In contrast to the fruits are vices—moral deformities or bad habits—that distort God's image and result in evil actions.

Here is a list of spiritual fruits and moral vices with a scriptural passage to describe each:

Spiritual fruit	*Moral vices*
love (Jn 13:35)	sexual promiscuity (1 Cor 6:18)
joy (Jn 3:29)	idolatry (1 Cor 8:6)
patience (perseverance/ long suffering) (Eph 6:18)	sorcery/witchcraft (Rv 22:15)
kindness (Acts 28:2)	hatred (1 Jn 2:9)
goodness (Mt 12:35)	jealousy (1 Cor 3:3)
faithfulness (3 Jn 5)	selfishness (Phil 2:3)
gentleness (Mt 11:30)	heresy/factions (Ti 3:9)
self-control (1 Cor 9:25)	drunkenness (Rm 13:13)

Do one of the following:

- ▪ Read and copy into your journal at least five biblical verses from each category.
- ▪ Make a collage of virtues and vices. From the newspaper, cut out articles or photos that depict at least three virtues and three vices. In a light-colored marker, print the name of the virtue or vice on the article. Then, arrange and glue the articles to a piece of poster board.

▪ *discuss* ▪

1. The media is often accused of focussing more on negative news than positive news. Do you think this is true? Why or why not?

2. What are some types of news stories you think the media should focus on? Why?

We Believe the Holy Spirit Proceeds from the Father and the Son

The article of faith "he proceeds from the Father and the Son" is an important one for many reasons. For one, it led to a division in Eastern and Western Christianity in 1054. The Roman church had added the expression "and the Son" (*filioque* in Greek) to the Nicene Creed without seeking approval for such a change at an ecumenical council. Though there were other issues involved, this *filioque* controversy resulted in the Eastern *schism*, or split, that still continues today.

This Nicene Creed article is also important because it attests to the doctrine of the Blessed Trinity and underscores the relationship among the three persons of the Trinity. The doctrine of the Trinity is central to Christian faith. It, like other articles in the Creed, is *dogma*, or core teaching of the church. The doctrine of the Trinity is a strict mystery that human reason cannot grasp on its own. That people have any knowledge of the Trinity is only because God in the persons of the Son and the Holy Spirit have revealed it to them.

The Trinity in the New Testament

The clearest gospel reference to the Trinity occurs at Jesus' baptism. The Holy Spirit descended upon Jesus in the form of a dove. A voice from heaven said, "You are my Son, the Beloved; my favor rests on you" (Mk 1:11). Thus, all three divine persons are present at Jesus' baptism: God the Father (heavenly voice), God the Son (Jesus), God the Holy Spirit (the dovelike form). The closing words of Matthew's gospel strongly attest to the Blessed Trinity. Before ascending to

heaven, Jesus said: "Go, therefore, make disciples of all nations; baptize them in the name of the Father and of the Son and of the Holy Spirit" (Mt 28:19).

Belief in the Trinity finds its roots in the first Christians' experience of Jesus. His life, death, and resurrection revealed to them one God who exists in a relationship of three persons: Father, Son, and Holy Spirit. St. Paul expressed this early belief when he ended a letter to the Corinthians with the following blessing:

> The grace of the Lord Jesus Christ, the love of God and the fellowship of the Holy Spirit be with you all (2 Cor 13:13).

Salvific Trinity.   When the church reflects on God as it experiences God in Jesus, it is reflecting on the *Salvific Trinity,* God-for-us, as Creator, Redeemer, and Sanctifier. The one God is experienced as three distinct persons, each relating to people in a special way. God the Father creates everything and continues to give life and being to everything in creation. God the Son is Jesus, the one who lived on earth, taught of the Father's love, and won eternal salvation for humankind by dying on the cross. God the Holy Spirit is the Love of God that was promised by Jesus to always remain with the church. The Spirit is the source of unity, courage, truth and love for all humanity. The Salvific Trinity is one way for humans to put into words a mystery that can never be fully comprehended.

Immanent Trinity.   Whereas Salvific Trinity reflects a human understanding of God, Immanent Trinity refers to God as God is in himself. God is three distinct persons: Father, Son, and Holy Spirit but the term *person* cannot be thought of in the usual way. "Person" in the Trinity refers to distinctions between the members. Thus, there are not three separate consciousnesses, intelligences, or wills in God. *There is only one simple divine being.* When one person of the Trinity acts, the other two persons also act. Each person is *distinct* but does not act separately from the others. God is one, a community-in-unity.

God acts as one, though people *appropriate* certain actions to each of the persons. For example, the church has traditionally attributed creation to the Father, redemption to the Son, and sanctification to the Holy Spirit. These are the *missions* of each of the three divine persons. But even in these actions all three persons are fully present to one another and act as one. For example, in creation, each person performs the common work according to unique personal properties or traits. Thus, the church taught at the Second Council of Constantinople, "for one is the God and Father *from* whom all things are, and one is the Lord Jesus Christ, *through* whom all things are, and one is the Holy Spirit *in* whom all things are." God loves people with the same love and knows them with the same knowledge.

Relationships among the Persons of the Trinity. The differences in the three Persons of the Trinity are in their *relationships*. Traditional Catholic teaching explains the relationships this way:

> **The Father.** The first person of the Trinity is absolutely without origin. From all eternity he "begets" the Son, the second person of the Trinity. The Son proceeds from the Father. There was never a time when the Son did not proceed from the Father.
>
> **The Son.** You can think of the Father's begetting the Son as God knowing himself perfectly. The Father expresses himself perfectly to himself, and this is the Son, the Word of God. Thus, the Son is the Father's perfect, divine expression of himself. They are one, yet distinct.
>
> **The Holy Spirit.** The relationship of the Father and Son is a perfect relationship. The Father and Son love each other with an eternal, perfect, divine love. This love *proceeds* from the Father and the Son and is the third person of the Trinity, the Holy Spirit. The Holy Spirit proceeds from **both** the Father and the Son as the perfect expression of their divine love for each other. Thus, the Holy Spirit is the Spirit of Love between the Father and the Son; the Spirit binds them into a community of unity.

In a classic expression of faith, the Athanasian Creed

expresses the relationships of the three persons of the Trinity this way:

> The Father is not made by anyone, nor created, nor begotten. The Son is from the Father alone, not made, not created, but begotten. The Holy Spirit is from the Father and the Son, not made, not created, not begotten, but proceeding. . . . The entire three Persons are co-eternal with one another and co-equal, so that . . . both Trinity in Unity and Unity in Trinity are to be adored.

Trinitarian Imagery

The doctrine of the Trinity is an absolute mystery. We need God's divine revelation to know that the *one* God is a relationship of three divine persons—Father, Son, and Holy Spirit. To help communicate this mystery of the Trinity, St. Patrick used the famous image of a shamrock—one leaf consisting of three petals. St. John Damascus used the following two analogies:

> "Think of the Father as a root, of the Son as a branch, and of the Spirit as a fruit, for the substance of these is one. Or, the Father is a sun with the Son as rays and the Holy Spirit as heat."

A modern analogy uses the image of a woman. Though one person, she has simultaneous, though different, relationships to others. For example, this one person is a mother, a wife, and a daughter. Still another way to think of Trinity is that the Father is the source of life, the Son is the expression of God's wisdom, and the Holy Spirit is the bond of love in God and for all people.

Christian art has used many images to try to express the mystery of the Triune God. For example, the equilateral triangle symbolizes the equality in nature of the three divine persons. The sides unite to form one figure, suggesting the one and inseparable essence of God.

The equilateral triangle with the Chi-Rho (first two letters of "Christ" in Greek) suggests that the Lord Jesus has led us to a true knowledge of God. He is the beginning and ending of our existence: Alpha is the first letter in the Greek alphabet, Omega is the last letter (see Rv 22:13).

Here is another Trinitarian symbol. In the space provided below, write a possible interpretation of it.

_____

_____

_____

_____

_____

The Holy Spirit
Has Spoken Through the Prophets

Today, God's Spirit speaks to individual people in many ways—through the beauty of nature, through the words of friends and acquaintances, and through the triumphs and tragedies of their personal life. The Holy Spirit also teaches each generation through the "signs of the times." Advances in science and new cooperation among nations are examples of signs that can help to advance justice and build God's reign. The Holy Spirit is especially active through the church: in the inspired scriptures, in Tradition, in the teachings of church leaders, and in the words and symbols of the sacraments. The Holy Spirit also intercedes for the church through prayer, guides its missionary activity, and reveals the life of God through the witness of all people who cooperate with God's plan of salvation.

The prophetic voice. The Holy Spirit has always been at work in human history. In a special way, the Spirit "spoke" to the Chosen People. These lessons are recorded in the Hebrew scriptures. Prophets like Moses, Isaiah, Jeremiah, and Ezekiel tried to call the kings and people back to fidelity to God's covenant. But too often the leaders put their faith in power, money, and armies. The people worshipped false gods, ignored the Law, and scorned the weak and the poor.

The Spirit spoke to the hard-hearted Israelites by promising them a new and final covenant with God (see Jer 31:31, Ez 36:26–27). Jesus, of course, was the prophet *par excellence* who initiated this final age. He spoke perfectly for God because he and God are one. Jesus said:

> "Do you not believe
> that I am in the Father and the Father in me?
> What I say to you I do not speak of my own accord;
> it is the Father, living in me, who is doing his works"
> (Jn 14:10).

The Spirit speaks today to the spiritual descendants of the Jews, the Christian community. The letter to Hebrews affirms:

> At many moments in the past and by many means,
> God spoke to our ancestors through the prophets; but
> in our time, the final days, he has spoken to us in the
> person of his Son (Heb 1:1–2).

The Holy Spirit invites you to a deeper relationship with God through knowing Jesus and by putting his words into action.

Conclusion

A truth of the Christian faith is that God is alive in you! When you allow the Spirit to come into your life through sanctifying grace, you become an important presence of God in the world for others. You help to bring about the reign of God and become instruments of God for other people. Life in the Holy Spirit **is** about sharing God's love. Recall the story of Miguel's gift to his father.

The ways people choose to share God's love are as unique as people are themselves. For a minute, think about the nicest thing you have ever done for someone else. Something that no one else is aware of. Why did you do it? What did you learn? How did the experience make you feel?

There are many ways the Holy Spirit's presence can be witnessed daily in your life; God's Spirit is with you in your joy, sorrow, anxiety, and contentment. Through prayer, you can remain in touch with the movements of the Spirit and find new ways to share the Spirit of God with others.

■ *focus questions* ■

1. List and briefly describe the seven gifts of the Holy Spirit.

2. Why do you think the Holy Spirit has been the neglected person of the Holy Trinity?

3. Identify *ruah*. Discuss two other images of the Holy Spirit found in Hebrew scriptures.

4. Give two examples of how the Holy Spirit was present in Jesus' life on earth.

5. What is the meaning of the term *Paraclete*? What was Jesus' promise concerning the Paraclete?

6. What was the meaning of the wind and fiery tongues at Pentecost?

7. How is the Holy Spirit different from an angel?

8. Distinguish between the meaning of *sanctifying grace* and *actual grace*.

9. In what sense can the term *grace* apply to the Holy Spirit?

10. Define the term *virtue*.

11. List and define the four cardinal virtues.

12. What is God's greatest gift to us? Why?

13. List the fruits of the Holy Spirit.

14. Define *filioque*. What is the significance of this term in church history?

15. Cite one scriptural basis for the doctrine of the Trinity.

16. What is the difference between *Salvific Trinity* and *Immanent Trinity*?

17. What are the missions of the three persons of the Trinity?

18. Discuss several ways the Holy Spirit speaks to people today.

19. What is one way you can share God's love with another?

▪ *exercises* ▪

1. Prepare a witness talk on the role of the Holy Spirit in your life. Arrange to give your talk to a youth group or confirmation preparation class.
2. Develop your own symbol for the Blessed Trinity. Use any form of art medium to communicate it to others.

Prayer Reflection

The following advice was written on the back of a prayer-card. It was composed by the archbishop of Malines, Belgium, Cardinal Désiré Mercier. Its title is "A Secret of Sanctity." Read his words. What do you think of his advice?

I am going to reveal to you a secret of sanctity and happiness. If every day during five minutes, you will keep your imagination quiet, shut your eyes to all the things of sense, and close your ears to all the sounds of earth, so as to be able to withdraw into the sanctuary of your baptized soul, which is the temple of the Holy Spirit, speaking there to the Holy Spirit saying:

O Holy Spirit, soul of my soul, I adore You. Enlighten, guide, strengthen and console me. Tell me what I ought to do and command me to do it. I promise to be submissive in everything that You permit to happen to me, only show me what is Your will.

If you do this, your life will pass happily and serenely. Consolation will abound even in the midst of troubles. Grace will be given in proportion to the trial as well as strength to bear it, bringing you to the gates of Paradise full of merit.

This submission to the Holy Spirit is the secret of sanctity.

▪ *reflection* ▪

Write about one time the Holy Spirit has clearly guided your life in a particular direction.

▪ *resolution* ▪

Pray Cardinal Mercier's prayer daily for the next two weeks.

▪ *vocabulary* ▪

Look up the meaning of the following words in the dictionary. Transcribe the definitions into your journal.

charism   sanctification
dogma   vice

chapter 4

The Church: Christ's Body

"You are salt for the earth. You are light for the world. . . . [Y]our light must shine in people's sight, so that, seeing your good works, they may give praise to your Father in heaven."

—Matthew 5:13–14,16

Have you ever had to explain to someone why you believe in God? Or, something that may be even more difficult, why you go to church? The conversation might go something like this:

You: I go to church on Sunday because I want to worship and honor God.

Them: I'm a believer too! But I don't have to prove it by hanging around a church.

You: But God wishes us to reserve a day . . .

Them: Hey, I spend Sunday morning at the lake admiring nature. Or I read my Bible at home.

You: Jesus gathered friends to be his followers. We, the church, are an extension of that first group.

Them: The people that go to church are a bunch of hypocrites . . .

You: You mean a bunch of sinners. Forgiven sinners!

The bottom line question to any conversation like the one above is, "Can I be a Christian without joining the church?"

Theoretically, it may be possible. But it would be like being:

■ a football quarterback without a team.

■ a dancer without music.

■ an author without readers.

■ a golfer without clubs.

■ a soldier without an army.

■ a lawyer who refuses to go to court.

Jesus established the church to be a benefit to his followers and to be a way of salvation for all people. The Second Vatican Council taught:

> All are called to belong to the new People of God. . . . This People, while remaining one and unique, is to be spread throughout the whole world and must exist in all ages, so the purpose of God's will may be fulfilled (*Lumen gentium*, No. 13).

In other words, the church is not optional for Christians. Jesus intended for his followers to witness the good news of salvation to the world. Participation in a church which is unified in Christ's name, truthful to his life, open to all, and faithful to the principles established by him and his apostles is the means to accomplish Jesus' mission. Christians consent to this when they state their belief in one, holy, catholic, and apostolic church—an article of the Nicene Creed.

What Would Jesus Think?

How did Jesus imagine the church? What do you think Jesus expects of the church today? Below you will find eight brief descriptions of the church. Rank them in the order (1–8) which you think best describes what Jesus wants the church to be. For example, the number one represents for you the most effective description of the church.

The church is:

_____ 1. a human organization with carefully defined roles that deal with religious affairs.

_____ 2. a group of people who commit themselves to work wholeheartedly for justice.

_____ 3. a family that exists primarily to take care of the needs of its members.

_____ 4. a community of believers whose primary task is to proclaim the good news of Jesus.

_____ 5. a place where like-minded believers worship God through Jesus Christ.

_____ 6. Jesus Christ present in the world through those who believe in him and do his will.

_____ 7. Roman Catholics under the leadership of the pope and the bishops.

_____ 8. a community of faith committed to loving God above everything and serving fellow humans.

▪ *discuss* ▪

1. Explain why you ranked the descriptions of church as you did.
2. What is one negative description you have heard of the church? Where do you think this description originates?
3. Imagine Jesus' whispering in the ear of the pope concerning the future of the church. What did Jesus say?

journal ▪

1. Write your own description of the ideal church. Do you think the church currently meets your standard? Explain.
2. What has been your best experience of church? What has been your worst experience of church? Write examples to illustrate each of these experiences.

The Church Is a Mystery

The fathers at the Second Vatican Council used many images to describe the church. For example, they said that the church is:

- a sheepfold whose one and necessary door is Christ.
- a flock whose shepherd is Jesus.
- a tract of land which the heavenly vinedresser cultivates.
- God's building of which the apostles are the foundation.
- the heavenly Jerusalem.
- our Mother.
- the spouse of the spotless Lamb. (See No. 6 in *Lumen Gentium, Dogmatic Constitution on the Church.*)

That the council fathers needed so many ways to try to describe the church is not surprising. The church is a home to both the human and divine. Christ lives in the church through the power of the Holy Spirit. The union of the human with the divine makes the church a *mystery*.

St. Augustine defined mystery as "a visible sign of some invisible grace." Pope Paul VI explained the mystery of the church in a similar way: "The church is a reality imbued with the hidden presence of God." Therefore, to call the church a mystery is to proclaim that the invisible, almighty God continues Jesus' saving activity through the people who are members. In actuality, no one description or image can perfectly describe the deep mystery of the church.

The English word *church* itself translates from the Greek *ekklesia* which means "those called apart." God calls Christians apart to assemble as one and proclaim to others the good news of Jesus Christ. The church is a *community* called to be a *sign* and *servant* of God's kingdom which is here now but will fully blossom only when Christ comes again. Prepared for in the Old Testament when God elected Israel as the Chosen People, Jesus himself founded the church when he preached the gospel and the coming of the kingdom. The church is a sign of the future reign of God already present to us in mystery.

According to the Catechism

The Catechism of the Catholic Church describes the church in the following ways:

Everyone is called to belong to the *People of God*. Christ is the head; the Holy Spirit dwells in each member giving them dignity. People become members through baptism and the Spirit. The law of love guides God's People whose mission is to be salt of the earth and light of the world and whose destiny is the kingdom of God (No. 782).

The church is the *Body of Christ* of which Jesus is the head and the people are the members. All members of the Body should work to resemble Jesus, their head. In this Body there is unity in diversity.

The church is also the *Temple of the Holy Spirit*. St. Augustine taught as the soul is to the human body, so the Holy Spirit is to Christ's Body. The Spirit is in the head, in the collective body of the church, and in each member. The Spirit gives gifts or charisms (special graces) that enable the church's members to live Christ's life and accomplish the mission of inviting all people to embrace God's kingdom.

■

What Are Some Models of the Church?

To highlight various features of the church and its mission of service to others, theologians have identified certain *models* that help describe the church in a more systematic way. A model is a standard of excellence, something to be strived for. As you read about these "models of church" note the strengths of each and the challenges they present to Christians today. Ask yourself how your own experience of church corresponds with these models.

1. **The Church Is a Community.** A loving family enjoying a holiday meal, a sports team working hard for a common victory, neighbors coming together to help the victims of a tornado—all of these examples give a sense of unity and common purpose. They convey a feeling of what it means to be a community. A community's success is dependent on the common and shared effort of its members; yet the individual talents of each member must be noted and appreciated. The model of church as community or "mystical communion" works in a similar way.

   The image of *Body of Christ* captures this model well. The members of the church form one body with Jesus as the head. As St. Paul wrote:

   > For as with the human body which is a unity although it has many parts—all the parts of the body, though many, still making up one single body—so it is with Christ (1 Cor 12:12).

   The documents of the Second Vatican Council explain:

   > The head of this body is Christ. He is the image of the invisible God and in him all things came into being. He has priority over everyone and in him all things hold together.

■ *discuss* ■

1. How can this model benefit all people?
2. What can you do to help the church bring this model to fullness?

He has shared with us his Spirit who, existing as one and the same being in the head and in the members, vivifies, unifies, and moves the whole body. This he does in such a way that his work could be compared with the function which the soul fulfills in the human body, whose principle of life the soul is (*Lumen gentium*, No. 7).

The Spirit gives each member of the church unique talents and gifts both to build up Christ's body and to help share Christ with others.

Strengths of the community model:	**Challenges** of the community model:
■ an emphasis on the church as a living organism with a shared life, tradition, and story ■ an acknowledgement of common fellowship ■ a reliance on the power of the Holy Spirit	■ to become a lively community of faith at all levels: home, parish, diocese, and universal church ■ to cooperate with the Holy Spirit in order to allow the risen Christ to accomplish the work of salvation through the lives of church members

2. **The Church Is a Proclaiming People.** This model of church has roots in the history of the Chosen People, the Israelites. In God's covenant with Israel, God wished to sanctify and save not only individuals, but individuals formed into a loving, witnessing community. The Hebrew scriptures relate how Yahweh taught, preserved, and cherished this people. God's special care foreshadowed the formation of the new people of God formed through the blood of Jesus Christ. The new covenant or testament calls all people to become one in the Holy Spirit.

The new people of God, the church, are those who receive baptism and acknowledge that Jesus Christ is Lord and Savior. A major task of the church under this model is to be a *herald* of Christ's gospel. A herald is an official messenger. Jesus instructed his disciples to go to "all the nations" to preach the good news of salvation and baptize in the name of the Father, and of the Son, and of the Holy Spirit. He said:

"Anyone who listens to you listens to me; anyone who rejects you rejects me" (Lk 10:16).

Thus, all members of the church are expected to proclaim the good news of salvation through their words and actions.

Strengths of the Proclaiming People model:

- God's Word is highlighted in the life of the Christian community
- God's Word forms the people
- church members are entrusted with sharing God's Word with all

Challenges of the Proclaiming People model:

- to be willing to grow in personal understanding of the faith so that it can be better explained to others
- to witness Christ in both words **and** deeds and to recall that actions always speak louder than words.

▪ *discuss* ▪

1. What do the following words of Jesus have to do with being a proclaiming people? "It is not anyone who says to me, 'Lord, Lord,' who will enter the kingdom of Heaven, but the person who does the will of my Father in heaven" (Mt 7:21).

2. Are you more comfortable sharing your faith with words or actions? Explain.

3. **The Church Is a Sacrament.** By definition, a sacrament is a visible sign of an invisible grace. It is also an outward sign that both points to and brings about some deeper reality. These definitions apply perfectly to Jesus, God's prime or first sacrament. Jesus is God-made-man, the almighty Son of God who became a human being. To experience Jesus is to experience God.

The most common way to experience the risen Jesus today is through his body, the church. As Vatican II teaches, the church is the sacrament of Christ:

> By her relationship with Christ, the church is a kind of sacrament of intimate union with God, and of the unity of all mankind, that is, she is a sign and

instrument of such union and unity (*Lumen gentium*, No. 1).

The church itself is an outward sign of Jesus' presence. It contains both a divine and human aspect. Though visible, it has a spiritual dimension. Christ said that to see him is to see the Father (Jn 14:9). In a similar way, it can be said that to see the church is to see Jesus. This places tremendous responsibility on Christians to be authentic signs of Christ through their worship, fellowship, and service of all people. By actively sharing in Christ's prophetic, priestly, and kingly ministries, the church helps to bring about unity among all people and union between people and God.

In fact, the church itself **is** the basic sacrament of Christ Jesus; the seven ritual sacraments **belong** to the church. The seven sacraments are individual actions of the church through which Jesus touches people in key moments of their lives. For example, a person's birth is celebrated with baptism; and the choice of a particular vocation is celebrated with either matrimony or holy orders.

Strengths of the Sacrament model:
- the church is a visible sign of God's love for all people
- the church embodies the values of the seven sacraments; for example, in welcoming, forgiveness, and healing

Challenges of the Sacrament model:
- the community must make the invisible Lord recognizable to others
- to celebrate the sacraments and to share sacramental values through the events of daily life

▪ *discuss* ▪

1. In what way could someone recognize Jesus in your words and actions?
2. Which sacramental values are most difficult for you to live? Why do you think this is so?

4. **The Church Is an Institution.** Any community that wants to accomplish certain tasks must assign roles to its members. It must also recognize lines of authority. Every organization, therefore, must have institutional aspects

to it. Catholics believe that Jesus organized the institutional church with Peter and the apostles who were to act as shepherds, or pastors (see Mt. 16:15–19). Today the pope and bishops are church leaders. They exercise their Christ-given authority by (1) *teaching* the authentic message of the gospel, (2) *sanctifying* through the administration of the sacraments and other means of holiness, and (3) *governing* through loving service of others.

Strengths of the Institutional model:
- clear lines of church authority are defined
- the magisterium (pope and bishops) keep Christ's truth before the people, see that there is access to the sacraments, and utilize the gifts of individuals to help effectively serve those in need
- organization is provided to help run schools, hospitals, foreign missions, and the like

Challenges of the Institutional model:
- to avoid the trappings and temptations of human power
- to keep focused on Christ's mission of preparation for the next world as the church attempts to function in this world

■ *discuss* ■

1. Describe some common anti-institutional biases people have toward the church.
2. What is another institution you belong to? How is its organization similar to the church's? How is it different?

5. **The Church Is a Pilgrim.** Life on earth is filled with adventures, friendships, good experiences, and bad experiences. Most people sense, however, that this life is not the final destination. Rather, it is like a way station to a newer, greater life. The church, too, is on its way to a better life—to the fullness of God's kingdom. Vatican II teaches:

"Like a pilgrim in a foreign land, [the church] presses forward amid the persecutions of the world and the consolations of God," announcing the cross and death of the Lord until He comes (*Lumen gentium*, No. 8).

The church reminds all people of their status as exiles or wanderers in this world and of Christ's promise of eternal life in the next. The risen Christ, together with the Holy Spirit, gives the church the strength to overcome any internal or external afflictions that may plague it along the way. Like the captain of a ship at sea, Jesus helps steer the church through dangerous waters.

Strengths of the Pilgrim model:
- offers Christians the hope of eternal life
- provides courage to help Christ's followers persist in this world
- consoles its members by assuring them that Jesus and the Holy Spirit are in control of the church and its mission

Challenges of the Pilgrim model:
- to not allow the desire for life in the next world to obscure the needed duties and real joys of this world
- to avoid the danger of being insulated to the point of ignoring the need to reach out to non-Catholics

■ *discuss* ■

1. What do you consider to be your main task while living in this world?
2. When have you witnessed people who focus greatly on the next world but avoid the needs of this world?

6. **The Church Is a Servant.** A popular image of the church today is that of servant. People tend to admire leaders who live and work among them rather than functioning from an aloof position. The church attempts to follow in the footsteps of Jesus. Jesus came as one "not to be served but to serve, and to give his life as a ransom for many" (Mt 20:28). At the Last Supper, Jesus showed his apostles the meaning of leadership by washing their feet. He instructed them to do the same:

"Anyone who wants to become great among you must be your servant, and anyone who wants to be first among you must be slave to all" (Mk 10:43).

Strengths of the Servant model:
- serves as a reminder that service is necessary for Christians
- helps to define the church's mission: to heal, reconcile, feed the hungry, give drink to the thirsty, welcome the stranger, clothe the naked, comfort the sick, and visit the imprisoned

Challenges of the Servant model:
- to remember that love, not political gain or earthly standards, is the only possible motive for followers of Jesus
- to back up the words that are preached with the active love of service

■ *discuss* ■

1. Share an example of how service can lead to greatness.
2. What do you admire about someone who is a servant leader?

How Are You a Model of the Church?

The church is a mystery of Christ's love for the world. Having both a human and a divine dimension, the total richness of the church cannot be fathomed. Models of the church help you to see the presence of Christ and the Holy Spirit in the church. For example:

Body of Christ Jesus is the head of the Christian body; you are a member who helps to do his work and share his life.

Proclaiming People The Lord forms the church into a people, and the Spirit enables you, a member, to preach the gospel.

Sacrament Jesus is present as the invisible grace or gift of God's love. He uses you to be an instrument and sign of the unity he intends for everyone.

Institution The Lord promised his presence to church leaders to help them teach, govern, and sanctify in truth. You cooperate with their leadership.

Pilgrim The Spirit is the ever-present guide on your earthly journey.

Servant The Spirit of love remains in the church empowering you to love and to serve by imitating the Lord Jesus Christ.

▪ *journal* ▪

Read the following New Testament passages that list various images of the church. In your *journal*, summarize each image and write what it says about the meaning of church.

1. Ephesians 5:29–30   2. Luke 9:1–6   3. 1 Peter 2:11
4. John 10:1–10   5. 1 Corinthians 3:9

▪ *activity* ▪

Your local church community, the parish, must reflect all models of the church in its ministry. Imagine that you are a member of the financial committee of your parish council. Your parish budget includes a $50,000 surplus for special projects. Various parish groups have requested the following amounts for worthy causes.

With a small group, (1) decide how you would spend the budget, (2) discuss which model of the church most influences your budgetary decisions, and (3) summarize and share the results of your discussion with the rest of the class.

- The church roof needs repairs—$20,000.
- An inner-city parish requests help for its soup kitchen—$10,000.
- The St. Vincent de Paul Society needs money to help the unemployed of the parish—$15,000.
- The parish needs to refurbish an old, unused classroom for a religious education resource center—$25,000.
- The aged and infirm of the parish and local community need a meals-on-wheel program—$30,000 to get the program underway.
- The youth of the parish need a youth minister and program. The estimated annual cost—$25,000.
- The diocese requests each parish to support a new mission in Latin America—$10,000 annually.
- The parish needs a part-time liturgy coordinator to enhance the quality of parish liturgical celebrations—$10,000.
- The school convent, which houses two nuns, needs major repairs—$40,000.
- The evangelization commission wishes to print up and distribute a booklet for non-Catholics in the area—$5,000.

- Working mothers in the parish want to begin a day-care center—$35,000 to get started. (The program would be self-sustaining after the first year.)
- The education committee requests: $30,000 for grade-school tuition help for poor students; $20,000 to begin a scholarship fund for poor students to attend Catholic high schools.

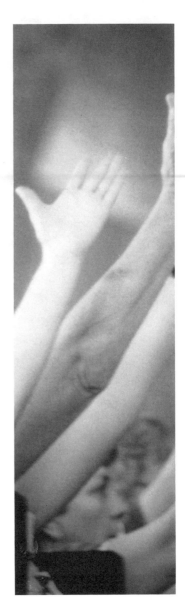

We Believe in One, Holy, Catholic, and Apostolic Church

The Nicene Creed lists the church's belief in four *marks* or *signs*. The church is one, holy, catholic, and apostolic. These marks strengthen the faith of believers as well as awaken the faith of non-believers.

Like the church itself, these four marks are paradoxical. They point to the *divine* element in the church, but the imperfect, human element remains. Paradoxically, Jesus and the Spirit are present and working through a visible community of imperfect humans.

For example, the church is *holy* because it has been sanctified by God. Yet sinners are members of the church. The church is *one* yet the various Christian churches are not united after centuries of differences. The church is *catholic* and thus open to all people, yet individual Christians display prejudice and narrow-mindedness which most often discourages non-believers. How, then, can these marks be explained?

The church is one. To say the church is one means that it is the *one* Body of Christ sustained and enlivened by the Holy Spirit who works through it. This unity expresses itself most beautifully in the Mass. Through the shared communion at eucharist Christ Jesus enables people of many different backgrounds and lifestyles to come into union with God and with each other. This unity is present within the local parish community, the area diocese, and the universal church itself.

This oneness of the church—from local to universal—reveals itself in three ways:

1. **The church has a unity in faith or creed.** Catholics profess the same creed or beliefs. The Nicene Creed, recited at Sunday Mass, is an example of a way this is done. The magisterium has Christ's authority to teach the creed and its meaning to the faithful, thus helping to preserve unity of faith.

2. **The church has one moral code.** The one moral code is based on writings and teachings like the Ten Commandments, the Beatitudes, Christ's commandment to love God and neighbor, and the teachings of the magisterium.

3. **The church has unity of worship (or cult).** For example, Catholics around the world, though speaking different languages, celebrate the same eucharist. The scripture readings heard at Mass are the same in each local parish worldwide. Likewise, the practice of the other sacraments, the divine office, and other rites and prayers are unified from place to place.

The church, though one Body, has different members. Thus, unity does not mean *uniformity*. Although Catholics believe the same truths, seek guidance from the same moral directives, and celebrate the same liturgy, there is room for variety and local custom. The Holy Spirit gives different gifts to the Body's members. The celebration of Mass in the local vernacular language is a good example of Christian unity in diversity.

Christ is the principle of unity in the church. At the Last Supper, he prayed:

> "May they all be one, just as, Father, you are in me and I am in you, so that they may also be in us, so that the world may believe it was you who sent me" (Jn 17:21).

He appointed Peter and his successors, the popes, to be the symbol and servant of unity. When threats to unity occur in the church, Catholics look to the pope for guidance and leadership.

■

Church Law

Church law includes those precepts and rules which help form the life of the Christian community. Another term for church law is *canon law*. Church laws help to promote Christian unity and build up Christ's body. Catholics are required to respectfully observe church laws. The key church laws, known as the *Precepts of the Church*, include the following:

1. *Keep holy the day of the Lord's resurrection and the holy days of obligation.* Catholics attend and participate at eucharist every Sunday and holy day of obligation. Also, Sunday is to be set aside as a day of relaxation, thanksgiving, and renewal. Unnecessary work is to be avoided on Sundays.

2. *Lead a sacramental life.* Catholics who are in the state of grace should receive the *eucharist* frequently. The minimum requirement is once a year, during the Easter season.

   Catholics should celebrate the sacrament of *reconciliation* to experience the forgiving touch of the Lord, to help conquer sinful habits, and to grow in holiness. A Catholic must go to confession whenever he or she is in the state of mortal sin.

   To become fully initiated members of the Christian community, Catholics receive the sacrament of *confirmation*. If confirmed after the age of reason, a study of the Catholic faith must be included as preparation. After confirmation, Catholics should continue their study of the faith and use their individual gifts to advance the gospel of Jesus Christ.

   Catholics should celebrate the *anointing of the sick* whenever seriously ill or before a major operation. Catholics who marry should follow the *marriage* laws of the Catholic community.

3. *Do penance and strive for holiness.* Catholics take seriously Jesus' command to "take up your cross and follow me" (Mk 8:34). In the Sermon on the Mount (Mt 5–7), Jesus taught three mutually enriching paths to holiness: prayer, fasting, and almsgiving (charity to the poor). Catholics are called to choose their own appropriate ways to carry out these commands, usually on a once-a-week basis. Friday has traditionally been a day of penance. Minimally, Catholics must observe the prescribed days of fasting and abstinence which occur during the season of Lent.

4. *Strengthen and support the church.* Service is a require- ment to bear the name *Christian*. As full members of Christ's body, Catholics must support the local church community and worldwide church by offering their tal- ents and time to serve the human family in some way.

▪ *discuss* ▪

1. Explain how each of these precepts promotes church unity.
2. If you were to add one rule to help build church unity, what would it be? Why?
3. List three ways teenagers can help support the local church.

———————— ▪ ————————

The church is holy. The church is holy not because of its members who are sinners, but because of Jesus, the leader who is "the holy one of God." However, Jesus' holiness al- lows anyone who cooperates with the Holy Spirit to become a saint, that is, to become holy as God is holy.

The word *holiness* describes God as a being of perfect love. Holy persons are those who love God above everything and their neighbor as themselves.

The way a person goes about being holy is to live as Jesus did. This means to participate in the sacraments and to live out sacramental values through daily actions. For example, baptism empowers Catholics with the gift of the Spirit. The sacrament of reconciliation offers forgiveness of sin and empowers Catholics to forgive others. And the eucharist is a preeminent way to become Christ-like: when you receive Christ you become Christ.

There are other means which assist people in becoming holy. These include reading scriptures, studying the church teachings found in the writings of the church Fathers, read- ing the lives of the saints, remaining up-to-date concerning the teachings of the magisterium of the church, living the spiritual and corporal works of mercy, and praying daily.

"Being holy" often gets a bad rap. Holy people are often associated with goody-goody types who never have any kind of fun. St. Irenaeus, a second century Father of the Church, disagreed. He said that "the glory of God is the person fully alive." Being holy means being whole. Whole people commit themselves to being the people God intends them to be.

Saint is another name for a holy person. The Apostles' Creed proclaims the church's belief in a "communion of saints," that is, a communion of the holy. The community of holy persons includes those living on earth and those who have died and are in heaven or purgatory.

You, too, are called to be a saint. Thomas Merton, a famous Cistercian monk and writer of the twentieth century, argued with his friend about the possibility that he, a sinner, could possibly become a saint. His friend told him, "All that is necessary to be a saint is to be one. . . . All you have to do is desire it" (from *The Seven Storey Mountain*).

God wants you to be what you are created to be. Holiness is a major mark or distinction of your being. Christ calls *everyone* to sanctity. This is the meaning of the Christian vocation or calling.

Thomas Merton

The church has produced many models of extraordinary holiness through its two thousand years. These saints are often recognized through the official process of *canonization* that certifies their heroic virtue and living in fidelity to God's grace. The canonized saints can intercede on your behalf and also inspire you to imitate their commitment. These Christian heroes—ordinary people like you—used the means of grace found in the church to become Christ-like. Their examples challenge the church to be true to Christ's gospel and to show that holiness can be everyone's vocation.

Works of Mercy

The spiritual and corporal works of mercy are traditional ways for Christians to grow in holiness. Propose a plan to help high school youth concretely put each of these works into practice. Discuss your plan with a classmate.

Spiritual Works of Mercy
1. Counsel the doubtful.
2. Instruct the ignorant.
3. Admonish sinners.
4. Comfort the afflicted.
5. Forgive offenses.
6. Bear wrongs patiently.
7. Pray for the living and the dead.

Corporal Works of Mercy
1. Feed the hungry.
2. Give drink to the thirsty.
3. Clothe the naked.
4. Visit the imprisoned.
5. Shelter the homeless.
6. Visit the sick.
7. Bury the dead.

■ *journal* ■

Find a quotation of a saint that speaks of the Christian call to holiness. Record it in your journal. Write a personal prayer for holiness based on this quotation.

The church is catholic.   St. Ignatius Antioch, a bishop and martyr, was the first (in A.D. 107) to use this adjective to describe the church. Catholic means "universal," or "open to all." The church *is* catholic because Christ is present in it. The church *must* be catholic because of Jesus' command to be open to all and to become the community united in him. Before ascending into heaven, Jesus instructed his apostles:

> "All authority in heaven and on earth has been given to me. Go, therefore, make disciples of all nations; baptize them in the name of the Father and of the Son and of the Holy Spirit, and teach them to observe all the commands I gave you" (Mt 28:19–20).

The church is catholic or universal in the following three ways:

1. **The church is always open to all people of any race, language, nation, ethnic group, or gender.** Poor and rich, learned and unlearned, and young and old alike are welcomed into Christ's family. Because Christ requires the church to be open to all, the church must be *missionary* (from the Latin word, "to send"). Just as Jesus was sent on a divine mission of love, so too the church is sent to love others and to help all people enter into the life of union with the Blessed Trinity.

2. **The church is universal in the sense of being *orthodox*, a word meaning "true teaching."** The church continues to teach faithfully *all* that Christ himself taught, whether it is popular or not. The same *essential* faith and worship can be found among many different types of people: those who are geographically separated, those who are culturally separated by racial and ethnic diversity, and those who are temporally separated by 2,000 years of history.

3. **Catholic also means *fullness*.** The church believes that all the baptized have access to the fullness of a faith relationship with Jesus Christ. Also, the *seven* sacraments represent the full means of achieving holiness and perfection that Christ left his church. The number seven symbolizes perfection.

To be Catholic means having a welcoming attitude toward other people. St. Paul instructed the early church to "test everything and hold on to what is good" (1 Thes 5:21). Catholics must be open to others, acknowledging and appreciating the truth and goodness in those who are different. Catholics should also share lovingly with all people the good news of Jesus that all are invited to the heavenly banquet.

The church is apostolic. The church is apostolic because it is built on the foundation of Peter and the other apostles. Everything that is essential in the church was founded by Jesus and passed on through the apostles. The church hierarchy today—especially the bishops and the pope—directly succeeds the apostles through the sacrament of holy orders. Thus, the apostles continue to teach, sanctify, and guide the church through the college of bishops and the pope.

The church is also apostolic because it professes the same doctrine and Christian lifestyle first taught by the apostles. Through the ages, Jesus has remained with the church preserving the gospel and the essential teachings. Before ascending to heaven he said,

> "And look, I am with you always; yes, to the end of time" (Mt 28:20).

Today the church continues to proclaim the same faith that the apostolic community proclaimed: "Jesus is Lord!

■ *journal* ■

Read Luke 14:7–14. What does this parable say about being Catholic? Write a paragraph to explain.

Repent and believe. Reform your lives. Accept baptism in the name of the Father, and of the Son, and of the Holy Spirit."

How is the apostolic nature of the church preserved? Jesus gave Peter teaching authority (see Mt 16:18–19) which has been passed on to the pope and the bishops. This teaching authority also helps preserve church unity when conflicts arise. For example:

- **Magisterial teaching.**   Catholics recognize the right of the pope, bishops—and to a lesser extent, priests—to teach in Jesus' name. Normally this is done through the ordinary magisterium of the church. This type of magisterial teaching can be found in papal encyclicals, pastoral letters, sermons, and the like. Magisterial teaching aims at correct proclamation of the gospel, the building up of Christian love and service, and the administration of the sacraments and other spiritual and temporal benefits of the church.

- **Infallibility.**   Catholics believe that, on essential matters of faith and morals, church teaching is *infallible*, or "without error." This teaching is based on Jesus' promise to be with the church always. Although the individual bishops are not infallible, collectively they can proclaim Christ's revelation concerning belief or morality. This type of teaching occurs especially when the world's bishops gather and meet with the pope at an ecumenical council.

- **Papal infallibility.**   The pope speaks infallibly when he teaches *ex cathedra*, that is, "from the chair" of St. Peter. To be an *ex cathedra* teaching, it must be a teaching by the pope in his role as the visible head of the whole church, be a teaching addressed to all Catholics, be a definitive proclamation on a matter of faith or morals, and be an unchangeable decision in which the pope has used his full authority. This kind of teaching is rare. The last time the pope issued a teaching that was *ex cathedra* was in 1950 when the doctrine of the assumption of Mary into heaven was proclaimed by Pope Pius XII. Papal infallibility refers solely to the pope's power or gift as

Bishops may teach infallibly when they are in union among the other bishops and with the pope, they teach authentically on a matter of faith and morals, and they agree on a single viewpoint as the one which the faithful must hold conclusively (*Lumen Gentium*, No. 25).

∎ *research* ∎

1. What value do you see of having a final arbiter (the pope) on matters of faith and morals? Study the organization of another Christian church. Find out how the church settles doctrinal disputes. Compare and contrast the differences between this denomination and the Catholic church.
2. Define *collegiality*. Find out how collegiality plays a part in the church's making important decisions.

successor of Peter to correctly teach Christ's revelation, especially when that revelation is under attack, thus confusing God's people. Like all gifts of the Holy Spirit, infallibility is a gift for the church, meant to build up Christ's Body. It helps give the church access to the truth of Christ.

The Communion of Saints

The communion of saints includes all believers, both those living and those who have died. It embraces the church on earth (pilgrim church), the blessed in heaven (church in glory), and the deceased undergoing purification in purgatory (the church suffering).

The doctrine of the communion of saints flows from the belief that the Spirit of Jesus Christ unifies all people. The bond of Jesus' love makes the church one. As members of the same Body, Christians rely on the prayers and good works of each other. St. James wrote: "The heartfelt prayer of someone upright works very powerfully" (Jas 5:16). Prayers of the living also help those who have died and are undergoing purification in purgatory. Finally, the church believes that the saints in heaven take an active interest in those on earth or in purgatory. The saints offer prayers for their salvation.

The church's liturgical calendar highlights the communion of saints on the feast of All Saints (November 1) and on the memorial of All Souls (November 2).

Belonging to the Church

Why should you belong to the Catholic church? Rank these reasons in their order of importance to you, with "1" being most important and "8" being least important.

_____ a. I belong to the church because of my parents.

_____ b. The church's sacramental life, especially the eucharist, means a great deal to me.

_____ c. I believe everyone should belong to some religion. Why not the Catholic faith?

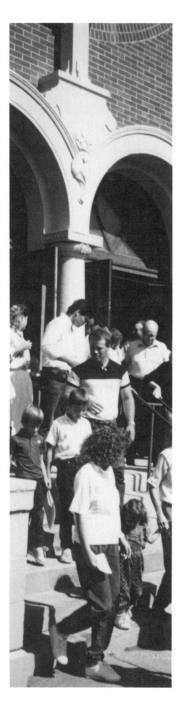

——— d. I find Jesus in the church.

——— e. I find a sense of community, care, and fellowship in the church.

——— f. Church membership helps keep my faith in God alive.

——— g. The church helps me learn how to love and serve others.

——— h. In all honesty, I don't know why I belong. I never thought about it that much.

■ *discuss* ■

1. Which of these reasons did you rank most important? least important? Why?
2. What is the most important benefit you get from being a Catholic?

Conclusion

A story is told of a teacher who said that he was going to write the word "CHURCH" on the blackboard. He then printed, "CH . . CH." The students told him that he left out two letters at the center of the word—"U-R." The teacher responded to the youngsters, "You are correct." "*You are* the heart and at the center of the church."

This story is a reminder that Christ's church needs all of its people. The church relies on you and your many God-given gifts to build up the Body of Christ. Jesus needs you to be his helpful hands, his feet that go out of the way to help others, his forgiving words spoken, his compassionate eyes.

In summary, you and all of the baptized are the church. The church is Christ's presence in the world proclaiming in word and deed the good news of salvation and helping to lead others to the loving God.

▪ *focus questions* ▪

1. Why is belonging to the church not optional for Christians?

2. How is the church a mystery?

3. Explain the image of the church as the Body of Christ.

4. What is a major challenge of the model of the church as a proclaiming people (herald)?

5. What is a sacrament? *Who* is the first sacrament? What does it mean to call the church a sacrament?

6. What is one strength of the institutional model of church?

7. What is meant by the church as pilgrim?

8. How did Jesus give an example of the servant model of the church at the Last Supper?

9. What are the four marks of the church? How are the marks of the church paradoxical?

10. Explain how the church is one in creed, code, and cult.

11. What are the key Precepts of the Church which Catholics are instructed to observe?

12. How does a person become holy?

13. What is another name for a holy person?

14. List the spiritual and corporal works of mercy.

15. Define *catholic*.

16. How is the church apostolic?

17. Define *infallibility*. On what do Catholics base this belief?

18. Under what conditions does the pope teach *ex cathedra*?

19. When was the last time a pope issued an *ex cathedra* teaching? What was the occasion?

20. Identify these terms:
    canon law
    canonization
    magisterium

■ *vocabulary* ■

Look up the meaning of the following words in the dictionary. Transcribe the definitions into your journal:

admonish   paradoxical
enhance   refurbish

■ *exercises* ■

1. Research the process of canonization in the Roman Catholic church. Briefly summarize the requirements of each step leading to sainthood.

2. Report on Chapter 2 of the *Dogmatic Constitution on the Church* from the Vatican II documents. The theme of this chapter is the church as the People of God.

3. Jesus was a servant leader. Design and carry out a project in which you model Jesus' servant leadership. For example, you may wish to (1) collect food for the needy, (2) begin a tutoring program for younger students, (3) help old people with household chores in your neighborhood, (4) organize a coffee and donut social after Mass, (5) participate in a pro-life awareness day, or (6) visit homebound parishioners or those in nursing homes.

Prayer Reflection

The Lord's Prayer reminds us to "forgive those who trespass against us." Forgiveness is essential in order for the Christian community "to be Christ for others." Try the following prayer of love and forgiveness for someone who has hurt you.

1. What is your attitude about forgiveness? Is it "I can forgive, but not forget" or "I want to forgive, but I can't"?

2. Next, examine any resentment you have toward the person who has hurt you. Get it out in the open. Imagine the other person standing in front of you. Tell the person why you are hurting inside.

3. Then, look at the situation from the other person's point of view. How did you contribute to the painful situation? Might the other person be hurting, too? Do you feel compassion for him or her?

4. Finally, put yourself in the presence of Jesus. See him hanging on the cross. Picture yourself and the person who has hurt you standing below the cross. See Jesus looking at both of you. Hear him speak words of forgiveness. See

the Lord loving this person. Ask the Lord to help you love this person, too. Ask him to give you the strength to forgive. Stay with this scene until you feel some of your anger begin to slip away. The Lord loves both you and the person who has hurt you.

▪ *reflection* ▪

Can you forgive your enemy? Will you?

▪ *resolution* ▪

Extend a gesture of friendship to the person who was the subject of your prayer of forgiveness. Ask the Holy Spirit to inspire you to think of a meaningful way to approach a reconciliation.

chapter 5
Human Destiny

[Jesus] then opened their minds to understand the scriptures, and he said to them, "So it is written that the Christ would suffer and on the third day rise from the dead, and that, in his name, repentance for the forgiveness of sins would be preached to nations."

—Luke 24:45–47

In This Chapter

You will study topics related to the final articles of the Nicene Creed, including:

■ baptism for the forgiveness of sin

■ resurrection of the dead

■ life in the world to come

A young boy lived with his grandfather near the top of a mountain in the Swiss Alps. The boy would often go outside, cup his hands around his mouth, and shout "HELLO!" He delighted in hearing the echo of his voice come back to him from the valley walls, "HELLO...Hello...hello...hello..." Then he would yell out, "I LOVE YOU." Back would come the echo, "I LOVE YOU...I Love You...I love you...love you."

One day the grandfather needed to reprimand the boy for misbehavior. The boy was embarrassed, sad, angry. He went outside, shook his fists, and bellowed out, "I HATE YOU!" How ashamed he was when the rocks and boulders across the mountainside hurled back the retort: "I HATE YOU...I Hate You...I hate you...hate you" (from *Growing Strong in the Seasons of Life* by Charles Swindoll).

Life is a lot like echoes. You receive what you give. The old saying, "what goes around, comes around" is rather accurate. If you want others to like you, then you too must be likeable. If you want patience and understanding, then you must tolerate and forgive others.

Jesus taught that acts of kindness done for others—even a person's most secret acts of mercy (see Mt 6:4)—will be rewarded. Your human destiny, that is, where and how you will spend eternity, is very much connected to how you live while on earth. Heaven is the echo of a life lived for Jesus. Oppositely, hell is the echo of alienation for those who die apart from God and others.

Thinking about the End

Though faith is a tool that allows Christians to imagine what death and its aftermath is like, death remains perhaps the greatest of mysteries. What do you think about death? Read the following statements. Circle the number that best reflects your opinion about that statement.

> 1—strongly agree
> 2—agree
> 3—don't know
> 4—disagree
> 5—strongly disagree

1. Some people are so afraid of death that they never begin to live.

   1   2   3   4   5

2. Death does not scare me; dying does.

   1   2   3   4   5

3. Death is the golden key that opens the palace of eternity.

   1   2   3   4   5

4. Let death be daily before your eyes, and you will never entertain any abject thought, nor too eagerly covet anything.

   1   2   3   4   5

5. Since death ends it all, grab everything with gusto while you are alive.

   1   2   3   4   5

6. Live each day as though it were your last.

   1   2   3   4   5

7. "Whoever keeps my word will never see death" (Jn 8:51).

   1   2   3   4   5

8. Italian proverb: "A good death does honor to a whole life."

   1   2   3   4   5

▪ *discuss* ▪

Which statement is closest to how you view death? Why? Share your own statement or proverb that expresses your belief about death.

▪ *journal* ▪

Write a testimony of your life that could be read at your funeral. This is more than a eulogy which lists your accomplishments. A testimony explains what you believed about life, what you held as important. Who would read this testimony? You might wish to write it from his or her perspective. Suppose you knew that you only had a week to live. What would you do in the next seven days? Compose a brief self-portrait that you would like a best friend to read at your funeral Mass.

▪

We Acknowledge One Baptism for the Forgiveness of Sins

It was the week before confirmation and Father John, the pastor, visited the high school students who were to be confirmed. "On Saturday," he said, "I expect each of you to come to afternoon confession. It is most appropriate for you to celebrate the sacrament of reconciliation before your confirmation."

The group hemmed and hawed, looking nervously at one another. Many of them had not been to confession in quite a while.

The pastor continued, "Of course, Randy, you will not need to come for reconciliation." Now, everyone else really began to protest.

Randy would be receiving all three sacraments of initiation at the confirmation Mass—he would be baptized, confirmed, and have first communion. The kids all knew that. "When you are baptized, your sins are forgiven," Father John smiled. "Randy can celebrate the sacrament of reconciliation later."

A boy named Howard spoke up. "Father, I choose that option too. I'll be re-baptized if I have to." Everyone laughed.

Father John waved off Howard as he headed out the door. "See you all on Saturday," he said. "Remember, confessions are in the afternoon from 3 to 5."

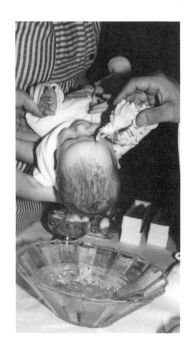

One baptism.   Father John's reminder to Randy and the rest of the confirmation group, and Howard's simple—if not silly—request teach some important truths connected with the Catholic belief in "one baptism for the forgiveness of sins."

First, the Catholic church believes in **one** baptism. Through water, a person is initiated into the Christian life. A formula is recited: "I baptize you in the name of the Father, and of the Son, and of the Holy Spirit." The church accepts as valid baptisms celebrated in most other Christian denominations. So, if a person later decides to join the Catholic faith, he or she would not need to be "re-baptized" as Howard suggested.

For the forgiveness of sins.   When people are baptized, they renounce sin. In infant baptisms, the parents and godparents do this for the baby. Baptism into Christ brings death to sin and rebirth into the life of the Spirit. Peter preached "baptism for the forgiveness of sins" at Pentecost. He said:

> "You must repent . . . and every one of you must be baptized in the name of Jesus Christ for the forgiveness of sins, and you will receive the gift of the Holy Spirit" (Acts 2:38).

For this reason, it would have been unnecessary for Randy to have confessed his sins prior to being baptized. Baptism is the proper place to renounce sin and begin life anew.

But what about post-baptismal sins? Some Christian denominations believe so strongly in the power of baptism to forgive sins, that they believe that this one time public confession of sin is enough. The Catholic church holds that Jesus not only provided the church with baptism for forgiveness of sins, but he also gave the church the authority to remit sins committed after baptism. Jesus gave this gift to the apostles, through Peter. Jesus said:

"Receive the Holy Spirit. If you forgive anyone's sins,
they are forgiven; if you retain anyone's sins, they are
retained" (John 20:22–23).

The sacrament of penance, or reconciliation, is a "second baptism" in which the church proclaims again Christ's forgiveness of the *contrite* sinner. Contrite sinners sincerely regret the evil they committed against God or others and firmly intend to avoid sin in the future. They also agree to do penance, that is, something to make up for their sins, amend their lives, and repair any injuries that they may have caused.

More about sin. Sin is a power that St. Paul said "you must not allow to reign over your mortal bodies and make you obey their desires" (Rm 6:12). Forgiveness of sin is necessary for a person's salvation; only Christ's love can overcome sin.

What is the definition of sin? Traditionally, the church has distinguished between two kinds of sin, *original sin* and *actual sin*. Here is a description of each:

Original sin is the term used to describe the disobedience of Adam and Eve. Although the "forbidden fruit" story in Genesis 3 is symbolic, the nature of the "original sin" was a deliberate act of disobedience against God. All humans have inherited the effects of this first sin: alienation from God, self, others, and creation. The worst spiritual effects of original sin are separation from God's love and the resulting loss of sanctifying grace. The worst physical effects of original sin are physical suffering and death.

The church holds that the perfect life and loving sacrificial death of Jesus Christ have conquered the power of original sin. Through Jesus, God has redeemed all people, offering forgiveness of sins and birth into a new life. It is this life of grace that God bestows on those who are baptized.

The freedom from original sin does not guarantee freedom from all sin. God's gift of free will makes it possible for people to continue to choose to do evil. Christians remain in need of the support, encouragement, and prayers of fellow Christians. The church provides many helps—primarily the sacraments—to fortify Christians in the life of grace.

Actual sin is personal, individual sin. A traditional definition of actual sin is "an act, word, or desire contrary to eternal law." "To commit a sin" means to do something evil, knowingly and willingly. Actual sin offends reason, truth, and right conscience and damages a person's relationships with God, others, and self.

Types of actual sins include:

- **freely chosen bad attitudes or inordinate desires.** Prejudice is an example of a bad attitude. Lust is an example of an inordinate desire.

- **failures to act.** Examples include sins of *omission*, like failing to help the poor.

- **inappropriate actions or words directed against God, neighbor, or self.** Examples include sins of *commission* like stealing, cheating, lying, or a misuse of sex.

Actual sins differ in their degree of sinfulness. *Venial* sins *partially* reject God; they are "pardonable" sins that do not permanently damage a person's relationship with God. Venial sins do not destroy sanctifying grace, friendship with God, charity, or eternal happiness. The theft of a small item, a sarcastic word, or not praying regularly are examples of venial sins.

The danger of all sin is that a person can become attached to it. Repeating the same sinful acts can give a foothold to vices or bad habits that can turn you away from love. These vices, especially the so-called deadly or capital vices—*pride, envy, anger, sloth, greed, gluttony, and lust*—can lead a person to more serious occasions of sin.

Mortal sin is also known as "deadly sin." Mortal sins include attitudes, desires, actions or non-actions that destroy a person's relationship with God and others. To be a mortal sin, a sin must meet certain conditions. It must involve:

- **a grave or serious matter.**   For example, murder, adultery, and apostasy are gravely wrong actions.

- **sufficient reflection.**   This means that a person is fully aware of the seriousness of the proposed action, yet does it anyhow.

- **full consent of the will.**   In other words, the action is done freely and not under the influence of limiting factors like force, fear, or blinding passion.

Mortal sin results in the loss of love and deprives the sinner of sanctifying grace. To return to a state of grace, a person must repent and confess the mortal sin in the sacrament of reconciliation.

■ *journal* ■

Read the story of the woman caught in adultery from John 8:1–11. Then, do one of the following:

1. Rewrite this story from the viewpoint of the woman or one of her accusers.
2. Write of a time when someone forgave you. How did you feel? How did this forgiveness affect your relationship with that person?

The Salvation of All Through Jesus Christ

The article of the Nicene Creed which professes faith in "baptism for the forgiveness of sins" raises the question of whether God saves non-Christians.

Because of a traditional church teaching that stated "outside the church, there is no salvation," some thought that only baptized Catholics could go to heaven. The original intent of this phrase was not to say that God does not save non-Catholics. Rather, its purpose was to emphasize the central role of the church in God's plan of salvation. The church **is** necessary for salvation because **Jesus** is necessary for salvation. Jesus is the High Priest, the one mediator between God and all people. As the Acts of the Apostles states:

> For all of the names in the world given to men, this is the only one by which we can be saved (Acts 4:12).

What is the role of the church in salvation? The church is the ordinary way for people to attain salvation through faith, baptism, and a life of discipleship. Jesus founded the church to lead people to him, and to be a *sign* and *instrument* of his salvation. As people seek salvation, they will be drawn to Christ and membership in his Body.

Jesus himself taught the need for faith and baptism (see Jn 3:5). The church teaches that anyone who knew "that the Catholic church was made necessary by God through Jesus Christ, [and] would refuse to enter her or to remain in her could not be saved" (*Lumen Gentium*, 14).

What about those people who have not heard the gospel? And others who have received only a partial or distorted picture of Jesus by Christians who do not live what they preach? The church teaches that God is a God of mercy. In ways that we cannot fully comprehend, Jesus' saving grace touches the hearts of those who live loving lives or conscientiously follow the truth as they know it. God wants to save all people. St. Thomas Aquinas explained:

> Divine care supplies everybody with the means necessary for salvation, so long as he on his part does not put up obstacles.

The Second Vatican Council also taught that God's grace can touch all:

> Those can also attain to everlasting salvation who through no fault of their own do not know the gospel of Christ or his church, yet sincerely seek God and, moved by grace, strive by their deeds to do his will as it is known to them through the dictates of conscience. Nor does divine Providence deny the help necessary for salvation to those who, without blame on their part, have not yet arrived at an explicit knowledge of God, but who strive to live a good life, thanks to his grace. Whatever goodness or truth is found among them is looked upon by the church as a preparation for the gospel. She regards such qualities as given by him who enlightens all men so that they may finally have life (*Lumen Gentium*, 16).

Thus God's kingdom includes all who are mysteriously drawn to it through the workings of the Holy Spirit. Non-Christians must seek the kingdom of God as they know it. As with a Christian vocation, the non-Christian's vocation is to live as lovingly as he or she possibly can.

We Look for the Resurrection of the Dead

Recall the survey on the meaning of death that you took at the beginning of this chapter. Your questions about death may have been different than those of your classmates, but the one thing you do have in common is that everyone does have questions.

Death is the one inevitable event that faces everyone. It points to the common human destiny. The poet John Donne wrote: "Do not send to know for whom the bell tolls. It tolls for thee. No man is an island unto himself."

The Nicene Creed states that "we look for the resurrection of the dead." The good news of our Christian faith is that with death comes a new type of life. Jesus taught:

"I am the resurrection.
Anyone who believes in me, even though that person
    dies, will live,
and whoever lives and believes in me
will never die" (Jn 11:25–26).

Every religion tries to make sense out of the ever-present reality of death and the afterlife. Christians believe that if they imitate Jesus in his love of others, then death does not need to be feared. Also, thinking about your own death can help you resolve to live a more purposeful life today. Reflecting on your eternal destiny can help you commit yourself to live more lovingly in the present. The philosopher Jean Jacques Rousseau commented, "When a man dies he clutches in his hands only that which he has given away in his lifetime."

■

How Death Is Viewed in Scriptures

The development of the Christian understanding of death can be traced in the Hebrew and Christian scriptures and the documents of the church. For example, the Book of Ecclesiastes teaches that it is natural to die: "There is a season for everything...A time for giving birth, a time for dying" (Eccl 3:1–2). Yet, scripture also says that death is a penalty for sin. God did not originally intend for people to die. St. Paul writes:

> It was through one man that sin *came into the world,* and through sin death, and thus death has spread through the whole human race because everyone has sinned (Rom 5:12).

Had Adam and Eve not sinned, people would be immune from bodily death. However, the good news of the gospel is that Jesus Christ has rescued you from your natural fate. According to the documents of Vatican II:

> It is in the face of death that the riddle of human existence becomes most acute. . . .
>
> Although the mystery of death utterly beggars the imagination, the church has been taught by divine revelation, and herself firmly teaches, that man has been created by God for a blissful purpose beyond the reach of earthly misery. In addition, that bodily death from which man would have been immune had he not sinned will be vanquished, according to the Christian faith, when man who was ruined by his own doing is restored to wholeness by an almighty and merciful Savior (*The Church in the Modern World,* No. 18).

Jesus shows the way to accept death. In the garden of Gethsemane, Jesus himself was anxious about his own impending death. He prayed:

> "*Abba* (Father)! For you everything is possible. Take this cup away from me. But let it be as you, not I, would have it" (Mk 14:36).

Jesus' "Let it be as you, not I, would have it" shows his final act of total self-giving to the Father. As his followers, Christians try to imitate him. Though it is natural to fear dying, in faith Christians recite with Jesus, "Father, *into your hands I commit my spirit*" (Lk 23:46).

Death is a profound mystery. But Christian faith reveals that Jesus Christ has conquered death. Faith in Christ guarantees everlasting life for the believer. This is the cornerstone of the Christian faith. Wrote St. Paul:

> If there is no resurrection of the dead, then Christ has
> not been raised either, and if Christ has not been raised,
> then our preaching is without substance, and so is your
> faith   (1 Cor 15:12–13).

Still, questions persist about what actually happens at the time of death. How and when does the person who has died experience resurrection? Many of these questions involve the Christian belief in *judgment*, that is, that Christ will judge the merits of each person's life to determine how he or she will spend eternity. Much of this teaching originates from these words of St. Paul:

> For at the judgment seat of Christ we are all to be seen
> for what we are, so that each of us may receive what
> he has deserved in the body, matched to whatever he
> has done, good or bad (2 Cor 5:10).

In the Hebrew scriptures judgment is something that belongs to God, something that God handles fairly. The Law was the Chosen People's code of judgment. When the people refused to live up to the terms of the covenant, God's judgment was against them. Still, Yahweh was seen as a God who defended all people, especially the poor and lowly.

In the New Testament, God has handed all judgment to the Son:

> "Thus as the Father raises the dead and gives them
> life, so the Son gives life to anyone he chooses, for the
> Father judges no one" (Jn 5:22).

Judgment, then, is tied to a person's faith in Jesus and the way he or she keeps Jesus' teachings. One way to consider the "day of judgment" is to think of it as a person's permanent decision to accept or reject Jesus Christ. This type of judgment occurs here and now. A person who chooses Jesus should live today in response to God's laws and the needs of others. Each day demands new actions that show how a person has chosen to live as a follower of Christ. But scripture also reveals another judgment, at the end of time. This will be a final judgment when there will be final victory over evil. The final judgment will occur at the end of time when Christ returns in glory. Here is some more information about each of these beliefs:

Particular Judgment.   The church teaches that each person will immediately appear before God after death for a *particular or individual judgment*. Jesus himself told us about this type of judgment in the parable of Lazarus and the rich man (see Lk 16:19–31). The story points out that after death an individual judgment awaits everyone. The result of this judgment will be either an eternal union or separation from God.

Vatican II's *Dogmatic Constitution on the Church* reaffirms this teaching:

> For before we reign with the glorious Christ, all of us will be made manifest "before the tribunal of Christ, so that each one may receive what he has won through the body, according to his works, whether good or evil" (2 Cor 5:10).

At death, the time of trial is over. The particular judgment reveals each person for who he or she is: someone who has lived a life of service or someone who has lived a life of self-centeredness. The poet Dante Alighieri wrote this about the time of judgment:

> If you insist on having your own way, you will get it. Hell is the enjoyment of your own way forever. If you really want God's way with you, you will get it in heaven.

In other words, the person who lives a good life should not fear judgment. God is for you, not against you!

> "In all truth I tell you,
> whoever listens to my words,
> and believes in the one who sent me,
> has eternal life;
> without being brought to judgment
> such a person has passed from death to life" (Jn 5:24).

You should not be surprised when you stand before God's judgment seat. You will know well enough if you are God-centered or self-centered. At the particular judgment Jesus will judge you lovingly, mercifully, and justly. Jesus' judgment will simply be a declaration of what is the truth about our acceptance or rejection of him.

▪ *exercise* ▪

Cartoons, comics, and the like often make light of the abbreviation *R.I.P.* Actually, its meaning is a short prayer to remember those who have died. The Latin *requiescat in pace* means "May he/she rest in peace."

You may have also seen a skull bone used to represent death. In fact, in many medieval paintings a skull sits on the desk of a monk. The monk is contemplating the skull and what it represents. The artist may also have added the words *Sic transit gloria mundi* which means, "Thus passes the glory of the world." The skull is a reminder that time speeds quickly by. What the world holds important may not be so in God's eyes.

Let these Latin phrases help you reflect on your own life. What will be your epitaph? An epitaph is an inscription that is written on a gravestone to sum up the life of the person buried there. Draw a model of the gravestone. Write your own epitaph on your gravestone.

▪ *journal* ▪

1. Imagine you were to die today. Write five personal qualities that you could offer to Jesus at your individual judgment that show how you have lived a Christian life.

2. Imagine you were to die at the age of eighty-five. Note five major achievements that you hope you will be able to offer to Jesus to show that you were a faithful disciple during your life.

General or Last Judgment. The general or last judgment will take place at the end of time. Then, God's saving plan will be clear to everyone who has ever lived. Christ will fully reveal each person's true relationship before God. As judge, Jesus' goodness, justice, mercy, and peace will establish God's reign in all its glory. Everyone will acknowledge and marvel at the Lord's majesty.

■ journal ■

Read the parable of Lazarus and the rich man in Luke 16:19–31. Rewrite this parable using modern-day characters and setting.

Matthew's gospel provides a vivid image of the final judgment. Christ will sit in judgment of both the just and unjust:

> "When the Son of Man comes in glory, escorted by the angels, then he will take his seat on his throne of glory. All nations will be assembled before him and he will separate people one from another as the shepherd separates sheep from goats" (Mt 25:31–32).

The criteria of this last or general judgment is simple: how well you have loved God with your entire being and your neighbor as yourself:

> "For I was hungry and you gave me food; I was thirsty and you gave me drink; I was a stranger and you made me welcome; lacking clothes and you clothed me, sick and you visited me, in prison and you came to see me" (Mt 25:35–36).

Christ's Second Coming.   The last judgment is associated with the Second Coming of Christ. The church believes that Jesus will come again at the *parousia*, a Greek word for "presence" or "arrival." At Christ's Second Coming, everyone who has ever lived will recognize Jesus as "Lord of all."

Christ's Second Coming will mark the time when God's reign will be fully established on earth. The world has a foretaste of this time now because Jesus has already inaugurated God's reign. God's loving grace is already bringing salvation to those who choose to accept it. Also, Christians help to build Christ's kingdom through their love and good works.

God's kingdom is here now, but there are many forces that remain opposed to God's saving will. God's reign has not taken root in the hearts of all. However, the Christian hope in the Second Coming enables the church to look forward to the day when Christ's work *will* be complete. On that day, human history will come to a definite close and Jesus Christ will come again. Humanity will be as God always intended. The visible universe and all of creation will be transformed to their original states, sharing in the glory of the risen Christ.

We Believe in Life in the World to Come

The Christian belief in "life in the world to come" points to a life lived waiting for the Lord's return. Jesus told a story of a man who left home and placed his servants in charge. The servants in the story had no idea when the man would return. The message was clear:

> "Be on guard, stay awake, because you never know when the time will come" (Mk 13:32).

St. Paul uses a vivid image of the Roman triumphal procession to describe the Lord's Second Coming. When the trumpet of God blasts, God will take both living and dead up into the clouds "to meet the Lord in the air" (1 Thes 4:16–17). Also, Paul writes of humanity's share in the resurrection of Christ:

> He who raised up the Lord Jesus will raise us up with Jesus in our turn, and bring us to himself—and you as well (2 Cor 4:14).

What does a share in the resurrection entail? Catholics believe in:

- the resurrection of the body,
- the resurrection of all the dead, both those who merit reward and those who merit punishment,
- the existence of heaven, hell, and purgatory.

The following sections provide more information about each of these beliefs.

The resurrection of the body. Christians believe that God will raise the bodies of the faithful at the end of time and transform them to share in the glory of Christ's resurrection. Many other religions believe in an afterlife, but few hold that the body is raised. Rather, they usually teach of some type of spiritual form of existence. Christian belief goes much deeper in teaching that the whole person—body and soul—will survive death.

Respect for the Body

The belief in a resurrected body underscores the profound respect that people should have for their bodies and the bodies of others. To be a *human* being is to have a *body* and soul which come from God and eventually return to God. The body is essential to being a person. Respect of the body is a way to show respect for God.

From the earliest years, Christians have speculated on the nature or quality of resurrected bodies. "What will they be like?" many have wondered. St. Paul addressed this question in the First Letter to the Corinthians:

> Someone may ask, how are dead people raised, and what sort of body do they have when they come? How foolish! What you sow must die before it is given new life; and what you sow is not the body that is to be, but only a bare grain, of wheat I dare say, or some other kind; it is God who gives it the sort of body that he has chosen for it. . . .
>
> What is sown is perishable but what is raised is imperishable; what is sown is contemptible but what is raised is glorious; what is sown is weak, but what is raised is powerful; what is sown is a natural body, and what is raised is a spiritual body (1 Cor 15:35–37, 42–44).

The most important quality of the resurrected body is immortality; those who have been raised will never die again. Paul lists other attributes that help describe the nature of the resurrected body: imperishable, glorious, powerful, and spiritual. Christian theology has interpreted these traits in the following ways:

1. Glorified bodies will never feel pain.
2. Glorified bodies will reflect the beatific vision, that is by "seeing God."
3. Glorified bodies will not be hindered by material creation; for example, they will be able to move about easily and swiftly.
4. Glorified bodies will be controlled by a person's spirit or soul.

Related to the belief in the resurrection of the body is the belief that God will transform material creation in Christ. This means that God has created a suitable environment where the resurrected, glorified bodies of the faithful will thrive for eternity.

■ ■

The resurrection of the dead.   Christians believe in the resurrection of **all** the dead, both those who have done good and merit eternal reward and those who have died separated from God and deserve punishment. Christians believe that heaven is eternal life spent in union with God and all those who share in God's life. Hell is eternal separation from God.

The existence of heaven and hell take very seriously the reality of human freedom. When freedom is used properly, people choose an eternal destiny spent in joyous union with God. If, on the other hand, a person's choices are based on selfish motives, God will likewise respect that decision. A person who chooses self over God has chosen hell. God respects human freedom and allows people to make the choice between good and bad.

■ ■

One Person's Heaven Is Another's Hell

Many stories are told to try to capture the differences between heaven and hell. One story comes from a legend which tells of a man who dreamed of both heaven and hell. In his first dream he found himself in a magnificent palace where countless millions gathered around eight-foot high tables overflowing with food. However, there was a problem. The spoons they had were long enough to reach the food but way too long to put the food into their mouths. Despite this, everyone was extremely happy and satisfied because they used their spoons to feed their neighbors and friends.

The man's second dream was like the first. Again, there was a very tall table replete with delicious food. But the people were upset, angry, frustrated, and bitter. Why? They tried to feed themselves. So fixed in their selfish mind set, it never occurred to them to feed those around them.

Can you understand the fine, but definite line between heaven and hell?

Heaven.   Heaven is the celebration of eternal life with God and all who have shared God's life. Jesus said:

> "I have come
> so that they may have life
> and have it to the full" (Jn 10:10).

The eternal life of heaven will bring happiness beyond what anyone can imagine:

> [God] "*will wipe* away all *tears from their* eyes; there will be no more death, and no more mourning or sadness or pain. The world of the past has gone" (Rv 21:4).

In heaven, all desires for truth, wisdom, goodness, beauty, peace, justice, companionship, understanding, and love will be fulfilled.

Though heaven brings people in *union* with God and all of God's creations, all individual identities will be maintained. Each person is transformed through the love of Jesus into unselfish images of God. While on earth, Jesus prayed for this to happen:

> "May they all be one,
> just as, Father, you are in me and I am in you,
> so that they also may be in us" (Jn 17:21).

Those who die in God's friendship and grace and are perfectly purified are like God. As a result, in heaven they will possess the *beatific vision* that will enable them to "see" God face-to-face—intuitively, directly, intimately, plainly, and personally perceiving God as God actually is. This "seeing" of God is what brings perfect happiness. God made all people to share the divine life; God destined all people for eternal happiness. Heaven is the final, perfect, human fulfillment, that state of being that makes each person what God intends of them.

Hell.   Hell is defined as eternal separation from God. Hence, a central truth of hell's reality is that *it is an eternal life alienated from God and God's love.* This alienation extends to all interpersonal relationships; hell also involves eternal separation from everything that it is good. In hell there is grief over eternal punishment, physical and spiritual pain, and despair of salvation.

The existence of hell is a doctrine of Christian faith. Jesus refers to hell several times in his teaching. For example, in Mark's gospel, Jesus warns:

> "It is better for you to enter into the kingdom of God with one eye, than to have two eyes and be thrown into hell where *their worm will never die nor their fire be put out*" (Mk 9:47–48).

Christians believe that hell exists because God made people as free beings. Hell is a reality because God respects human freedom, a freedom that can pridefully refuse God's grace, love, and mercy. Through grace, love, and mercy, God continuously invites all people to join the divine family. But a person is free to reject that invitation by living a selfish, heartless, and unloving life.

Although Christians believe in a hell, no one knows for sure who, if anyone, is in hell. Although the church has never explicitly pointed to any human as being in hell, it has proclaimed that countless people are in heaven. Jesus said, "Do not judge, and you will not be judged" (Lk 16:37). A significant work of Christian charity is to pray for others that they may accept Jesus and turn from their sinful ways.

■ ■ ■

■ *activities* ■

1. C.S. Lewis wrote in *The Screwtape Letters*:
   "The safest road to Hell is the gradual one—the gentle slope, soft underfoot, without sudden turnings, without milestones, without signposts."

   Discuss with a classmate what these words mean. Is Lewis correct? Offer evidence to support your reasoning. Then, use any form of art medium to describe your own view of hell.

2. Read the parable of the weeds (Mt 13:24–30, 36–43) and the parable of the net (Mt 13:47–50). Write your interpretation of these parables. Share your interpretation with the class.

3. C.S. Lewis contrasted heaven and hell using images like these:

Hell is…
- an unending church service without God.
- grey and so are its inhabitants.
- full of clocks and telephones.
- sex without pleasure.

Heaven is…
- God without a church service.
- full of colors and all colors of people.
- full of only those possessions you gave away on earth.
- pleasure without sex.

Create some of your own images to contrast heaven and hell. You may write these images in your journal. Share these images with the class.

━━━━━━━━━ ∎ ━━━━━━━━━

Purgatory.   The church teaches the existence of purgatory, that is, a place or state of purification as preparation for entrance into heaven. Purgatory is necessary because only a clean, or pure, person can enter heaven. A person who dies faces God's infinite love. To embrace this all-loving God, he or she must let go of all imperfections.

Purgatory comes from the Latin word for "purification" or "cleansing." What needs cleansing are venial sins present at death and any punishment due those sins. This process of purification can also take place in this life. When you work at ridding yourself of sin and self-centeredness, you are undertaking a process of purification. But this process is long and often painful. To become other-centered, more loving, and Christ-like takes a lifetime of growing in holiness.

The pain involved in the purification process comes from letting go of **all** selfish attachments when passing to a new life with God. But those in purgatory are also joyful and peaceful because they know that they will one day be in union with God in heaven. Thus, purgatory involves a paradox: joy and peace while in a state of suffering and purification.

The church has not defined the exact nature of purgatory. And the church has not officially declared what kind of "place" purgatory is or "how long it lasts." Space and time images are just that—images that try to describe the mystery of eternal life.

The best scriptural basis for the doctrine of purgatory occurs in 2 Maccabees 12:40–46. This passage encourages prayers **by** the living **for** the dead so that the dead can be released from their sin. The church teaches that the prayers of the living, especially in the eucharist, can help those undergoing purification. The church also recommends alms-giving, indulgences, and works of penance to help those in purgatory. The doctrine of the communion of saints underscores this unity between all Christians—in heaven, on earth, and in purgatory.

Conclusion

"Amen" is the traditional way Christians end their prayers. The Nicene Creed also concludes with "Amen," a resounding, "Yes" that means, "I agree." In Hebrew, *Amen* comes from the same root as the word for "believe." Thus, when you say "Amen" at the end of the Nicene Creed, you are making an act of faith, proclaiming the truth of what you pray and celebrate. It is a summary of your beliefs in the articles of the creed.

In a similar way, death is a kind of "Amen" to a person's life. For Christians who have "fought the good fight," death enables them to present themselves to God as the finished story of a loving disciple.

The Christian beliefs about human destiny and the "last things" can assure you that God has the last word. Your end in this life is but the birthday to an eternal life with the Lord. The doctrines of the resurrection of the body, judgment, and eternal life teach that everything you do, or fail to do, has significance. If you choose Jesus and stay close to him in this life, then you can truly take comfort in these words of St. Paul:

> Death, where is your victory? Death, where is your sting? The sting of death is sin, and the power of sin comes from the Law. Thank God, then, for giving us the victory through Jesus Christ, our Lord (1 Cor 15:55–57).

focus questions

1. Does a person who is already a member of another Christian faith have to be baptized upon becoming Catholic? Explain.

2. What are three signs of a *contrite* sinner?

3. What is original sin? What are some of its effects?

4. Define *actual sin*. Discuss three general types of actual sin.

5. Distinguish between venial and mortal sin.

6. Cite the scripture example that showed that Christ gave the church the power to forgive sins.

7. Can non-Catholics and non-Christians be saved? Explain.

8. How did John Donne's words point to the common human destiny?

9. Why do Christians believe that death should not be feared?

10. Distinguish between the *particular* and the *general* judgment.

11. How will the world react to the Second Coming of Christ?

12. Define *parousia*.

13. Explain the Christian belief in the resurrection of the body?

14. Do Christians belief in the resurrection of **all** the dead? Explain.

15. Define *heaven*.

16. Define *hell*.

17. Why does God permit the existence of hell?

18. Why is purgatory necessary?

19. What is the meaning of the word *amen*? What does it mean when it is stated at the end of the Nicene Creed?

▪ *exercises* ▪

1. Research and report on what one of the following religions teaches about the afterlife: Judaism, Islam, Buddhism, Hinduism, or a native-American religion. Be sure to include mention of their beliefs about the resurrection of the body.
2. Research what the church teaches about reincarnation, limbo, and indulgences.

▬▬▬▬▬ ▪ ▬▬▬▬▬

Prayer Reflection

The "centering" method of prayer can help make you present to the Lord. It can bring God's presence to the center of your existence. Many spiritual writers tell how centering prayer can lead you to rest in the presence of the God who loves and sustains you. Here is one approach to this form of prayer:

Step 1: Find a quiet place to pray. Assume a comfortable position with your spine in a straight line. Then, relax by slowly inhaling and exhaling. Close your eyes. Become aware of God's presence within. Express your faith in words like these:

> Lord, I believe that you are present in me, at the very center of my existence, keeping me alive in your love. For this time with you, please be with me. Draw me close to you, Lord. Let me experience your presence and your love.

Step 2: After a minute or so, select a special word that makes you think of God and God's love. Recite this word over and over. The repetition will help keep distractions away. Choose a name, quality, or title that carries deep meaning for you. Here are some examples:

Jesus	Father	Spirit
Lord	Abba	Love
Truth	Life	Way
Savior	Yahweh	Protector

▪ *vocabulary* ▪

Look up the meaning of the following words in your dictionary. Transcribe the definitions into your journal.

beatific   tribunal

After a few minutes you can stop reciting the word as you become aware of the Lord at the center of your being. If distractions come your way (and they often do) return to the word to refocus on God and God's loving presence.

▪ *reflection* ▪

At the end of your time of prayer, thank the Father for being present to you. Tell Jesus of your love for him. Ask the Holy Spirit to remain with you. Slowly and meditatively recite the Lord's Prayer.

▪ *resolution* ▪

Spend ten to fifteen minutes on this prayer daily for the next two weeks. Note positive differences in your life as a result of this prayer.

PART 2

CODE

Though often presented as something more complex, Catholic morality can easily be described as *responsible Christian living*. Take a look at three key parts of this description:

1. **Christian morality is a response.** Christian life is a response to God's freely given love and offer of salvation through Jesus Christ. Salvation is a gift that cannot be earned. However, you can accept the gift by living according to God's will.

2. **Christian morality requires the "ability" to respond to God.** Because God made you in the divine image, you can both think and choose freely. Reason enables you to recognize God's voice, speaking to you in your conscience and encouraging you to choose what is good and true. Yet, your freedom makes you responsible for your own decisions and actions. When you say "yes" to God's love, then you act morally and allow God's life to live in you. When you reject God's love, then you act immorally and against God's plan.

   God gives you the *ability* to respond, to love in return. This ability to live a Christian life is also a gift. Thus, Christian morality does not rest primarily on your own talents, strengths, insights, or deeds. Rather, the Holy Spirit who comes to you at baptism is the source of your power to say yes to God and God's love.

   Focusing on morality as *response* and *ability to respond* highlights the covenant nature of morality. The God of three Persons—Father, Son, and Holy Spirit—continually reaches out to you and invites you to participate in God's own life. Christian morality is your part of the covenant relationship. It is your response to the gift of divine friendship.

3. **Christian morality is Christ-centered living.** Jesus is the model for a Christian moral life. His dwelling within you by the power of the Holy Spirit enables you to live a full life of love and service. He continues to teach you through the scriptures and through the teachings of the church. The heart of Jesus' message is summed up in the law of love:

   "You must love the Lord your God with all your heart, with all your soul, and with all your mind. This is

the greatest and first commandment. The second resembles it: *You must love your neighbor as yourself"* (Mt 22:37–39).

This section of the text will reflect on what it means to love God and neighbor, the very meaning of living a moral life. Specifically, you will be studying the *code* of Christian living, the ethical norms and rules that guide you in doing the right thing as an individual who lives in community. Chapter 6 will focus on conscience, the Beatitudes, and the Ten Commandments. Chapter 7 will highlight some of the major themes of Catholic social justice, that is, the application of the gospel to societal systems, structures, and institutions.

chapter 6
Christian Moral Living

"It is not anyone who says to me, 'Lord, Lord,' who will enter the kingdom of Heaven, but the person who does the will of my Father in heaven."

—Matthew 7:21

In This Chapter

You will study the following topics as they relate to Christian morality:

■ Conscience

■ Conscientious decision-making

■ Jesus, the moral guide

■ the Beatitudes

■ the Ten Commandments

A priest and a soapmaker were friends. One day while taking a walk in the city, the soapmaker asked the priest, "What possible good can religion be? After thousands of years of preaching goodness, truth, and peace, look at all the misery and sin in the world. If religion is supposed to be so beneficial for people, why should this be?"

For a while, the priest said nothing in reply. Shortly, they came to a school yard where some children were playing in the dirt. They were covered with grime. The priest then spoke up, "See those kids. You say that soap makes people clean, but still those children are filthy. I wonder how effective soap is after all."

The soapmaker protested, "But, Father, soap is of no value unless people use it."

"Precisely," replied the priest. "And so it is with religion" (adapted from *Stories for Sharing* by Charles Arcodia).

Faith and religion are useless unless they are put into practice. Only through living a Christian, moral life do faith and religion become credible. St. James made the connection between having faith and doing good works:

> How does it help, my brothers, when someone who has never done a single good act claims to have faith? Will that faith bring salvation? If one of the brothers or one of the sisters is in need of clothes and has not enough food to live on, and one of you says to them, "I wish you well; keep yourself warm and eat plenty," without giving them these bare necessities of life, then what good is that? In the same way faith: if good deeds do not go with it, it is quite dead (Jas 2:14–17).

Christian moral living is about true **human** living. To be moral is to be human. The corollary is that to be human

147

means to make sound moral decisions. According to the Second Vatican Council document:

> Our human dignity requires us to act conscientiously and with freedom. It requires us to rid ourselves of any slavery to our passions and to choose what is good. God's grace helps human freedom weakened by sin to achieve the good (*Pastoral Constitution in the Modern World*, No. 17).

God gives you the gift of conscience to help you decide between right and wrong. Conscience is not a separate entity standing outside of you and waiting to turn a thumbs down on any decision you make. Rather, conscience is the deepest part of you, the real and honest part of you that helps you to make good decisions.

The grace God provides to help you live morally is not limited to personal conscience. Jesus' life and teachings—especially the Beatitudes—are guides to help you to live a moral life. In the words of Pope John Paul II, the Beatitudes "are a sort of self-portrait of Christ, and for this very reason are invitations to discipleship and communion of life with Christ" (*The Splendor of Truth*, #16). The Second Vatican Council teaches that

> Jesus Christ is the key, center, and purpose of all human history. He shows us how to be fully human (*Pastoral Constitution in the Modern World*, No. 10).

Pope John Paul II adds, "Following Christ is thus the essential and primordial foundation of Christian morality" (*The Splendor of Truth*, #19).

In addition, the Ten Commandments of the Hebrew scriptures continue to shed light on how to love God and neighbor. They can help you to not only "do the right thing," but to be the person that God intends of you.

These graces—conscience, Jesus and the Beatitudes, and the commandments—can help to show that religion, like soap, really works when put into practice!

You Be the Judge

Think about what you already know about conscientious decision-making, the Beatitudes, and the Ten Commandments. Based on these graces, how would you judge the morality of the following situations? Use this scale:

1— This is wrong. It denies or diminishes what it means to be human.
2— I am not sure if this is right or wrong.
3— This is right in line with what it means to be human.

_____ 1. consulting and following the advice on an astrologer

_____ 2. using obscene gestures to show displeasure with someone

_____ 3. keeping $100 from a wallet with no identification that you found

_____ 4. habitually eating junk good and failing to exercise regularly

_____ 5. cheating on a test to even the score after a teacher treats you unfairly

_____ 6. spending money on superfluous things and never giving to the less fortunate

_____ 7. being sexually intimate with someone without the commitment of marriage

_____ 8. snooping in a brother or sister's room to see if he or she is using drugs

_____ 9. failing to defend a classmate from racial slurs made by others

_____ 10. always taking the easy way out when it comes to choosing academic courses and doing school work

▪ *discuss* ▪

1. Which items do you consider to be mostly moral? mostly immoral? Explain.
2. What additional information is needed to decide the morality of any of the situations listed above?

▪ *journal* ▪

Find an article in the newspaper that illustrates a good example of what it means to be human. Summarize the story in your journal. Write how the lesson of the story can be applied to people your own age.

Conscience

St. Thomas More was a lawyer and a friend of King Henry VIII of England. Nevertheless, when the king required his subjects to sign an oath of allegiance to him that declared the king the head of the church of England, thereby renouncing the pope and the Roman church, Thomas More refused. He was sentenced to imprisonment in the Tower of London. For fifteen months he ignored the pleas of his family and friends to relent and sign the oath. Finally, on July 6, 1535 he was to be executed. Prior to his beheading, More declared that he died for the Catholic church—that he was "the King's good servant, but God's first." Thomas More's conscience had spelled out the truth for him, and he had the courage to act on it.

Most people do not have to make life-and-death moral decisions. But each day some of the moral decisions you do make may have life and death implications. For example: "Should I ride in a car with a friend who has been drinking alcohol?" Also, "Should I have sexual intercourse?" Or, "Should I use steroids to help me improve my athletic skills?" How can making the wrong choice in each of these areas be life threatening? Life is filled with countless decisions—some more serious than others. In each important decision your conscience can be a help.

What is the meaning of conscience? *Conscience is a practical judgment of reason concerning whether an action or attitude is good or sinful, right or wrong, moral or immoral.* Put simply, conscience is the ability to discover God's will for your life. Your conscience enables you to carry on an inner dialogue with God. For Catholics, conscience is human intellect enlightened by God's word as taught by the church. Your conscience helps you to perceive and apply principles of morality to concrete actions and enables you to judge actions already or yet to be done. Thus, your conscience operates before, during, and after acting. It allows you to take responsibility for your actions.

The church teaches that there are two key principles to keep in mind when making a moral decision:

1. Properly form your conscience. (This is a lifelong task.)

2. Follow your conscience.

The following sections list some suggestions for incorporating these principles into your life.

Conscience formation.   Many factors can disrupt the effect a conscience has on helping a person distinguish between right and wrong. For example, *ignorance*, simply not knowing or never learning that something is right or wrong, can cause a person to make false judgments. *Emotions* can cloud a conscience. A person may cave in to the temptation to do what feels good, even though "feeling good" does not automatically mean the actions are right. *Conformity* to what others are doing can also lead someone to a wrong decision. Just because everyone else is doing something does not make it right.

Obeying one's conscience underscores the need to form it properly. Left to themselves, people make mistakes. Catholics need the help of Jesus and the guidance of the church to develop a sensitive and mature Christian conscience. The following are some important steps a Catholic should take in developing a mature conscience.

1. **Find the facts. What** is the issue? **Who** is involved? **Where? When? How?**

   The **what** question corresponds to the *moral object*, the matter of the human action. Some actions are so anti-human or against God that by definition they are always wrong. Examples include rape, murder, apostasy, and adultery.

   The **who, where, when,** and **how** questions correspond to the *circumstances* in which the acts are performed. Circumstances may increase or diminish the moral goodness or evil of certain acts. If the answer to one of the questions is improper (for example, driving a car 70 miles-per-hour in a school zone—the **where** question), then the proposed act is wrong.

   The **how** question relates to the means to be used to accomplish the goal. A solid principle of Catholic morality is: *A good end (outcome or purpose) does not justify evil means to attain it.* For example, you may not cheat (the **how** question) to attain good grades.

2. **Examine your motives.**   **Why** do you want to do this?

3. **Think of the possible effects.**   How will this action (or non-action) affect you, other people, and society? What if everyone did what you propose to do?

4. **Consider alternatives.**   Is there another way to act? Use your imagination to find alternatives.

5. **What does the law have to say?**   Law is not opposed to conscience; rather, it helps to form conscience. Whereas conscience is the subjective norm or related to specific states of mind, law is the objective norm. These types of laws need to be considered when making decisions:

   Natural Law is God's law written into the nature of things, the way things are made.

   Civil Law is the particular application of natural law for a given society. Many civil laws, like our traffic laws, help apply the natural law for the protection of human life.

   Divine Law is law revealed by God. The Sermon on the Mount and the Ten Commandments are classic examples of divine law, especially the law to love.

   Church Law is the particular application of divine law for the Christian community. The church teaches that Catholics must worship God weekly at the Sunday liturgy, for example. This law is a particular application of the third commandment—Remember to keep holy the Sabbath—for Catholics. You can find some other chief precepts of the church on pages 106-108 of this text.

6. **What is the reasonable thing to do?** Because you have been given a mind, you must use it in figuring out the moral way to act. Ask yourself what the reasonable decision is.

7. **What does your own experience and that of other people say about the issue?** Because you are a part of a society with a history, you must check out other responses to similar problems. If possible, seek the wisdom of others: parents, teachers, trusted adults, and the like.

8. **What would Jesus have done?** How does this action measure up to Jesus' yardstick of love? What does the New Testament have to say? Jesus is the absolute norm

of Christian morality. He is the one perfect human response to God. Seek out his will and follow his example before making a decision.

9. **What is the teaching of the church?** Catholics believe that the Holy Spirit lives in the church and both guides and empowers the baptized to live virtuous lives. In addition, Jesus continues to teach through the pope and the bishops united with him. Thus, sincere Catholics consider it a serious obligation to consult official church teaching on moral issues as well as to learn from competent theologians and other teachers in the church.

10. **Pray for guidance.** God will help you if you ask.

11. **Admit that you sometimes sin and might be wrong.** Humbly asking for God's forgiveness and resorting frequently to the sacrament of penance can help you develop a fine-tuned conscience.

Following your conscience.   The previous eleven steps lead to a most important twelfth step: **follow your conscience.** It is **always** wrong to go against a properly formed conscience:

> Everyone who knows what is the right thing to do and does not do it commits a sin (Jas 4:17).

Part of completing this step successfully means avoiding situations where past experience has taught you that strong emotions have a tendency to destroy your freedom to choose good. It also often means making the decision to do right even if it means going against what the majority is doing.

Finally, following your conscience is not a one time occurrence. Each new decision must be made in light of the same process. And, once a decision has been made, it must be occasionally reevaluated in order to see if all the same factors are present to still make it right. If not, your conscience may instruct you in a new way.

Jesus and the Beatitudes

Christian morality is intimately linked to the life of Jesus. It would be impossible for a Christian to form his or her conscience without knowing something about Jesus and his

teachings. Knowing **about** Jesus can lead to faith **in** Jesus. Such faith allows Jesus to guide a person's life.

Jesus' approach to morality can be described succinctly as the law to love. Jesus said:

> "This is my commandment:
> love one another,
> as I have loved you" (Jn 15:12).

Jesus preached love of God and love of neighbor. And, according to Jesus, there is no limit to love. The basic question of Christian morality is not "which laws must I follow" but "what can I do to love others the way Jesus did?"

▪ *journal* ▪

Read Matthew 5:14–16. How have you been light for others? Write five things you can do to love others the way Jesus did.

▪ *discuss* ▪

What was a difficult decision that you faced? Describe a process that helped you to make a good decision.

In fact, the Sermon on the Mount (Mt 5–7), presents Jesus as the new Moses who deepens the Mosaic Law. Jesus' disciples are called to discover a deeper, interior spirit of the Law. Christians are to put trust in God alone, to be the "poor in spirit" described in the first beatitude. Being a just and moral person means trusting in God's love and living out the values described in the Beatitudes. The Golden Rule sums up how a Christian should act:

> "So always treat others as you would like them to treat you" (Mt 7:12).

The word *beatitude* comes from the Latin word for "blessedness" or "happiness." The Beatitudes help Christians form those basic *attitudes* that Jesus' followers should have in relationship to God and to other people. As you study the Beatitudes, note how all of them reflect in some way the first—being "poor in spirit." You were made to know, love, and serve God as a way to enter eternal happiness. Jesus taught the Beatitudes to show you how to achieve your purpose.

The Beatitudes

How blessed are the poor in spirit:
the kingdom of heaven is theirs.
Blessed are *the gentle:*
they shall have the earth as inheritance.
Blessed are those who mourn:
they shall be comforted.
Blessed are those who hunger and thirst for
    uprightness:
they shall have their fill.
Blessed are the merciful:
they shall have mercy shown them.
Blessed are the pure in heart:
they shall see God.
Blessed are the peacemakers:
they shall be recognized as children of God.
Blessed are those who are persecuted in the cause
    of uprightness:
the kingdom of heaven is theirs.
                —Matthew 5:3–10

How blessed are the poor in spirit: the kingdom of heaven is theirs. The first beatitude is the announcement that God's reign has broken into human history. In these words, Jesus proclaimed the gospel to the poor. The "poor in spirit," known by their Hebrew name the *anawim*, were those without material possessions who placed their complete trust in God.

Think about what can happen to people who have few earthly possessions. Those deprived of material goods, power, prestige, and other signs of worldly success are in a position of openness before God. They know they must trust God completely for everything.

Jesus asks his disciples to have that same attitude. All trust and confidence must be placed in God alone. If you are poor in spirit you recognize that everything you have— your life, intelligence, education, possessions—are gifts from God. You show your gratitude when you share what God has given you. Generosity is a true sign that you recognize that God is your source and your destiny.

▪ *discuss* ▪

Who are the *anawim* in the world today? in your neighborhood? in your school? How can you reach out to these people? How can you be more like them?

Blessed are the gentle: they shall have the earth as inheritance. The word gentle means unassuming, tolerant, and patient. If you are gentle you work to solve problems without hatred, rancor, ill-will, or violence. You accept your dignity as a child of God.

▪ *discuss* ▪

What is something that irritates you? How can a gentle spirit help you deal with this irritation?

Blessed are those who mourn: they shall be comforted.   The third beatitude promises consolation in the midst of the most disheartening difficulties. The world is filled with much evil. You do not need to be bitter. Rather, you should express the virtue of hope by communicating in words and actions that God will conquer even the darkest problems. Hope expresses the belief that all sorrow will eventually be comforted.

▪ *discuss* ▪

Share five distressful realities in today's world. How can the virtue of hope bring consolation to these woes?

Blessed are those who hunger and thirst for uprightness: they shall have their fill.   In this beatitude, Jesus praises those who seek God by working for justice. At the end of Mass, the faithful are told to "go out to love and serve the Lord." Having received Jesus in Word and in the forms of bread and wine, Catholics must take Jesus and the gospel into the world to feed others. You do this when you treat others justly, making sure that everyone is treated with respect and given the basic necessities to live a genuinely human life.

▪ *journal* ▪

What do you hunger for most in life right now? How compatible is the "hunger and thirst for righteousness" with your desire?

Blessed are the merciful: they shall have mercy shown them. This beatitude echoes the petition of the Lord's Prayer: "forgive us our trespasses as we forgive those who trespass against us." Through Jesus, God forgives sins and accepts the baptized into the divine family as adopted children. In return, God asks Christians to extend mercy, love, and forgiveness to one another. When you forgive those who have hurt you (including your enemies), you are living the meaning of this beatitude.

▪ *resolution* ▪

Resolve to extend a word of friendship to someone who has hurt you.

Blessed are the pure in heart: they shall see God. The pure in heart have a single-hearted commitment to God. Nothing should distract you from God. Job, family, friends, and reputation are all good, but they should play secondary roles in your life. Seeking and accomplishing God's will are the primary duties of a disciple of Jesus Christ.

▪ *discuss* ▪

Share examples of how the consumer society distracts people from a single-hearted commitment to God.

Blessed are the peacemakers: they shall be recognized as children of God. Lives lived in love and peace are the twin signs of being God's adopted children. Christians have the duty to unite those who are in strife, disharmony, or opposition by helping them realize their common brotherhood and sisterhood with each other and with Jesus Christ.

How can you be a peacemaker? Consider taking these steps suggested by Quaker international peace worker Adam Curle:[1]

1. Acknowledge that the Spirit of God lives within every person you meet.

---

[1]Adam Curle, *True Justice: Quaker Peace Makers and Peace Making* (London: Quaker Home Service, 1981), pp. 56–63.

2. Learn to listen to others. Also, prayer helps you to recognize the dignity of others and to calm your own fears and anxiety so that you can be a better listener.

3. You must earn the acceptance of other people. You can do this by being willing to work side-by-side with them in common endeavors.

4. You must be persistent and never give in to discouragement. Recall St. Paul's description of love as patient. Peace and love go together, and peace is patience.

▪ *discuss* ▪

Apply these steps to a conflict you have had with a teacher, parent, or friend. How are they practical?

Blessed are those who are persecuted in the cause of uprightness: the kingdom of heaven is theirs.   There can be no greater sign of your union with Jesus than being willing to suffer for him. Jesus' words and deeds brought him misunderstanding and abuse. To be Christian means to be willing to stand up for deeply held convictions, even if this means rejection, abuse, or martyrdom. The reward which Jesus promises his sincere disciples is nothing less than God's kingdom and the eternal happiness it brings.

▪ *discuss* ▪

Share a time when you have been ridiculed because of your faith in Jesus Christ.

Beatitude Survey

Are you a Beatitude person? Answer "yes" or "no" to the following questions. Then rate yourself on the beatitude scale below.

Poor in spirit	_____ Is God #1 in my life?
Gentle	_____ Am I a gentle person, one who solves problems without ill-will?
Mourn	_____ When I see an unfair situation, do I try to help change it?

Hunger and thirst for uprightness	_____ Do I really want to be a holy person?
Merciful	_____ Do I forgive others when they hurt me?
Pure in heart	_____ Am I a person of integrity? Am I undivided in my loyalties?
Peacemaker	_____ Am I a person of peace who recognizes that the Lord lives in everyone?
Persecuted	_____ If it were a crime to be a Christian, would there be enough evidence to convict me?

Scale

7–8 "Yes" answers: You are a committed disciple!

5–6 "Yes" answers: You are developing a true Christian vocation.

3–4 "Yes" answers: You have been concentrating on your strengths.

0–2 "Yes" answers: How might you resolve your uncertainties?

The Ten Commandments

You might wonder what the Ten Commandments have to do with your life. "Aren't the Ten Commandments outdated? Haven't they been replaced?" you may ask. Some Christians even equate following the Ten Commandments to playing vinyl records after the invention of the compact disk. "Jesus gave a simple law to love," they say. "Isn't that all we need?"

Each commandment underscores key attitudes and actions which can help you to be a better person, a more loving person. The commandments also point out behaviors and attitudes which can damage loving relationships. In any case, the Ten Commandments are hardly obsolete. Jesus said:

> "Do not imagine that I have come to abolish the Law or the prophets. I have come not to abolish but to complete them. In truth I tell you, till heaven and earth disappear, not one dot, not one little stroke, is to disappear from

the Law until all its purpose is achieved. Therefore, anyone who infringes even one of the least of these commandments and teaches others to do the same will be considered the least in the kingdom of heaven; but the person who keeps them and teaches them will be considered great in the kingdom of heaven" (Mt 5:17–19).

How can the Ten Commandments improve the quality of your life? As you become a young adult, the Commandments can offer you new insights on the proper way to live and love. The first three commandments highlight the love of God; the last seven stress the love of neighbor. The following examination of each commandment will stress both the positive values you should strive for and the representative negative actions or attitudes that should be avoided.

From the Bible

The Ten Commandments are located in two places in the Bible: Exodus 20:2–17 and Deuteronomy 5:6–21. This summary is from the *New American Bible* translation.

I   I, the Lord, am your God. You shall not have other gods besides me.

II   You shall not take the name of the Lord, your God, in vain.

III   Remember to keep holy the sabbath day.

IV   Honor your father and your mother.

V   You shall not kill.

VI   You shall not commit adultery.

VII   You shall not steal.

VIII   You shall not bear false witness against your neighbor.

IX   You shall not covet your neighbor's spouse.

X   You shall not covet anything that belongs to your neighbor.

I, the Lord, am your God. You shall not have other gods besides me.   God loves you beyond what you could possibly imagine; God wants your love in return. The first commandment can help you put your life in order. In the Hebrew scriptures, Yahweh says, "I am a jealous God" (Dt 5:9). This means that a relationship with God should be your top priority. Putting God first can bring benefits. Prayer, sacrifice, and worshipful adoration of the one, true God can unite you with God. This union will result in an eternal life of happiness. The first commandment spells out the duty to believe in and witness to God (faith), confidently desire the blessed vision of God (hope), and love God above all creatures and things (love).

The first commandment warns of the danger of making something besides God the object of worship and devotion. This is known as *idolatry*, that is, worship of idols. The worship of sex, money, power, possessions, or prestige can be forms of idolatry. *Satanism* or devil worship is the most serious form of idolatry. Other types include:

- **Superstition.** It is a form of idolatry because it invests godlike powers in ordinary things.
- **Astrology.** It is the belief that the stars control the lives of people.
- **Divination.** This practice seeks to learn about the future from Tarot cards, ouija boards, fortune-tellers, or palm readers. The scriptures condemn divination as evil (see Dt 18:10–14).
- **Spiritism.** Trying to contact the dead through mediums and seances also violates faith in the one true God. Scripture likewise forbids this practice (see Lv 20:27).

You honor the first commandment when you gratefully acknowledge, worship, thank, and *trust* God who is the source of everything in existence.

You shall not take the name of the Lord, your God, in vain. The second commandment stresses the need to respect God's name and to practice religion with a spirit of humility. Some things are sacred, including God's name. Since a person's language reflects who he or she is, your language and attitude toward religion should be respectful. For example, it would be wrong to ask God to bring harm to another person. This is known as *cursing*. Cursing is a misuse of God's name because it tries to involve God in evil. Two other violations of the second commandment are *swearing* and *blasphemy.*

Swearing is the taking of an oath by invoking God's name to bear witness that one is telling the truth. Although Jesus told his disciples that they should be so truthful that oath-taking should be unnecessary (Mt 5:34–37), the judicial system has traditionally required swearing, as in the "swearing in" of a witness. Swearing is wrong when a person *perjures* him or herself, that is lies after taking an oath to God.

Blasphemy is abusive or disrespectful remarks made against God. Since Jesus is God, any scornful thought, word, or action directed against him can also be blasphemous.

The second commandment underscores the value of praying to God with humility and trust. Your prayers should reflect the trust you have in God's Word.

Remember to keep holy the sabbath day.   The Jewish sabbath is Saturday to commemorate the seventh day of creation when God rested from all the work that had been completed. The early church began to keep the first day of the week as holy. Sunday is the day of Jesus' resurrection.

For Catholics, Sunday is a day for worshipping God and attending to the needs of family, friends, and the Christian community. By worshipping God through participating in the eucharist, Catholics also show love for the Christian community. By being present at Mass, Catholics are saying that they need others on the Christian journey and that they are there to help others as well. In addition, the community's gathering at eucharist is a sign to the world of God's importance in the life of the church. Attendance at Sunday or Saturday evening Mass is also an *obligation* for Catholics according to church law.

Keeping Sunday holy also retains the original idea of Sabbath as a day of relaxation and renewal. Catholics are to refrain from unnecessary work, spend time with family, visit friends or relatives, enjoy nature's beauty, or renew their minds by reading a good book. All of these activities can help to re-energize a person's life so that he or she can be of greater service to others during the upcoming week.

Your Sunday Obligation

An obligation is a "binding promise or responsibility." As a Catholic, you are obliged to attend Mass on Sunday or Saturday evening and on all holy days. Church law states:

> On Sundays and other holy days of obligation, the faithful are obliged to assist at Mass. They are also to abstain from such work or business that would inhibit the worship to be given to God, the joy proper to the Lord's Day, or the due relaxation of mind and body. . . .
>
> The obligation of assisting at Mass is satisfied whenever Mass is celebrated in a Catholic rite, either on a holy day itself or on the evening of the previous day (*Canons 1247–1248*).

▪ *discuss* ▪

1. List some common reasons people give for missing Sunday Mass. Offer some suggestions for how these difficulties might be avoided.

2. What are some good Sunday activities that can help re-energize a person for the week ahead?

Holy Days

In addition to Sundays, Catholics in the United States celebrate the following holy days of obligation:

1. Solemnity of Mary, Mother of God (January 1)
2. Ascension Thursday (forty days after Easter)
3. Assumption of Mary into Heaven (August 15)
4. All Saints Day (November 1)
5. Immaculate Conception of Mary (December 8)
6. Christmas Day (December 25)

Honor your father and your mother.   The fourth commandment is about family life. It mirrors the loving relationship that God has with all people. For example, just as God loves all people, so human parents should love and care for their children. Two ways parents show their love is by educating their children and by giving them enough freedom so that they can grow in independence. Catholic parents are also responsible for having their children baptized and for nurturing their developing faith in Christ and the church.

Likewise, this commandment also instructs children to honor their parents. Honor implies giving parents obedience, courtesy, and gratitude. When parents are sick or need help, it is the responsibility of their children to care for them. Also, the fourth commandment requires that brothers and sisters show each other patience, friendship, and respect so that the family can be a harmonious place of love.

Finally, the fourth commandment has social implications. Respect is also due all proper church and other authority figures (teachers, employers, police, leaders) since all authority comes from God. In the civic order, this implies a moral obligation to pay taxes, exercise the right to vote, and serve the nation in its defense or in some other way. However, when societal laws conflict with God's will or God's law, then this obligation is removed.

■ *activity* ■

Make a list of ten "Teen Commandments," in other words reasonable rules and guidelines for living in a family. For example, "Always call home when you will be more than a half-hour late." Share your list with the class. Combine it into one class list. (Don't worry about sticking to exactly ten commandments.) Make copies of this final list. Share it with your parents.

You shall not kill.   The fifth commandment is the commandment of life. It encourages you to appreciate, care for, and love God's gift of life. It teaches that human life is of priceless value.

You can keep this commandment by doing things like getting proper exercise and rest, eating wholesome food, avoiding harmful substances like drugs, alcohol, and tobacco, and challenging your mind by learning new things. You also show respect for life when you promote, protect, and speak out for others, especially the weak and helpless.

This means supporting life—being pro-life, if you will, for all of life from beginning to end. One of the best ways to show you are pro-life is in the way you treat other people. Being pro-life also means to condemn all anti-life behaviors. These include:

- **Murder and suicide.** Murder is the unjustified taking of another person's life. Suicide is the taking of one's own life. Humans may never directly kill themselves regardless of their motives.

- **Unjust war.** Though the church permits a nation to engage in war in order to protect itself or the human rights of others, military action that involves nuclear, chemical, and biological weapons and does not discriminate between innocent people and military targets is a violation of the fifth commandment.

- **Capital punishment.** The American Catholic bishops oppose the use of the death penalty. In the United States, poor people and minorities who cannot afford costly legal appeals have been executed disproportionally to the rest of the population. Capital punishment also goes against Jesus' call for repentance and forgiveness.

- **Abortion.** Catholic opposition to abortion rests on the fundamental fact that human life begins from the moment of conception and thus deserves to be protected. The fifth commandment forbids any act that directly intends to kill an unborn human life.

- **Euthanasia.** Euthanasia comes from the Greek word meaning "easy death." *Direct* or *active* euthanasia ("mercy killing") is any act or omission of an act that causes the death of a seriously ill or dying person.

- **Kidnapping, acts of terrorism, and torture.** These are violent acts which are grave threats to human dignity. They are seriously immoral and condemned by the fifth commandment.

▪ *journal* ▪

The following New Testament passages teach something about how Christians should live. Read each passage and note one of the points it makes about the given theme.

Generosity	2 Cor 9:6–15
Judging others	Gal 6:1–5
Serving others	Mk 6:37–42
Good Samaritan	Lk 10:30–37
Greatest	Mk 9:33–37
Words and deeds	Jas 1:22–25
Rich man and Lazarus	Lk 16:19–31
Sexual immorality	Heb 13:4

■ *research* ■

What does the church teach about:

- medical experimentation on humans?
- under what conditions it is moral to donate one's organs?

Share your findings with the class.

You shall not commit adultery. You shall not covet your neighbor's spouse.   The sixth and the ninth commandments are commandments of fidelity, especially in the areas of marriage and sexual love. In the Song of Songs, God's love for the Chosen People is compared to the passionate love that a husband has for his bride. And in the Letter to the Ephesians, St. Paul refers to the church as the bride of Christ (see Eph 5:25–33). The love of a Christian husband and wife should reflect Christ's love for his church.

The prime virtue of God's covenant love is fidelity, or faithfulness. A Christian marriage, likewise a covenant of love, should reflect the selfless, faithful love of God. The Catholic community sees marriage as a way to grow in holiness.

Sexual intercourse (and all acts leading up to it) must express a total, unreserved commitment of love between a man and a woman. Such a commitment can take place only when a couple has publicly declared a lifelong devotion to each other, as in the sacrament of marriage. The sixth commandment forbids *adultery*, sexual intimacy engaged in by a married person with another who is not one's spouse. Adultery is a serious failure in the permanent commitment of a married couple who promised lifelong fidelity to each other.

The sixth commandment is to be observed by all Christians, not exclusively those who are married. As you know, the church teaching on sex vastly differs from the messages proclaimed by the media, popular society, and probably some of your peers. However, without the pledge of a commitment, sexual intercourse becomes nothing more than a biological act. The element of bonding, growing love is missing.

Sexual behavior also forbidden by the sixth commandment includes:

- **Fornication.** Sexual intercourse engaged in by unmarried people is defined by the term fornication.

- **Homosexual activity.** Objectively, homosexual genital activity is wrong because it frustrates the aims of sexual intercourse: unity between a husband and wife and the openness to the transmission of human life.

- **Masturbation.** The self-stimulation of one's own sexual organs is a misuse of God's gift of sexuality.

- **Pornography.** Sexually explicit material damages the dignity of those who are exploited in it—most often women or children—as well as those who create, sell, and use it for their sexual pleasure.

- **Prostitution.** This is a serious cheapening of the gift of sexuality and life itself for those who sell their bodies and those who pay for sex.

- **Rape.** A seriously, intrinsically evil act, rape (including date rape) violates another's sexuality through force or the threat of force. Similar evil acts are **incest** and **sexual abuse of children**.

Jesus said that evil intentions and actions like those described above come from the heart (see Mt 15:19). The ninth commandment is a reminder that sinful sexual activity comes from disordered hearts.

The term to describe this disorder is *concupiscence*, which refers to an abnormal sexual desire, or lust. Coveting others sexually is a form of concupiscence that allows strong, uncontrolled internal desires to turn others into objects of pleasure. Jesus described this sin when he said:

"But I say this to you, if a man looks at a woman lustfully, he has already committed adultery in his heart" (Mt 5:28).

Chastity is the God-given power that enables people to use the gift of sexuality in the right way. All Christians must live chaste lives, depending on their state in life. This includes people who are single, married, or committed to religious life. The virtue of *modesty* can help you to live a chaste life. Modesty in your choice of clothes and tastefulness in speaking about sexual matters, for example, can be a sign that your purity of action is in line with your pure thoughts.

▪ *journal* ▪

Choose and answer one of the following:

1. Why does pornography violate the ninth commandment?
2. How do sexually explicit song lyrics affect the morals of pre-teens or teenagers?
3. How do movies, advertisements, television programs, and other forms of media undermine the values of chastity?
4. What are appropriate guidelines for modest dress? Outline your proposal.

You shall not steal. You shall not covet anything that belongs to your neighbor.   The covetousness of things condemned in the tenth commandment often leads to the theft of those things which is prohibited by the seventh commandment. Covetousness is often motivated by greed, jealousy, or envy. The tenth commandment is a reminder to appreciate what you have been given and to desire not more things, but rather a more firm and trusting relationship with God. Jesus said:

"No one can be the slave of two masters: he will either hate the first and love the second, or be attached to the first and despise the second. You cannot be the slave both of God and money" (Mt 6:24).

The seventh commandment forbids stealing. Stealing means taking something from someone without his or her knowledge or consent. Such actions break down the honesty and trust which any social unit needs to function. The gravity of stealing depends on the value of the stolen object and the circumstances. For example, it would be slight matter for an office worker in a large company to take home supplies for personal use. However, it would be much more serious for someone to willfully steal a social security check from a poor, elderly person. Besides stealing, theft can also involve cheating, the misuse of personal talents, lack of stewardship for the environment, and the failure to share. Here is more information on each of these kinds of theft:

- **Cheating.** Cheating involves two wrongs: theft and lying. For example, people who cheat on a test not only take answers that do not belong to them (theft), but they claim the answer as their own (lying).

- **Misuse of personal talents.** Failure to use God-given talents is a form of theft because it deprives others of something that is good. For example, if a gifted pianist failed to perfect his or her talent, others would be deprived of the music, a good.

- **Lack of stewardship for the environment.** When the earth and its resources are not cared for, future generations are deprived of their rightful inheritance. Water and air pollution and even simple acts of littering are examples of environmental theft.

- **Failure to share.** Many people do not even have the basic necessities of life. A failure to share food, shelter, and other resources with those in need is a form of theft.

Is Gambling a Sin?

To gamble means to play games of chance for money or something else of value. In most places, there is some form of legal gambling. Even some churches use gambling to raise money for particular needs. There is nothing wrong with gambling if a person can control the desire and it is within his or her financial means. But out-of-control gambling can be sinful. It can lead to theft, lying, abuse of families, impoverishment, or gambling addiction.

▪ *journal* ▪

Read the following quotation. Write about what you think it means.

"The measure of a man's real character is what he would do, if he knew he would never be found out."—Macaulay

▪ *discuss* ▪

1. What do you think about gambling?
2. What are some kinds of gambling you have participated in? Could you imagine this form of gambling becoming addicting?
3. Share your position on government-sponsored gambling and church-sponsored gambling.

▪ *research* ▪

Research and report on *Gamblers Anonymous*, an organization that helps compulsive gamblers.

You shall not bear false witness against your neighbor. Jesus referred to himself as the Way, the Truth, and the Life. Being truthful is one way to imitate Jesus.

The opposite of being truthful is being a liar. Lying means communicating a known falsehood to another person. Evidence of lying abounds in our society: Politicians say one thing to get elected, then do another. Advertisers make false claims about their products. Witnesses perjure themselves in courtroom trials. Unfaithful spouses disregard their marriage commitment. Teens distort the truth about their whereabouts to their parents. One friend gossips about another. All these actions are wrong and forbidden by the eighth commandment.

Lying erodes the mutual trust which people need to live together in society. It frustrates the function of speech which is to communicate and share the truth with others. The letter of James warns about the damage lying can do:

> Nobody can tame the tongue—it is a pest that will not keep still, full of deadly poison. We use it to bless the Lord and Father, but we also use it to curse people who are made in God's image (Jas 3:8–9).

Despite the warning, you must learn to control your speech and tell the truth. As St. Paul writes:

> So from now on, there must be no more lies. *Speak the truth to one another,* since we are all parts of one another. *Even if you are angry, do not sin:* never let the sun set on your anger (Eph 4:25–26).

Conclusion

Love, of course, is the final word in Christian morality. Living a moral life means loving God above everything and your neighbor as yourself. Yet, loving others can be difficult and life is filled with many seemingly impossible choices.

The Beatitudes and the Ten Commandments give helpful guidance and direction on how to love. They can serve as guides to assist you as you make right choices by following your conscience. These helps, as well as the very life of Jesus itself, can lead you on the difficult but rewarding road of discipleship.

▪ *focus questions* ▪

1. How is Catholic morality about "true human living"?

2. How is faith without works empty?

3. How is Jesus a Christian's moral guide?

4. What is conscience? What are the two principles associated with a mature Christian conscience?

5. Discuss one factor that can cloud a conscience decision.

6. Outline some of the key steps you can take to develop a mature Christian conscience.

7. Distinguish between and among the following types of law: natural, civil, divine, and church.

▪ *discuss* ▪

1. Can you ever reveal a secret if someone swore you to secrecy? If so, what exceptions would you make? If not, why not?

2. Which of the following is most dishonest? least dishonest? Explain the reasons for your answers.
   a. cheating on a test
   b. shoplifting
   c. sneaking into a movie without paying
   d. protecting a friend by lying
   e. not giving a full effort at work

8. Finish this statement: "Christian morality is not about which laws I must follow, but..."

9. List the Beatitudes. Explain a key idea from each.

10. List the Ten Commandments and at least one value that underlies each of them.

11. Identify these terms: superstition, astrology, divination, and spiritism. How are they forms of idolatry?

12. Define: *cursing, swearing, perjury,* and *blasphemy.*

13. Why do Catholics worship God on the first day of the week?

14. Discuss how the fourth commandment supports family life.

15. What are some actions which the fifth commandment forbids?

16. Discuss several specific church teachings in the area of sexual fidelity.

17. What are some forms of stealing?

18. Discuss two ways people bear false witness. Why are they sinful?

▪ *exercise* ▪

Research one of the topics discussed in this chapter. For example, astrology, divination, capital punishment, pornography, shoplifting, or slander. Prepare a two-minute oral report on the topic for the class.

▪ *vocabulary* ▪

Look up the meaning of the following words in the dictionary. Transcribe the definitions into your journal.

concupiscence
covetousness
superfluous

Prayer Reflection

Jesus is the guide and model for living a Christian moral life. Catholics believe that Jesus' presence in the Blessed Sacrament can be comforting and can provide strength. Sit before the Blessed Sacrament. Pray this famous fourteenth-century prayer of adoration.

Anima Christi

Soul of Christ, be my sanctification;
Body of Christ, be my salvation;

Blood of Christ, fill my veins;
Water of Christ's side, wash out my stains;
Passion of Christ, my comfort be;
O good Jesu, listen to me:
In thy wounds I fain would hide,
Ne'er be parted from thy side;
Guard me, should the foe assail me;
Call me when my life should fail me;
Bid me come to thee above,
With thy saints to sing thy love
World without end. Amen.

▪ *reflection* ▪

When do you think of Jesus each day? When do you ask his help when tempted to do wrong?

▪ *resolution* ▪

Pray the *Anima Christi* prayer daily during the coming two weeks. Try to visit the Blessed Sacrament or receive holy communion at least one time in addition to Sunday.

chapter 7

Catholic Teaching on Social Justice

To do justice and to love kindness, and to walk humbly with your God.

—Micah 6:8 (*RSV*)

A young man fell asleep on the bus and missed his stop. For the first time in his life he found himself in the poorest section of town. He looked out the window and saw a young girl, dirty and in tattered clothes, begging for money on the street corner. The man was shaken. That night before he fell asleep he angrily prayed to God, "How, O Lord, can you permit such wretchedness? Why don't you do something."

During the night the young man had a dream. In it, God appeared to him and said, "You know that poor child you saw today? I did indeed do something about her. I made you."

As God sent Jesus to accomplish salvation for all people, so Jesus sends you to continue his work. As a Christian missionary (a word meaning "one sent"), your task is threefold. You must *proclaim* by word and example the gospel of Jesus. You must be a *sign* of the gospel by being a member of the church community. You must *serve* the gospel by helping to meet the basic needs of all. Working for *justice* is one way to accomplish all three tasks.

What is justice? The word justice equates with something that is fair, deserving, and right. There are various types of justice. For example:

■ *Commutative justice* requires basic fairness in all agreements and exchanges between individuals.

■ *Legal justice* concerns what citizens in fairness owe to the community (for example, the paying of taxes).

■ *Distributive justice* governs what the community owes its citizens based on their contributions and needs.

Social justice, on the other hand, deals with the obligations of individuals and groups to apply the Christian gospel to the systems, structures, and institutions of society. Social

175

justice "implies that persons have an obligation to be active and productive participants in the life of society and that society has a duty to enable them to participate in this way" (*Economic Justice for All*, #71).

Social justice is Christ's message come alive. Working for justice ranks with the celebration of the sacraments and the preaching of the gospel as an essential ministry in the church. As a Christian, you must do your part to apply Jesus' message to the structures, systems, and institutions of society. Social justice is also an essential *human* task. This is true because all human relationships—personal, cultural, political, and economic—take place in the social frameworks that social justice addresses.

This chapter will examine six key themes of Catholic teachings on social justice. These teachings explain the attitudes Christians should have toward social justice. Some related issues will also be presented. Justice is the minimal human and Christian response to others. As American novelist Herman Melville wrote:

> We cannot live for ourselves alone. Our lives are connected by a thousand invisible threads, and along these sympathetic fibers, our actions run as causes and return to us as results.

Finally, this chapter will suggest some activities that you can do to become involved in the church's social justice ministry.

What Does Justice Mean to You?

Use this scale to express your opinions on the following statements:

5—strongly agree
4—agree
3—don't know
2—disagree
1—strongly disagree

_____ 1. Society should give preferential treatment to members of disadvantaged groups when they apply to college and for certain forms of employment.

_____ 2. A Catholic should never fight in a war.

_____ 3. Rich nations should pay a form of tax to help poorer nations to develop.

_____ 4. Human rights have to be earned, not just granted to people.

_____ 5. Since laws rarely change attitudes, there is little value in passing civil rights legislation or anti-discrimination laws.

_____ 6. Larger political units (federal and state government) should *not* involve themselves in matters that smaller social units (local government, families, etc.) can handle on their own.

_____ 7. Workers whose jobs involve a key service (police, fire, medical staff, etc.) should *never* strike, regardless of their grievances.

_____ 8. Christians can never justify the possession of nuclear weapons.

_____ 9. A pro-life amendment that would outlaw both abortion and euthanasia should be added to the constitution.

_____ 10. There should be stricter national and international laws to protect the environment, even if they would negatively affect economic development.

_____ 11. All governments should reduce military spending and allocate the savings to programs for the poor.

_____ 12. Society has a moral duty to provide a minimum subsistence level for those who cannot take care of themselves.

_____ 13. Consumerism is a major societal disease. It makes people materialistic, selfish, and morally bankrupt.

—— 14. Every citizen has a basic right to minimum health care.

▪ *discuss* ▪

1. Defend two of your most strongly held positions.
2. How are your opinions on these issues similar to those of a parent or other significant adult in your life? different?
3. Provide a possible solution to one of the social dilemmas on the list.

Theme One: Life and Dignity of the Human Person

Catholic social teaching is rooted in the human person. Each person images and reflects God. And, through Jesus, each person is redeemed. All people have a basic dignity and are "capable of knowing and loving their Creator" (*The Church in the Modern World*, #12). In other words, your worth comes from *who you are* as God's creation, not *what you do*. Nor is your worth dependent on your race, gender, age, or economic status. The dignity of human creation is described in the Book of Psalms:

> Yet you have made him little less than a god,
> you have crowned him with glory and beauty,
> made him lord of the work of your hands,
> put all things under his feet (Ps 8:5–6).

When the Son of God took on flesh in the person of Jesus Christ, God raised human nature "to a dignity beyond compare" (*Redeemer of Humankind*, #8). Jesus offers each person the true human vocation, to be the person God intended of him or her. Catholic social teaching attempts to judge every policy, law, and institution according to how well they enhance human life and dignity.

From the Documents

Dignity.   At the center of all Catholic social teaching are the transcendence of God and the dignity of the human person. The human person is the clearest reflection of God's presence in the world; all of the Church's work in pursuit of both justice and peace is designed to protect and promote the dignity of every person. For each person not only reflects God, but is the expression of God's creative work and the meaning of Christ's redemptive ministry.

—*The Challenge of Peace*, #15

Issues

What are the issues? Here are some key issues affecting the life and dignity of the human person. First, note the problem. Then, begin to consider ways you can help to affect change:

- **Respect for the unborn.** Jesus modeled caring for the weak and helpless of society. Today, the unborn are an especially vulnerable group. Governments around the world permit the killing of thousands of unborn human lives daily through permissive abortion laws.

  Social justice in this area means that society must first recognize and then protect by law the basic right to human life. Thus, Christians and others who work to correct legal decisions which permit abortion are promoting God's work for justice in a significant way.

  Working for changes in laws is not the only thing that needs to be done. Women who are pregnant—especially young, poor, and unmarried women—must be shown other solutions to handling their pregnancies besides abortion. Prenatal and natal care, and post-pregnancy care for both mother and child must be provided. This may include helping to arrange for adoptions. Several Catholic organizations assist with these types of pastoral care.

- **Women in society.** Jesus affirmed the equality and dignity of women. Jesus freely associated with women which went against all standing cultural and religious practices of the day.

■ *discuss* ■

1. What are some current events from the news that illustrate a disregard for basic dignity?
2. How are people who disregard basic human dignity themselves dishonored? How do they dishonor God?

Church teaching likewise outlaws discrimination against women and affirms the human rights of all:

> With respect to the fundamental rights of the person, every type of discrimination, whether based on sex, race, color or social condition, language, or religion, is to be overcome and eradicated as contrary to God's intent (*The Church in the Modern World*, #29).

However, the church also cautions against views which would ignore or deny significant differences between the sexes, undermine marriage or motherhood, or erode family life. For example, Pope John Paul II wrote:

> The true advancement of women requires that labor should be structured in such a way that women do not have to pay for their advancement by abandoning what is specific to them and at the expense of the family, in which women as mothers have an irreplaceable role (*On Human Work*, #19).

■ **Respect for racial and ethnic groups.** Individuals and the structures of society often discriminate against people based on racial, national, ethnic, or religious difference. Though civil rights laws cannot change prejudicial attitudes by themselves, laws do serve to foster justice by protecting minority groups, by deterring those who might otherwise violate someone's rights, and by educating people to know right from wrong. Pope Paul VI wrote:

> Within a country which belongs to each one, all should be equal before the law, find equal admittance to economic, cultural, civic and social life and benefit from a fair share of the nation's riches (*A Call to Action*, #16).

A society must foster racial justice, especially in housing, education, health care, employment, and the administration of justice. Personally, each Christian must become better informed on the various differences between people, but more importantly look for concrete ways to promote Christian unity.

■ *activities* ■

What can you do? Use these suggestions as a starting point (or come up with one on your own). Complete one of the activities.

Write a report on what you did. Share your report with the class.

1. Write a letter to a legislator or one of the media expressing a pro-life position rooted in human dignity.

2. Participate in a pro-life rally.

3. Interview several people of different racial, ethnic, national, or religious backgrounds about how they perceive prejudice at your school. Share the results of your interviews. Discuss with the class what you can do to lessen prejudice in your school.

4. Evaluate radio and television advertisements aimed at teens. Discuss what message they are selling concerning self-esteem. Critique these messages considering the basic dignity of each human person.

5. Evaluate any pending tax legislation on the local, state, or national level to see what it is doing *for* and *to* people.

6. Share a way that you can treat one individual person with greater respect.

7. The United States bishops had difficulty completing a pastoral letter on women. Why do you think this was so? Read an article that sheds more light on this subject. Share some information from what you read.

Theme Two:
Rights and Responsibilities

People are endowed with basic human rights and corresponding duties according to their God-given dignity. The most basic human right is the right to life. This right includes entitlement to life's basic necessities: food, clothing, housing, health care, education, security, social services, and employment. Other rights are the freedom of conscience and religious liberty, the right to raise a family, the right to emigrate, the right to just treatment, and the right to a fair share of the earth's goods.

Every right has a corresponding duty and responsibility: to others, to family members, and to the larger society of which all people are members. In claiming his or her rights, each person must respect the rights of others and work for the common good.

From the Documents

Rights. Among the most important of . . . rights . . . [is] the right to life, an integral part of which is the right of the child to develop in the mother's womb from the moment of conception; the right to live in a united family and in a moral environment conducive to the growth of the child's personality; the right to develop one's intelligence and freedom in seeking and knowing the truth; the right to share in the work which makes wise use of the earth's material resources, and to derive from that work the means to support oneself and one's dependents; and the right freely to establish a family, to have and to rear children through the responsible exercise of one's sexuality. In a certain sense, the source and synthesis of these rights is religious freedom, understood as the right to live in the truth of one's faith and in conformity with one's transcendent dignity as a person.

—*The One Hundredth Year*, #47

Duties: The right to live involves the duty to preserve one's life; the right to a decent standard of living, the duty to live in a becoming fashion; the right to be free to seek out the truth, the duty to devote oneself to an ever deeper and wider search for it.

Once this is admitted, it follows that in human society one man's natural right gives rise to a corresponding duty in other men; the duty, that is, of recognizing and respecting that right. Every basic human right draws its authoritative force from the natural law, which confers it and attaches to it its respective duty. Hence, to claim one's rights and ignore one's duties, or only half fulfill them, is like building a house with one hand and tearing it down with the other.

—*Peace on Earth*, #29–30

▪ *discuss* ▪

1. List five rights you have as a student. What are their corresponding duties?
2. With the class, brainstorm a list of rights in each of the following categories: economic, political, cultural, social, and religious. Then, discuss corresponding duties to each of the rights.
3. Pope John Paul II wrote that religious freedom is the "source and synthesis" of other rights. What does this mean?

Issues

What are the issues? Here are some key issues connected with basic human rights and duties. Note the abuses to each right. Think about what can be done to guarantee these rights to all people.

▪ **Hunger.** One of the tragedies of the modern world is

that thousands of people continue to die of starvation each day. This is even more tragic considering that the farming countries of the world produce enough food to provide every person with a minimum but adequate diet. According to Arthur Simon:

> If the present world food production were evenly divided among all the world's people, with minimal waste, everyone would have enough. Barely enough, perhaps, but enough (*Bread for the World*, p. 18).

An obvious response to the problem of hunger is a more equitable redistribution of food to reach people in the poorer nations of the world. The difficulty comes in sifting through the various political and economic mazes which prevent this from occurring. Vatican II teaches a proper Christian response to the problem of hunger:

> Since there are so many people in this world afflicted with hunger, this sacred council urges all, both individuals and governments, to remember the saying of the fathers: "Feed the man dying of hunger, because if you have not fed him you have killed him" (*Church in the Modern World*, #69).

- **The aged.** Society too often neglects the elderly. The aged are often shuttled away from the mainstream of societal and familial life, and their wisdom, knowledge, and experience are not utilized. When possible, children of elderly parents should welcome them into their homes.

> Anyone who does not look after his own relations, especially if they are living with him, has rejected the faith and is worse than an unbeliever (1 Tm 5:8).

Society, furthermore, must help to care for the aged who can no longer take care of themselves.

- **The handicapped.** Discrimination against the handicapped is wrong, in that it pits the strong and healthy against the weak and sick. The church teaches that it is unworthy of Christians "and a denial of our common humanity, to admit to the life of the community, and thus admit to work, only those who are fully functional" (*On Human Work*, #22).

- **Crime and criminals.** People have the right to be protected from crime and criminals. Victims of crimes should be cared for. Efforts to help victims achieve justice should be supported. Societies should work not only for stricter laws and more law enforcement but also strive to root out the sources of much crime—poverty, injustice, and materialism.

  Prisoners also have rights. These rights include: protection from assault and access to proper food, health care, recreation, and education.

- **Migrant workers.** Migrant workers—usually farm workers who must move often from one place to the next—are frequently the victims of discriminatory attitudes which force them to live with the insecurity of low pay and improper housing. Emigrating to find work is sometimes a necessary evil, but "migration in search of work must in no way become an opportunity for financial or social exploitation" (*Laborem Exercens*, #23).

▪ *activities* ▪

What can you do? Use these suggestions as a starting point (or come up with your own). How can you help to guarantee more people are granted basic human rights? How are you personally responsible? Write or share a summary of your work.

1. Research and write a three-page report on either the causes of world hunger or the effects of hunger (malnutrition and undernutrition). Cite recent statistics on the problem.

2. Volunteer at a hunger center or sponsor a hunger awareness day at school.

3. Visit a nursing home or a homebound person from your parish on a regular basis. Keep a journal detailing each of your visits.

4. Research and report on the plight of migrant workers in your state.

5. Analyze your eating habits for one week. Note your consumption of unnecessary food and its cost. Cut back on this kind of food. Donate your savings to a hunger center.

6. Write a letter to or visit your grandparents or an older relative some time in the next week.

Theme Three: Call to Family, Community, and Participation

Families are the foundation of society. One strength of families is their ability to offer affirmations and love to individuals not for *what* they do or have but for *who* they are. In families, people learn values and how to act on them. The state must support families since it is families that support the various other social institutions.

Family members have both the right and responsibility to participate in and contribute to the political and economic realms of society at large. Likewise, the state and other political and economic institutions must promote the dignity and rights of individuals. Furthermore, governmental agencies should intervene to meet basic human needs when individual or family initiative is incapable of doing the job. The litmus test in judging political, legal, and economic institutions is deciding what they do *to* and *for* people and how people participate in them.

From the Documents

Primacy of Family.   The family, founded upon marriage freely contracted, one and indissoluble, must be regarded as the natural, primary cell of human society. The interests of the family, therefore, must be taken very specially into consideration in social and economic affairs, as well as in the spheres of faith and morals. For all of these have to do with strengthening the family and assisting it in the fulfillment of its mission.
—*Peace on Earth,* #16

The natural family, stable and monogamous—as fashioned by God and sanctified by Christianity—in which generations live together, helping each other to acquire greater wisdom and to harmonize personal rights with other social needs, is the basis of society.
—*The Development of Peoples,* #36

...The state has the duty of watching over the common good and of ensuring that every sector of social life, not excluding the economic one, contributes to achieving that good while respecting the rightful autonomy of each sector.

—*The One Hundredth Year*, #11

Issues

What are the issues? Here are some issues involved with family life and the family's participation in society at large. Consider the significance of each in the area of social justice.

■ **Children.** Parents have a vital role in God's creative plan. Cooperating with the Creator, they have the privilege of transmitting life and rearing children in a loving, stable family (*Church in the Modern World*, #50). In accord with God's plan, parents have the right to choose the size of their family, but selfishness can never be the determining factor. God designed marriage for the intimate sharing of love between a husband and wife and as the means to procreate human life. These two values—life and love—are the firm foundation for the larger society.

■ **Common good.** Catholic social teaching promotes the common good, that is, all the spiritual, social, and material conditions societies need for individuals to achieve full human dignity. The common good is "the sum of those conditions of social life which allow not only groups but also their individual members to achieve their own fulfillment more fully and more readily" than they could on their own (*Church in the Modern World*, #26).

Meeting basic needs like food, shelter, clothing, as well as receiving a decent education, worshipping God as one sees fit, and being able to participate in public life are some of the rights the common good embraces. The common good of one nation can never be independent of the world community. Thus, the wealthy nations must help the poorer nations to develop and refrain from policies that would diminish their economic or political freedom. The world is one community and national policies must promote the good of all.

All elements in a society (individuals, organizations, public agencies) must work to promote the common good. The state (government), however, has a unique role to preserve public order and, *as a last resort*, to intervene to promote justice.

> The common good that authority in the state serves is brought to full realization only when all the citizens are sure of their rights (*Redeemer of Humankind*, #17).

■ **The principle of subsidiarity.** Although the church supports the rights of governments to intervene with aiding human rights, it does not advocate doing so to the detriment of small social units. In 1931 Pope Pius XI wrote:

> The supreme authority of the state ought . . . to let subordinate groups handle matters and concerns of lesser importance (*Reconstruction of the Social Order*, #80).

The principle of subsidiarity holds that decisions in the social order should be made at the lowest reasonable level so that more people can freely and responsibly participate in the tasks of society. Only when an individual or smaller social unit cannot properly fulfill a task should the larger society take it up. Pope John Paul II wrote:

> A community of a higher order should not interfere in the internal life of a community of a lower order, depriving the latter of its functions, but rather should support it in case of need and help to coordinate its activity with activities of the rest of society, always with a view to the common good (*The One Hundredth Year*, #48).

For example, the state should not interfere with the parents' *primary* right and duty to care for their children. But when parents cannot adequately take care of their children because of extraordinary circumstance, then the larger society should step in and offer its help.

■ *activities* ■

What can you do? Use these suggestions as a starting point (or come up with your own) to help insure greater participation by more people in these areas of society. Complete one of the activities. Write or share a summary of your work with the class.

1. How does the student government at your school effect change? Do an objective analysis of its effectiveness.

2. Sponsor a career day at school by inviting in various representatives to share insights on their vocations. Develop a format for the students to ask questions and seek follow-up information.

3. List and discuss some social services that government agencies currently handle that should be taken care of by families or other local agencies.

4. Analyze a policy of the federal or state government based on how well it supports the common good of all people.

Theme Four: Dignity of Work and Rights of Workers

Besides helping to support people's basic needs, work also helps people to express their dignity and their participation in God's ongoing creation. People have the basic right to decent and productive work, fair wages, private property, and economic initiative. The church has consistently upheld workers' right to form unions and associations in their pursuit of their rights and dignity. Catholic teaching points out that the economy exists to help people, not vice versa.

From the Documents

Just remuneration for the work of an adult who is responsible for a family means remuneration which will suffice for establishing and maintaining a family and for providing security for its future. Such remuneration can be given either through what is called a family wage—that is, a single salary given to the head of the family for his work, sufficient for the needs of the family without the other spouse having to take up gainful employment outside the home—or through other social measures such as family allowances or grants to mothers devoting themselves exclusively to their families.

—*On Human Work,* #19

▪ *discuss* ▪

How could Pope John Paul's idea of a family wage be practically applied in today's job marketplace?

Issue

What is the issue? Examine the issue of employment and the right of all people to be able to work. How is this right met in today's economy? What can be done to insure that all people have a meaningful job?

▪ **Employment.** The church supports the right of every person to do productive work:

> The entire process of productive work, then, must be accommodated to the needs of the human person and the nature of his life, with special attention to domestic life and mothers of families, in particular, taking sex and age always into account. Workers should have the opportunity to develop their talents and their personalities in the very exercise of their work, while devoting their time and energy to the performance of their work with a due sense of responsibility, they should nevertheless be allowed sufficient rest and leisure to cultivate their family, cultural, social, and religious life (*Church in the Modern World,* #67).

In his encyclical *On Human Work,* Pope John Paul reiterated the church's position on the rights of workers to unionize and to strike. In this same letter, Pope John Paul criticized the world's two opposing economic systems, Marxism and capitalism. He rejected the Marxist emphasis on state ownership of material and property. He also warned capitalistic society for often neglecting the common good and for choosing economic profit and productivity over the rights of people.

▪ *activities* ▪

What can you do? Interview ten Christian adults currently in the work force. Make sure to interview both men and women representative of many different kinds of professions. Ask them these or similar questions. Note trends in the interviews. Write a summary of the interviews and share it with the class.

1. What do you consider a just wage for a job in your chosen career?

2. How did you choose your career? What kind of training did you need? What do you find most rewarding about your career?

3. What recourse do you have to deal with unjust situations as they might pertain to your work? For example, any type of job discrimination.

4. How does your occupation help your personal development? What contributions does your job make to helping other people?

5. What do you feel are the benefits of unions? Should people in your occupation have the right to strike? Explain.

Theme Five: Option for the Poor and Vulnerable

Catholic social teaching asks society these questions: How are your most vulnerable members doing? Have your hungry been fed? Have your thirsty been given something to drink? Have those without homes or families been welcomed? Have those who are naked been clothed? Have you visited your prisoners lately?

Of course, these are the same questions posed by Jesus in the last judgment scene from Matthew 25. Jesus' basic instruction: Put the needs of the poor and outcasts first. Today, modern democratic ideals and principles must be applied in order to guarantee the basic requirements of a life of dignity for all.

From the Documents

Love for the poor means justice. Love for others, and in the first place love for the poor, in whom the church sees Christ himself, is made concrete in the promotion of justice. Justice will never be fully attained unless people see in the poor person, who is asking for help in order to survive, not an annoyance or a burden, but an opportunity for showing kindness and a chance for greater enrichment. . . . [I]t is not enough to draw on the surplus good which in fact our world abundantly produces; it requires above all a change of lifestyles, of models of production and consumption, and of the established structures of power which today govern societies.

—*The One Hundredth Year*, #58

▪ *discuss* ▪

Defend or refute each of these statements. Cite examples to support your opinions:

- There is a job for anyone who really wants one.
- Schools are essentially the same. If students study hard, they can improve their state in life regardless of how poor they are.
- Homelessness should never happen in a rich society.
- Most welfare recipients are lazy.
- Poverty is the result of society ignoring the needs of the poor.

Issues

What are the issues? Meeting the needs of society's most vulnerable includes the following issues. As you read about each issue, think about how they are inter-related.

- **Poverty.** The American bishops defined poverty as "the lack of sufficient material resources required for a decent life" (*Economic Justice for All*, #173). The economy of the United States and many other wealthy nations is marked by an uneven distribution of wealth and income. Catholic social justice teaching does not require absolute equality in the distribution of income and wealth, but it does demand evaluation of current economic structures. Also, the church seeks an increased level of participation by all members of society in the economy.

    The American bishops' pastoral letter on the economy, *Economic Justice for All*, offers recommendations for curing some of the ills of poverty. These include raising the minimum wage for workers, adjusting the tax system to better meet the needs of the poor, and making a major commitment to education and the eradication of illiteracy. It also involves developing a plan whereby mothers of young children do not have to seek employment outside the home. Thorough reforms of the welfare system were also recommended. The bishops also called for each person to re-examine his or her attitudes concerning poverty:

> We ask everyone to refrain from actions, words or attitudes that stigmatize the poor, that exaggerate the benefits received by the poor, and that inflate the amount of fraud in welfare payments. These are symptoms of a punitive attitude towards the poor (*Economic Justice for All*, #194).

- **Consumerism.** The rampant buying and selling of goods and services, many of which are needless, is a plague of consumerism. The Christian calling is to turn away from greed and consumerism to make a wholehearted commitment to work for the development of every human being. Pope John Paul challenged people to examine their motives and re-evaluate their lifestyles:

> It is not wrong to want to live better; what is wrong is a style of life which is presumed to be better when it is directed toward "having" rather than "being" and which wants to have more, not in order to be more, but in order to spend life in enjoyment as an end in itself. It is therefore necessary to create lifestyles in which the quest for truth, beauty, goodness, and communion with others for the sake of common growth are the factors which determine consumer choices, savings, and investments (*The One Hundredth Year*, #36).

- **Developing nations.** The poorer nations of the world need to become free from internal and external oppression. Dependency on other nations often mires them in hopeless conditions. Development means establishing a process which enables nations to have a better chance at political, social, and economic self-sufficiency. The church teaches that developing nations have the right to control and direct their own process of development, though foreign economic and technical assistance are certainly a necessary part of the process.

Some suggestions for assisting developing nations include:

- reforming the existing international trade system;

- establishing a world monetary system that is not based on fluctuating exchange and interest rates that hurt poorer countries;

- sharing technological resources with developing nations;

- reviewing and correcting the operating methods and costs of existing international organizations (*On Social Concern,* #43–45).

▪ *activities* ▪

What can you do? Use these suggestions as a starting point (or come up with your own) to help you do your part to alleviate poverty and its related causes. Write or share a summary of your work with the class.

1. Note some advertisements in your favorite magazine. List at least ten possessions the ads claim help lead to your happiness. Summarize some of the methods the ads use to sell their products.

2. Note in your journal the six moral principles, Nos. 13–18, on which the pastoral *Economic Justice for All* is based.

3. Imagine that your family's income, after taxes, is only $15,000 per year. If you were the head of a household that included three people besides yourself, how would you budget necessary items for your family (use the items listed below)? Work out your family's budget for these items on a monthly basis. Then, determine what you consider to be a fair income for a family of four living in your neighborhood.

   - food
   - housing
   - clothing
   - medical expense
   - insurance
   - recreation
   - education
   - other

Theme Six: Human Solidarity

Human solidarity refers to the reciprocal network of relationships which link all humans to each other and to the environment. Whatever a person's national, racial, ethnic, economic, and philosophical origins, all people belong to one human family. This fact demands that people live in harmony with one another, supporting and caring for the common and particular needs of all.

Violent conflict and the denial of human rights to even one person affects and diminishes the entire human family. For Jesus, the love of God and the love of neighbor are one. Jesus prayed for human solidarity:

"May they all be one,
just as, Father, you are in me
   and I am in you" (Jn 17:21).

Human solidarity and solidarity with the environment encompasses issues like world peace, global development, protection of natural resources, and international human rights.

From the Documents

Peace.   Peace is more than the absence of war: it cannot be reduced to the maintenance of power between opposing forces nor does it arise out of despotic dominion, but it is appropriately called "the effect of righteousness" (Is 32:17). It is the fruit of that right ordering of things with which the divine founder has invested human society and which must be actualized by man thirsting after an even more perfect reign of justice.
   —*Church in the Modern World*, #78

Resources for Peace.   Enormous resources can be made available by disarming the huge military machines which were constructed for the conflict between east and west . . . But it will be necessary above all to abandon a mentality in which the poor—as individuals and as peoples—are considered a burden, as irksome intruders trying to consume what others have produced. The poor ask for the right to share in enjoying material goods and to make good use of their capacity for work, thus creating a world that is more just and prosperous

■ *discuss* ■

1. Share an example from the recent news of a conflict that was resolved peacefully.
2. Share an example from the recent news of a conflict that was resolved violently.

for all. The advancement of the poor constitutes a great opportunity for the moral, cultural and even economic growth of all humanity.

—*The One Hundredth Year*, #28

Issues

What are the issues? Successful human solidarity is based on how well people can get along with each other and with the rest of the environment. As you read these issues, rate how well you think solidarity is being observed in each of these areas.

- **Environment.** People are stewards of the environment (see Gn 1:28–30). This is a task that demands responsibility from all nations and all individuals. To be responsible in the area of the environment means that everyone must utilize careful planning, conservation, and an unselfish respect for the goods of this world. God wants each person to "communicate with nature as an intelligent and noble 'master' and 'guardian,' and not as a heedless 'exploiter' and 'destroyer' " (*Redeemer of Humankind*, #15).

    Industrial waste, deforestation, pollution resulting from a consumer society, and other abuses which affect the environment know no national borders. For example, the factories in America's midwest cause acid rain which affects Canada's lakes. The deforestation of the jungles of Brazil increase the rate of global warming. These and other issues like them are issues which must transcend national self-interest.

- **War.** Catholic teaching advocates the peaceful settlement of disputes. People and nations must do everything possible to avoid war and seek peaceful solutions to conflict. In extreme cases, though, nations may resort to force. For example, every nation has the right and duty to defend itself against unjust aggression. The principles of the church's just-war tradition permit war if **all** the following conditions are present:

    1. There must be a real and certain danger. If a situation threatens the life of innocent people, if basic human rights are violated, or if there is an imminent need for self-defense, then there would be just cause.

2. The right to declare a war of defense belongs to those who have the legitimate responsibility to represent the people and uphold the common good.

3. The rights and values in the conflict must be so important that they justify killing.

4. To be just, a war must be waged for the best of reasons and with a commitment to postwar reconciliation with the enemy. Needless destruction, cruelty to prisoners, and other harsh measures cannot be tolerated.

5. War must be a last resort. Nations must first try **all** peaceful methods to settle differences.

6. The odds of success should be weighed against the human cost of the war. This criterion prevents irrational use of force or hopeless resistance when either will prove futile anyway.

7. The damage the war will inflict and the cost it will incur must be proportionate to the good expected. For example, if a minor dispute would lead to a war that destroys many people, then the resulting conflict would violate this principle of proportionality.

Even if all the above criteria are present and nations declare war, the principles of proportionality and discrimination must govern the conduct of the war. The principle of discrimination requires that the combatants in a war make a distinction between aggressors and innocent people.

■ **Nuclear war.** The principles of proportionality and discrimination dictate that any attempt to exterminate an entire people, nation, or ethnic minority is unjust. Furthermore, any act of war aimed indiscriminately at entire cities or extensive areas and their populations is a crime against God and humanity. Both actions merit total condemnation. Likewise, the buildup of nuclear arms through a nuclear arms race is also wrong. Pope John Paul said:

Our future on this planet, exposed as it is to nuclear annihilation, depends on one single factor: humanity must make a moral about face (*address to United Nations University*, Hiroshima, Japan).

■ **Pacifism.** The church respects the personal conscience of those who enter the military service out of loyalty to their country. They "should look upon themselves as the custodians of the security and freedom of their fellow countrymen and women." When they carry out their duties properly, "they are contributing to the maintenance of peace" (*Church in the Modern World*, #79).

At the same time, the church respects pacifists, that is those "who forego the use of violence to vindicate their rights and resort to other means of defense which are available to weaker parties, provided it can be done without harm to the rights and duties of others and of the community" (*Church in the Modern World*, #78).

Furthermore, the church supports laws which support "conscientious objectors" who refuse to bear arms, "provided they accept some other form of community service" (*Church in the Modern World*, #79).

■ *activities* ■

What can you do? Use these suggestions as a staring point (or come up with your own) to help you understand more about human solidarity and its related issues. Write or share a summary of your findings with the class.

1. Research the causes of a given war (for example, the Persian Gulf war). Apply the just war principles. Give your opinion of the morality of the war you researched.
2. Write a report that lists the pros and cons of pacifism.
3. Research how local government in your area is handling one of these environmental issues: land, air or water pollution, waste disposal, or deforestation. Present an oral report summarizing its effectiveness or ineffectiveness.

Conclusion

Social justice translates simply into Jesus' command to love God and neighbor. True love of God and neighbor are one. Jesus said:

> Anyone who says "I love God" and hates his brother, is
> a liar, since whoever does not love the brother whom

he can see cannot love God, whom he has not seen. Indeed this is the commandment that we have received from him, that whoever loves God, must also love his brother (1 Jn 4:20–21).

The synod of bishops reiterated Jesus' words in their document, *Justice in the World*:

> Christian love of neighbor and justice cannot be separated. For love implies an absolute demand for justice, namely a recognition of the dignity and rights of one's neighbor. Justice attains its inner fullness only in love (*Justice in the World*, #34).

Catholic teaching on social justice ranges over a host of dilemmas and issues. Basically, the church cares about any issue that affects the quality of human life. The church recognizes that all people belong to one human family. In order for the dilemmas and issues to be solved, each person must do his or her part to love God and neighbor.

How does love of God and neighbor translate into practical action? On a personal level you can be just in your dealings with others. You can also:

- respect all life, since true peace flows from an awareness of the worth and dignity of each human person.

- learn to forgive and ask for forgiveness.

- work to solve your own problems in a nonviolent way.

- keep abreast of current issues affecting social justice, select one of the issues, and act upon it.

Finally, everyone can make it part of their human task to pray for world peace and justice for all. Only through these good works and prayer, can true social justice hope to be accomplished.

▪ *focus questions* ▪

1. What is your task as a Christian missionary?

2. What are the differences between legal, commutative, distributive, and social justice?

3. Why is social justice an essential human as well as Christian task?

4. Cite one statement from a key church document concerning social justice. List the author and key themes.

5. What is the vocation that Jesus intends for all people?

6. Why are the unborn an especially vulnerable group today?

7. Share the church's teaching in each of these areas: justice for women, justice for the unborn, and justice for minorities.

8. List five basic human rights and their corresponding duties.

9. What are the responsibilities society has toward the hungry, the aged, the handicapped, criminals, and migrant workers?

10. What is the basic unit of society? Discuss two ways the larger society can help this basic unit.

11. Define the *common good.*

12. Define the *principle of subsidiarity.*

13. What are three basic rights of workers?

14. Define *consumerism.* What makes it wrong?

15. What are some violations of human solidarity in today's world?

16. Briefly summarize the principles of a "just war."

17. Define the "principle of proportionality" and the "principle of discrimination" as they pertain to war.

18. Why does the church condemn nuclear war?

19. What is the relationship between justice and love?

■ *exercise* ■

Research and prepare a report on a contemporary or historical leader in Catholic social justice. You may use one of the following suggestions or choose one of your own.

> St. Vincent de Paul
> St. Louise de Marillac
> St. John Baptist de LaSalle
> St. Elizabeth Ann Seton
> Archbishop Oscar Romero
> Dorothy Day
> Mother Teresa of Calcutta

■ *vocabulary* ■

Look up the meaning of the following words in the dictionary. Transcribe the definitions into your journal:

allocate
punitive
remuneration

Prayer Reflection

First, put yourself in the Lord's presence. Thank God for the good in your life: for example, your parents, friends, education, material possessions, talents, and faith.

Next, try to imagine what you will do with your life in regards to your future career, spouse, children, accomplishments, and possessions.

Finally, remaining in God's presence, project yourself to the last judgment. You, with every other person who has ever lived, are standing before God's judgment seat. Now, slowly and meditatively read Jesus' story of the last judgment from Matthew 25:31–46.

- What will you answer the Lord when he asks if you fed the hungry, gave drink to the thirsty, welcomed the stranger, clothed the naked, visited the sick and the imprisoned?

- What will you say when he asks what you did to help the least of your brothers and sisters?

▪ *reflection* ▪

What have you done for Christ? What are you doing for Christ? What will you do for Christ?

▪ *resolution* ▪

Make a commitment to do something specific in the coming week to make your family, school, or community a more just place to live.

PART 3

CULT

Imagine this scene: It's opening night at the theatre. A single actress moves on stage. The curtain rises and she looks out to a vast sea of darkness. She is ready to begin her lines, but she feels like screaming out to the darkness instead:

1. Is anyone there?
2. Is anyone listening?
3. Does anyone care?

Through the ages, those who seek meaning in life have thrown these questions to the skies. Christians, of course, confidently believe that Jesus answers each question with a resounding "Yes!"

1. "Yes, wonderful children I am here. You may find me hidden in your hearts, in each other, in my biblical word, in my church, in my sacraments, in the beautiful creation my Father created, in the poor in your midst."

2. "Yes, beloved sisters and brothers. I am listening. However, my question to you is: 'Do you take the time to pray to me, to listen to the Spirit in your heart, to read the signs of my presence all around you?'"

3. "Yes, sons and daughters of my loving Abba, I do care. And I proved my love by dying so you could live. And I remain with you to this day. You will experience my love in a special way through the seven wonderful signs you call sacraments."

In the first two sections of this text, you studied the church's *creed* and *code*. In this section you will look at the church's *cult*, a word that refers to a definite form of worship or religious observance. The focus will be on prayer and the rich liturgical and ritual tradition of the Catholic church, especially the seven sacraments.

Chapter 8 will examine how the Catholic community celebrates Jesus' presence in the sacraments. Chapter 9 uncovers new and traditional ways to meet God in prayer. You will study the petitions of the Lord's Prayer and look at the examples of Jesus and Mary as model pray-ers.

What are some key terms you will need to know as you begin this section of the text? First, *worship* is defined as "a natural response for those who wish to praise, thank, petition, and ask God for forgiveness." A person can worship

God alone. But Christians place a high value on communal worship because Jesus said, "For where two or three meet in my name, I am there among them"(Mt 18:20). By worshipping God in Christian community, you celebrate your Christian identity and all that God has done for you.

Liturgy refers to the official public worship of God by the church. The word liturgy comes from the Greek word for "people's work." The celebration of the eucharist and other sacraments are the primary examples of the church's liturgy.

Liturgy is organized into *ritual*. All rituals bring a recognizable order to certain words, actions, and symbols to create a meaningful celebration for a particular group. Thanksgiving meals, Independence Day celebrations, and sports rallies are examples of rituals. They use words (greetings, memorable songs, cheers), gestures (flag waving, parades, hugs or handshakes), and symbols (team mascot, flag, special menu, flowers) to communicate and celebrate. The seven sacraments are the key rituals of the church. They all celebrate Jesus' paschal mystery. They all contain a past, present, and future dimension. Sacramental liturgies are really celebrations because they include a guest of honor who is none other than Jesus Christ. Jesus comes to the church through the sacramental liturgies at the key moments of life. Liturgy—the ritual re-enactment and retelling of the Christian story—is a joyful part of the Catholic story because the risen Jesus joins the church when it assembles to remember him and his good news.

chapter 8

Sacraments: Signs of God's Love

Whatever was visible in our Redeemer has passed over into the sacraments.

—St. Leo the Great

A special feature in the maternity wings of many hospitals today is something called the "Baby Brigade." Volunteers who join this group agree to hold, cuddle, caress, and feed the many infants who remain in hospitals awaiting adoption. The regular staff simply does not have the time to give these infants the loving attention they need. Medical science has proven that human touch and the interaction of human words does help newborns to learn to trust their new world as a safe and warm place and to develop as healthy and well adjusted human beings. The Baby Brigade helps to fulfill this need. It is a sign of love.

All human beings need signs and symbols to express and deepen mysteries like love. Whether you realize it or not, you need things like smiles, humorous cards, hugs, sympathetic words, kisses, handshakes, gifts, and other signs to remind you that you are indeed loveable. You also need to use these kinds of gestures and symbols to communicate your love to others. To be a human being is to belong to a "People Brigade" whose primary task is to share love and the symbols of love with others.

Jesus understands the human need to be reminded that someone loves and cares for you. *Sacraments* are special symbols of God's love, important signs of grace and divine friendship. Sacraments are also central to the Catholic identity as a Christian community. They are a key way God is present to the church in ordinary life. The sacraments are God's way of sharing a hug that you can really feel or a kind word that you can really hear.

Looking at Love

Far more than a store-bought greeting card or even the warm embrace shared between a couple in love, the sacraments are powerful signs that are a means to transmit God's love and life to all people. In order to understand the sacraments, think about what love means to you. Reflect on the meaning of love and the signs of Christ's presence in your own life by responding to the following:

1. I think love can mainly be described as (check two):

   _____ a commitment   _____ a feeling   _____ sharing

   _____ instinctual   _____ spiritual   _____ life-giving

   _____ other: _____

2. How do you experience the presence of God? Check any examples which have been a way for you to meet God.

   _____ gazing at a sunset   _____ praying alone in your room

   _____ helping someone   _____ receiving holy communion

   _____ listening to meaningful   _____ accepting or giving
          music lyrics   forgiveness

   _____ praying with others   _____ holding a newborn infant

   _____ talking about your faith   _____ watching young children
                                            at play

   _____ taking a hike   _____ meditating alone before the
                                            Blessed Sacrament

   _____ experiencing the joy of friendship _____ other: _____

3. Share a symbol of love that is most meaningful for you.

   _____

4. Share a symbol of you at your best. What is something that captures the *real* you?

   _____

▪ *journal* ▪

1. What do the words *I love you* mean to you?

2. Share an experience that lets you know that Jesus really loves you.

What Is a Sacrament?

A *sacrament* is an "efficacious symbol," a special sign that effects what it symbolizes and symbolizes what it effects. What does this mean? One of the clearest ways to understand this definition of sacrament is to see how it relates to a traditional understanding of Jesus and the church.

Recall that one way to describe Jesus **is** sacrament. Jesus not only signifies God's love, he **is** God's love. His teaching, his healings and other miracles, and his sacrifice on the cross all symbolize the love God has for all people. But Jesus is more than just a symbol of God's love; he is God-made-human, Love-made-flesh.

The church is also a sacrament, an efficacious symbol of salvation. The community of believers offers a foretaste of what it will be like to live forever in God's kingdom. Yet, the church is already the kingdom, made up of people who, through baptism, have been saved by the life, death, and resurrection of Jesus. The risen Jesus lives and works among the people who make up the church.

The seven individual sacraments are special actions of Christ working in the church. They too are effective, symbolic actions which not only point to God's life but actually convey it to the members of the church. They bring about what they point to. For example, the waters of baptism not only represent new life, they actually bring about new life for the baptized in union with God. The eucharist not only signifies the sharing of a common meal, but actually and really brings about a union among those who participate and with the risen Jesus.

A sacrament makes the mystery of God's love—that is, grace—visible. The fifth-century church father St. Augustine of Hippo defined sacrament as a "visible sign of an invisible reality, a visible sign of invisible grace." Through the sacraments, people both *perceive* and *receive* invisible grace.

Jesus is the primary visible sign of invisible grace. The church is also sacramental because it continues Jesus' work of salvation. And, Jesus has given the church the seven sacraments to help Christians grow in friendship with him. The seven sacraments help to make visible the spiritual life that has been given to the church by Jesus. The seven sacraments are baptism, confirmation, eucharist, reconciliation, anointing of the sick, holy orders, and marriage. According to the Vatican II documents, the purpose of the seven sacraments is:

> to sanctify [people], to build up the body of Christ, and finally, to give worship to God. Because they are signs, they also instruct. They not only presuppose faith, but by words and objects they also nourish, strengthen, and express it (*Constitution on the Sacred Liturgy*, No. 59).

Sacraments are efficacious signs of grace, instituted by Christ and entrusted to the church. Through them divine life comes to us.

What Does the Church Teach About the Sacraments?

Official church teaching about the seven sacraments includes the following points:

- *Jesus Christ instituted the seven ritual sacraments.* The origins of the seven sacraments can be traced to Jesus. This does not mean that the historical Jesus prescribed each sacrament as it is celebrated today. It *does* mean that God's action, not human action, accounts for the Christian sacraments.

- *Sacraments are symbols of sacred realities.* Sacraments are efficacious signs because Jesus himself works through them.

- *Sacraments confer grace.* Sacraments confer the grace they signify, deepening God's life in those who participate in them.

- *Three sacraments—baptism, confirmation, and holy orders—confer a character.* A sacramental "character" is a particular sacrament's lasting effect. It is a seal by which Christians share in the priesthood of Christ and participate in the church's life according to their particular office, function, or state in life. Because the character is lifelong, these three sacraments are received only once.

- *God's action in the sacraments does not depend on the intention or purity of the minister.* Although the minister of the sacrament should be holy, God can still work through the sacraments despite human sinfulness. Divine grace is much more powerful than human weakness.

- *For believers, sacraments are necessary for salvation.* The Holy Spirit makes those who live a sacramental life sharers in God's nature by uniting their lives to that of Jesus Christ.

Sacraments of Initiation: Baptism, Confirmation, Eucharist

What comes to mind when you hear the term "initiation"? Do you think of an oath to be pledged, as if entering scouting? Or, maybe you associate initiation with instruction. A basketball player must **learn** the team's plays as part of becoming a member of the team. You might also think of a ceremony. A soldier **receives** a medal or badge after basic training to represent how he or she is now a full member of the nation's army.

The process of initiation into the Catholic church also involves instructions, pledges, and ceremonies. In the rite of Christian initiation of adults, also known as RCIA, the men and women who come to the church inquiring about the faith are led through a process in which they become *catechumens*, a Greek word to describe a person who receives instruction. There are four major parts to the RCIA process. They are:

1. *Evangelization.* Hearing the gospel of Jesus Christ leads a person to an initial conversion in which the Holy Spirit opens their hearts to examine the Christian faith community.

2. *Catechumenate.* During this period, the catechumens study more carefully the Catholic faith.

3. *Purification and Enlightenment.* It is a period of purification, penance, and intense spiritual preparation that takes place during Lent and concludes at the Easter vigil liturgy when those who have been "elected" by the church are baptized, and confirmed, and receive the eucharist for the first time.

4. *Mystagogia.* During the Easter season, the new Christians—called neophytes—reflect more deeply on their new identity as full members of the church.

The RCIA process represents the traditional way that adults entered the church in its earliest days. The Second Vatican Council renewed this process for adults today. But what about you? Most likely you were baptized as an infant,

■ *journal* ■

Read the following passages which point out the scriptural roots of the seven sacraments. Summarize each teaching. What do these passages teach you about the meaning of each sacrament?

Sacraments of initiation
baptism (Rm 6:3–11)
confirmation (Acts 19:1–6)
eucharist (1 Cor 11:17–34)

Sacraments of vocation
marriage (Jn 2:1–12)
holy orders (Ti 1:5–9)

Sacraments of healing
reconciliation (Lk 15)
anointing of the sick (Jas 5:14–15)

received first communion in second grade, and recently celebrated confirmation or will celebrate it soon. This detailed initiation process may have little to do with your personal experience.

Yet, these three sacraments are also celebrations of your initiation into the Catholic church. You too have been instructed, taken a pledge of faith, and received the sacraments. Though you may not have received them in the order of baptism, confirmation, and eucharist, and your reception of each sacrament may be spread out over time, these three sacraments are the means by which all Catholics—including you—become fully initiated members of the faithful.

Baptism.   The first sacrament of initiation, baptism is the way a person first enters into life in union with Jesus and the Christian community. "To baptize" means "to plunge or immerse in water." The essential action of baptism consists in immersing the candidates in water or pouring water on their heads while reciting these words: "I baptize you in the name of the Father, and of the Son, and of the Holy Spirit."

The effects of baptism can be summarized as follows:

> Baptism incorporates us into Christ and forms us into God's people. The first sacrament pardons all our sins, rescues us from the power of darkness, and brings us to the dignity of adopted children, a new creation through water and the Holy Spirit. Hence we are indeed called the children of God (*The General Introduction to the Rite of Christian Initiation*, No. 2).

Through baptism, a person symbolically enters into the mystery of Christ's death and resurrection. The church calls the baptized to convert from a life of sin (for infants this means original sin) and to accept a new life of redemption in Jesus Christ. Baptism also provides the gift of the Holy Spirit to help Christians to live as Jesus intended.

Understanding the meaning of the baptismal symbols can help you to uncover more of the sacrament's meaning. *Water* is the primary symbol of baptism. Water is a paradoxical symbol in that it can bring both purification and new life as well as destruction and death. Baptismal water represents the death of an old life to sin and a rebirth to a new life in Christ.

The rite of baptism includes two anointings with *oil*. Oil is a sign of both healing and royalty. Baptismal anointing with oil means that a person has become the "anointed one" of the Messiah. The person is empowered by the Holy Spirit to take on Jesus' own roles of prophet (to speak for him), priest (to act as his mediator), and king (to lead by serving).

At the Easter vigil, after the adults are baptized they often replace an old, off-color gown with a new *white garment*. Likewise, most infants are dressed in white at baptism. White, the color of purity, is a reminder that the sacrament brings a new life, a fresh start in Christ.

The *lighted candle* is another baptismal symbol. The celebrant lights a small candle from the Easter candle and gives it to the baptized or their parents or godparents. They are reminded that they have been given the light of Christ and are entrusted to keep it burning. The gathered community of faith may sing a baptismal song such as: "You have put on Christ, in him you have been baptized. Alleluia, alleluia."

The person's given *name* is also important. Christians traditionally take the name of a saint who will become their patron through life. Finally, the *minister* and the gathered *community of faith* symbolize the church's welcoming spirit and answer to Jesus' command to "go, therefore, make disciples of all nations; baptize them in the name of the Father and of the Son and of the Holy Spirit" (Mt 28:19).

Confirmation. Adults celebrate confirmation at the Easter vigil liturgy immediately after their baptism. Usually, it is the pastor of the parish who confers the sacrament on adults. In the Roman church, those who were baptized as infants are confirmed some time between the ages of seven and 18. In that case, the bishop is the usual celebrant. The bishop's presence underscores the church's apostolic traditions and its unity among all members.

The rite of confirmation is always most appropriately celebrated within the Mass, right after the liturgy of the Word. Each candidate comes before the bishop and is anointed with oil. The bishop traces the sign of the cross on the candidate's forehead, and says "Be sealed with the gift of the Holy Spirit." The candidate replies "Amen."

The sacrament of Confirmation has three principal effects. They are:

1. **To confer and seal the fullness of the Holy Spirit.** The sealing conforms the Christian more perfectly to Christ

■ *research* ■

1. What is the origin of your name (either your first name or middle name)?
2. Find out if there is a saint who bears your name. When did this saint live? What qualities of the saint do you admire?

and enables him or her to better serve the church and the world. Like baptism, confirmation imprints a permanent spiritual mark; thus, it can only be received once.

2. **To provide the strength to live as Christians.** "To confirm" actually means "to ratify or strengthen." Confirmation perfects the graces of baptism. In confirmation, a person restates the baptismal promises and becomes more fully incorporated into Christ and the church. This new life is witnessed by Christian faith in words and deeds.

3. **To deepen the power of the gifts received in baptism.** The traditional seven gifts of the Holy Spirit—wisdom, understanding, right judgment, courage, knowledge, reverence, and wonder and awe—are imparted at reception of the sacrament. The number seven suggests perfection or fullness.

Eucharist.   The sacrament of eucharist is the culminating point of Christian initiation. Its function as a sacrament of initiation is most clearly seen in the Easter vigil. After being baptized and confirmed, the neophytes take an active role in the rest of the liturgy. Their intentions are specifically included in the prayer of the faithful. Representatives from the group of neophytes may bring the offertory gifts to the altar as the liturgy of the eucharist begins.

Being present at the liturgy of the eucharist is a new experience for the neophytes. As catechumens they had been dismissed from Mass after the liturgy of the Word. Now, in full communion with the church, they take part in the sacrifice of the Lord's Supper and recite the Lord's Prayer with the rest of the faithful. At communion, the neophytes receive the body and blood of Christ for the first time.

For those baptized as infants, first eucharist generally takes place before confirmation, at about age seven. Prior to the twentieth century, boys and girls did not receive first eucharist until early adolescence. Also, even when eligible, Catholics rarely went to communion. Pope Pius X (1903–1914) thought that practice was wrong and he sought to change it. He encouraged frequent reception of communion. And, he permitted children to receive the eucharist at the age of reason.

■ *journal* ■

Read the following scripture passages about the Spirit. Summarize the key point of each passage in your journal.
Role of the Spirit:
  Romans 5:1–2, 5–8
  and 8:14–17
Gifts of the Spirit:
  1 Corinthians 12:4–13
  and Galatians 5:16–25
Answering the Spirit:
  Ephesians 4:1–6,
  Matthew 16:24–27,
  and John 15:18–21, 26–27

The importance of the sacrament of eucharist in the life of the church can be appreciated by its many titles and descriptions. Among them are:

1. **Eucharist as Thanksgiving.** The Greek word *eucharistein* from which "eucharist" derives means "giving thanks." One of the best reasons for celebrating eucharist is to show gratitude for God's many blessings, especially the gift of Jesus' death on the cross.

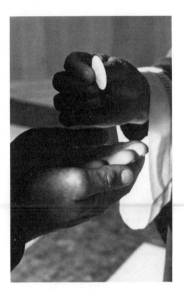

2. **Eucharist as Sacred Meal.** Meals are an intimate symbol of companionship. Sharing the eucharist is the most important thing the Christian community does together and for one another. One of the reasons that it is so important to attend Sunday Mass is that the Christian community is not complete if even one person is missing. Also, the image of sacred meal foreshadows the scriptural image of the heavenly banquet that will take place at the end of time.

3. **Eucharist as the Holy Sacrifice of the Mass.** The eucharist represents Christ's sacrifice on the cross. To commemorate the eucharist is to have a share in this sacrifice. The *altar* is a key part in this definition. It is both the altar of sacrifice and the table of the Lord. It symbolizes Christ's presence as both the victim offered for redemption and as heavenly food.

4. **Eucharist as Blessed Sacrament.** The eucharist is the prime sacrament. As the last initiation sacrament, the eucharist incorporates Catholics into the full body of the church. As the Blessed Sacrament, the eucharist is different from the other sacraments in that it is not only a sacrament to be received, but one to be adored before, during, and after reception. Jesus remains present in the Blessed Sacrament as long as the properties of the blessed bread and wine remain unchanged.

5. **Eucharist as Holy Communion.** The word *communion* describes the unity the sacrament brings between Jesus and those who participate in the celebration, and also the unity among the participants themselves. Receiving holy communion brings these benefits: it preserves, increases, and renews baptismal graces, forgives venial sins, and helps to preserve the recipient from future mortal sin. Holy

communion also brings unity and impels further unity between all Christians.

6. **Eucharist as Real Presence.** Jesus said: "Whoever eats my flesh and drinks my blood lives in me and I live in that person" (Jn 6:56). Jesus' words underscore the Catholic belief in the real presence of Christ in the eucharist. To say that Jesus is *really* present means that his presence is not merely subjectively in the mind of the believer; he is objectively in the eucharist. Exactly how Jesus is present in the consecrated bread and wine is a mystery. The church has traditionally used the term *transubstantiation* to express that at the consecration of the Mass, the reality (substance) of the bread and wine changes into the reality of Jesus—his risen, glorified body and blood. Those who receive Jesus in either the "species" of the consecrated bread or the "species" of the consecrated wine have received the whole Christ. He is present in both species. Catholics also believe that Jesus is really present in the community of believers (including the priest) and in the word of God, as recited in the readings at Mass.

7. **Eucharist as Liturgy.** Recall that the term *liturgy* means "the people's work." All the sacraments are liturgical rituals, but the preeminent liturgy is the eucharist. Sunday is the day when the community of the faithful gathers to participate in liturgy and hence celebrate Jesus' victory over sin and death.

The Mass

The term "Mass" comes from the words of dismissal in the Roman rite, "Ite missa est," "Go, you are sent." *Missa* literally means "dismissal." *Missionary* is a related word. The term *Mass* is a reminder that the Christian mission in life is to live Jesus' Passover, in other words to become for the world "the body given" and "the blood poured out."

The Eucharistic Liturgy

The Mass consists of the introductory rites, the liturgy of the word, and the liturgy of the eucharist. In the liturgy of the word the faithful hear God's word and derive nourishment from it. The liturgy of the eucharist celebrates the death and resurrection of Jesus. Listed below are the parts of the Mass:

Introductory Rites

Entrance: The Mass begins with the singing or recitation of a song.

Greeting: The priest and people make the Sign of the Cross. The priest greets the people, and they respond.

Penitential Rite: The priest and people acknowledge their sinfulness and ask God's forgiveness.

Hymn of Praise (not always part of the Mass): The "Glory to God" is sung or recited.

Opening Prayer: The priest offers a prayer of petition for the worshipping community.

Liturgy of the Word

Readings: The first reading is from the Old Testament; the second from the latter part of the New Testament; the third from one of the gospels. Psalm verses are recited between the first two readings and alleluias are sung before the gospel.

Homily: The celebrant or deacon relates the readings to everyday life.

Profession of Faith (not always part of the Mass): Together the people acknowledge their common beliefs.

General Intercessions: The community's petitions for the needs of the church, the world, public authorities, individuals and the local community are presented.

Liturgy of the Eucharist

Preparation of the Altar and Gifts: The gifts of bread and wine are brought forward in procession, the altar is prepared, and a prayer is said over the gifts.

Eucharistic Prayer (Canon): There are several eucharistic prayers the church uses on different occasions. The eucharistic prayer includes the words Jesus said at the Last Supper and the memorial acclamation, and concludes with the doxology, a prayer of praise to the Trinity which is sung or recited by the celebrant.

Communion Rite: This part of the Mass includes the Lord's Prayer, the prayer for deliverance, the prayer for peace (after which the sign of peace is exchanged), and the breaking of the bread while the Lamb of God is sung or recited. After the reception of communion, the priest offers a prayer of petition on behalf of the community.

Concluding Rite: There are often announcements followed by the words of blessing and dismissal.

Those parts of the Mass which change with the feast or liturgical season are called the *Proper of the Mass.* Those parts of the liturgy which remain the same are called the *Ordinary of the Mass.*

■ *exercise* ■

Locate the scripture readings to be used during the liturgy of the word for the coming Sunday. Read and summarize each of these readings in your journal. Then, outline a short homily based on the readings. Hint: look for a central theme in the first reading and the gospel. Apply this theme to people your own age. Finally, share your homily with your classmates.

■ *discuss* ■

What are some common excuses teens give for missing Sunday Mass? Which do you consider valid? invalid? Explain.

The Liturgical Year

Sunday is the foundation and core of the entire *liturgical year.* The preeminent Sunday of all is Easter Sunday. On every Sunday of the year the church commemorates the day of Jesus' victory over sin and death.

The other days and seasons of the liturgical year focus on various mysteries of redemption. The seasons of the liturgical year are *Advent, Christmas, Lent, Easter,* and *Ordinary Time.*

Sacraments of Healing: Reconciliation and Anointing of the Sick

Of life's many deep questions, the one concerning the presence of suffering is certainly among the most perplexing. As you observe the cruelty and injustice that takes place in this world, you have probably called out with many who have come before you, "Why does God permit suffering? Why do people have to suffer?"

Suffering, of course, is directly related to sin. Each is intimately tied to God's gift of free will. In order for God to have made people perfectly free, the possibility of humans choosing to do evil always existed. Suffering is the result of sinful choices.

Nevertheless, the question of suffering remains a difficult one, and people continue to wonder about its answer. In John's gospel, Jesus' disciples pose him a question about a man born blind from birth: "Rabbi, who sinned, this man or his parents, that he should have been born blind?"

Jesus' answer was surprising: "Neither he nor his parents sinned. He was born blind so that the works of God might be revealed in him" (Jn 9:2–3).

This answer was the only thing close to an explanation for suffering that Jesus ever offered. Usually when he encountered a person in need of either physical or spiritual healing, all Jesus did was heal the person or forgive his or her sins. In the cure of the paralytic (see Mk 2:1–12) Jesus did both. To show that he had been given the power to forgive sins he said to the man "I order you: get up, pick up your stretcher, and go off home."

The sacraments of healing—reconciliation and anointing of the sick—continue Jesus' work of healing. These sacraments do not provide answers to why people must hurt, why people must suffer. Rather, they seek simply to heal the hurt, heal the suffering that people are feeling.

Reconciliation. In baptism, a person is reconciled with God; his or her sin, both original sin and personal sin, has been removed. Yet, temptations to choose evil do not disappear. Though a person belongs to Christ, he or she still sins. Sin remains a part of human nature. When a person sins, it damages his or her relationship with God and with other people. Even after baptism there remains a need for conversion and reconciliation.

The Christian life involves constant conversion, that is reforming one's life from wrong to right, from sinful ways to Christ-like ways. The sacrament of reconciliation is the official way the church offers forgiveness for sins after baptism. It is an important sign that helps sinners to convert and renew their friendship with God. Its two main effects are obtaining forgiveness for sins and bringing about reconciliation with the church.

Catholics are required to confess serious sins of which they are aware, telling what they have done and how often, at least once a year. The sacrament of reconciliation is the only means for Catholics conscious of mortal sin to be reconciled with God and the church. Though the church does not strictly require sacramental confession of venial sins, it is strongly recommended. Frequent recourse to the sacrament can help you uproot sin from your life.

The sacrament is known by various names. It is called the sacrament of *penance* or *conversion* because it is an outward sign that a sinner means to convert and make better choices, as well as make satisfaction, or penance, for previous sins. It is called *confession* because the telling of sins to a priest is an essential part of the sacrament. It is called the sacrament of *forgiveness* since God grants pardon and peace to sinners through the words of absolution. Finally, *reconciliation* means "coming back together." This term for the sacrament emphasizes the need for the sinner to repair the harmed relationships with God and others that the sins have caused.

The sacrament of reconciliation includes three acts of the penitent: contrition, confession, and satisfaction (penance). It also includes an action of the priest: absolution. Also, an important preliminary step of the penitent is an *examination of conscience*, or prayerful reflection of the areas of sinfulness in his or her life. Reviewing the Sermon on the Mount, Ten Commandments, and Christ's injunction to love God, neighbor, and self are ways to aid one's examination of conscience. Here is further explanation of the acts of the penitent and priest:

1. *Contrition* means "heartfelt sorrow and aversion for the sin committed along with the intention of sinning no more" (*Decree on Penance*, No. 6). Contrition is the heart of the *conversion* which rights the person's relationship with God.

2. *Confession* is an **external** sign of **interior** sorrow.

Through confession the penitent meets the Christian community in the person of the priest and faces his or her own sinful condition in the eyes of God. By confessing, the penitent forces sin out into the open, thus emphasizing its social nature. Confession also displays an outward sign of God's mercy.

3. *Act of satisfaction (penance).* With true conversion comes the desire to make up for your sins, amend your life, and repair any injuries you have caused. The priest assigns a penance—for example, prayers or good works—to help correct the harm done or to serve as a spiritual remedy for the sins.

4. *Absolution.*   Absolution means "to free." The words of absolution assure the penitent that he or she is free from sin. The formula, "I absolve you," the imposition of the priest's hand, and the Sign of the Cross are powerful signs of God's healing and forgiveness.

Why Confess?

The sacrament of reconciliation was instituted by Christ. Jesus empowered the church to continue his ministry of reconciliation when he commanded the apostles (and their successors) to forgive sin in his name:

> "Receive the Holy Spirit.
> If you forgive anyone's sins,
> they are forgiven;
> if you retain anyone's sin,
> they are retained" (Jn 20:23).

The sacrament can enable you to experience Christ's saving touch. Participating in the sacrament of reconciliation typically results in a peaceful conscience and spiritual joy. Here are four other reasons for going to confession. Mark + if you think this is a good reason for you or a ? if you are not sure. Share any other good reasons for going to confession that you can think of with a classmate.

_____ Confession helps me face the truth about myself: "I am a sinner."

_____ I need Christ to reassure me of his love and forgiveness.

_____ I need to experience reconciliation with God, the church, others, myself, or creation.

_____ I need to grow in holiness.

■ *journal* ■

What would you would tell a non-Catholic friend about the sacrament of reconciliation? Write a few paragraphs of explanation.

———————————— ■ ————————————

Anointing of the Sick. Healing was a major part of Jesus' earthly ministry. He cured the blind, made lame people walk, cleansed lepers, and brought the dead back to life. Once, his disciples brought all of the friends they knew who were suffering from diseases to Jesus. He laid his hands on each as he cured them (see Lk 4:41).

After his resurrection, Jesus said that one of the signs his disciples would be known by was that "they will lay their hands on the sick, who will recover" (Mk 16:18). Anointing and praying for the sick was commonplace in the early church. These words from the Letter of James provide the scriptural basis for the sacrament:

> Any one of you who is ill should send for the elders of the church, and they must anoint the sick person with oil in the name of the Lord and pray over him. The prayer of faith will save the sick person and the Lord will raise him up again; and if he has committed any sins, he will be forgiven. So confess your sins to one another to be cured (Jas 5:14–16).

The sacrament has undergone many changes. By the ninth century, the clergy had become the ordinary ministers of the sacrament. By the Middle Ages, the sacramental action of anointing was reserved, for all practical purposes, only for those who were dying. The name for the sacrament at that time was *extreme unction*, that is, "the last anointing" before death. Penance and the reception of a final eucharist (known as *viaticum*—"food for the way") preceded the sacramental anointing. This practice of anointing **only** those near death continued until recent times.

With the reforms of Vatican II came a renewal of the sacrament as one for all those who are seriously ill, not just those near death. The sacrament of anointing of the sick is appropriate for the elderly, for those facing major surgery, as well as for the dying. The sick person may repeat the sacrament if, after recovery, he or she falls ill again or if the original condition worsens.

Today's rite reintroduces the important sign of the *laying on of hands*, a symbol of Jesus' touch and the outpouring of the Spirit of strength, love, and forgiveness. The priest also *prays over the sick person*, invoking the church's faith. Finally, in the Roman rite, the priest *anoints the forehead and hands of the sick person with the blessed oil*. Anointing symbolizes healing, strengthening, and special dedication to God.

The sacrament of the anointing of the sick is administered by bishops and priests but includes the prayerful support of the Christian community (the family, friends, and parish community of the sick person). Communal anointings of the sick during the Mass, for example, sensitize the parish to respond lovingly to the needs of those who are sick.

Today's rite also underscores the need for the sick person to overcome the alienation caused by sickness and suffering. It helps and challenges the sick person to grow to wholeness through the illness, to identify with the sufferings of Jesus Christ, and to enter more fully into the paschal mystery.

The sacrament of the anointing of the sick has several effects:

- It wipes away sin and its remnants if a person has not been able to obtain forgiveness through the sacrament of reconciliation.

- It brings about spiritual healing by strengthening the sick and dying during their suffering.

- It restores physical healing when this will help the person in his or her condition before God.

- It unites the anointed person more closely to Christ's redemptive passion.

Finally, when this sacrament is received before death, it strengthens the recipient for the moment of death and the passing from this world to the next. The reception of a final eucharist—viaticum—gives nourishment for the final journey, a sacrament of passover from this life to eternity with God.

■ *journal* ■

The following scripture passages list examples of times that Jesus healed the sick. Write a summary and your comments for each.

Jn 4:46–54   Mk 1:29–31   Jn 5:1–15
Lk 7:1–10   Mt 9:18–26   Lk 17:11–19

Sacraments of Vocation: Marriage and Holy Orders

The word *vocation* literally means "calling." A vocation is a call or summons to a particular way of life. At baptism, you accepted your primary vocation, the vocation to Christian life. Within the Christian vocation there are several more specific ways to live and thrive using your talents. You may have heard of a musician or writer describe their activities as "their vocation." The word aptly describes things that people do that are personally satisfying and of service to others. There are many different kinds of vocations. The church celebrates two vocations—marriage and holy orders—with sacraments.

The Catechism of the Catholic Church calls marriage and holy orders "the sacraments in service of communion" because they contribute to an individual's personal growth as well as helping to meet the needs of the church at large. Here is a closer look at these two sacraments of service:

Marriage. Today, most people eventually marry. The sacrament of marriage has been described as a *covenant*, the choice of a man and woman to commit to a life together of love and friendship.

The sacrament of marriage elevates an ordinary human relationship into an extraordinary reality that reflects the love between Jesus and the church. St. Paul described the union between a husband and wife as that between the head (Christ) and the body (the church):

> Husbands should love their wives, just as Christ loved the church (Eph 5:28).

There are three aspects to the definition of marriage as covenant. They are:

1. **The sacrament of friendship.** The marital relationship between a man and woman is based in friendship. "Becoming friends" is the first task of two people who desire intimacy; it is also an ongoing task that develops in new ways through the life of the relationship. The Book of Genesis states the need for man and woman to be together (see Gn 2:18). The complementary nature of males and females reveals that God made man and woman to be together physically, emotionally, and spiritually. The sacrament of marriage symbolizes this complementary friendship through things like the empathy, understanding, forgiveness, and sexual union that a husband and wife share.

2. **The sacrament of life and love.** The sharing of sexual intercourse has two purposes: It is for the *procreation* of children and it serves as a *unitive* expression of love between wife and husband. According to the Book of Genesis:

> God created man in the image of himself,
> in the image of God he created him,
> male and female he created them.
> God blessed them, saying to them,
> "Be fruitful, multiply, fill the earth and subdue it"
>   (Gn 1:27–28).

The sacramental grace of marriage helps a couple raise and educate their children, perfect their love, and strengthen their unity.

3. **The sacrament of covenant relationship.** The sacrament of marriage is a true covenant relationship. It mirrors the unconditional love that God has for all people for all time. Unconditional love results in unity, indissolubility, and openness to new life. In marriage, this translates to "total fidelity" and an "unbreakable oneness between them" (*The Church Today*, #48).

The sacrament of marriage is unique among the sacraments in that it is the only one conferred by the participants. The man and woman confer the sacrament on each other by expressing their consent to marry before the church in the person of the minister (priest or deacon) and the community of faith (family and friends). They pledge their commitment to one another using these or similar words from the rite of marriage:

> I promise to be true to you in good times and in bad, in sickness and in health. I will love you and honor you all the days of my life.

The church does not recognize civil divorce as a means for dissolving the pledge of commitment made in marriage. This is based on the teachings of Jesus (see Mt 19:4–8) and the rules and practices of the early church (see 1 Cor 7:10–11). Only the death of one of the partners can dissolve a valid, sacramental, Christian marriage.

Statistics show that divorce occurs today in roughly half of all marriages, Catholic and otherwise. Usually, divorce is the result for couples who are not willing or who are not able to work out their differences. People who are divorced and do not remarry outside of the church may continue to live a sacramental life and participate in the church. Many parishes offer special support groups for those who are divorced.

Sometimes, the church will rule that a marriage was never a sacramental union. In that case, the marriage court of the church will declare the marriage "null," meaning that a sacramental marriage never existed. Common grounds for an *annulment* include the inability to provide full consent at the time of marriage and the lack of true freedom by one or both partners. If the church grants an annulment, and the reasons for the annulment no longer exist, the individuals are free to enter a sacramental marriage in the future.

▪ *activities* ▪

1. Write ten rules for preparing for a happy marriage. (Examples: "Learn how to be a friend." "Practice self-control.") Share your list with the class. Record a list of

the best rules. Share them with an engaged couple. Ask for their comments.

2. Interview a Catholic couple who have been married for many years and another who have recently married. Ask each couple to share five essential ingredients for a successful marriage. Report your findings to the class.

Holy Orders.   The common Christian vocation given at baptism is to serve others in Christ's name. Christ, the one high priest and minister, has shared his priestly power with all Christians. Baptized Christians exercise the common priesthood when they participate, each according to his or her vocation, in the church's mission as priest, prophet, and king.

For some time in their lives all people live out the Christian vocation as single people. Some choose to commit to a single life in order to have more time to devote to a special cause. A teacher devoted to his or her job and students would be an example of a person living out the Christian vocation as a single person. As described, marriage is another way men and women may serve God through relationships with their spouse, children, and all they meet. Traditionally, a "religious vocation" meant those who chose to take vows based on the gospel counsels of poverty, chastity, or obedience. Though the definition has expanded to include single and married Christians, *brothers* and *sisters* (men and women who live in religious communities) and the *ordained ministers* (deacons, priests, and bishops) have chosen to make public, total commitment to serving people by working for God's kingdom.

The ordained ministry is celebrated in the sacrament of holy orders. It recognizes a second type of priesthood in the church which is *essentially* different from the common priesthood of baptism: the *ministerial or hierarchial priesthood* of bishops and priests.

Holy orders is the sacrament of Christian ministry. Through the laying on of hands by bishops, holy orders confers gifts on the ordained that help them to preach the gospel, teach the faith, and serve as models of Christian life. There are three levels of holy orders: *episcopacy, presbyterate,* and *diaconate.*

The bishop receives the fullness of holy orders, episcopacy. Traditionally the bishop is the successor of the apostles. He is the overseer of the local church community and a symbol of church unity. Episcopal consecration confers on the bishop the offices of teaching, governing, and sanctifying. A bishop's chief responsibilities are to preach the gospel, to see to the administration of the sacraments, and to serve the needy in a diocese, or district.

Bishops ordain presbyters, or priests, to help them carry out their duties. Priests have many roles in the church, but you are probably most familiar with them as administrators of the sacraments at a local parish.

At a third level in the hierarchy of orders is the diaconate. In recent times the permanent diaconate has been restored. Married men may serve in this role. The primary role of deacons is service. Deacons cooperate with the bishop and priests in liturgical celebrations, in the distribution of communion, in preaching the gospel, in witnessing and blessing marriages, in presiding at funerals, and in the social work of the church.

Like baptism and confirmation, the sacrament of holy orders imparts a "character" on the men who receive it. This character permanently marks the ordained man as a deacon, priest, or bishop.

▪ *journal* ▪

Read the following passages about the roles of deacons in the early church. Note your findings in your journal.

1 Tm 3:8–13   Acts 6:1–4
Acts 7   Acts 8:4–13

What Are Sacramentals?

"Sacramentals" resemble the sacraments. They are objects, actions, prayers, and places which help people to remember Christ's presence. Sacramentals prepare Christians for the sacraments. The spiritual value of sacramentals depends on a person's own personal faith and devotion. Examples of sacramentals include:

- *Actions*: blessings (for example, of persons, meals, objects, and places) which praise God; genuflections before the blessed sacrament; the sign of the cross; bowing one's head at the name of Jesus; church processions.

- *Objects*: candles used in prayer or worship; holy water; statues and icons; holy pictures; blessed ashes used on Ash Wednesday; palms used before Holy Week; rosaries; relics; incense; vestments; scapulars; church buildings; crosses; religious medals.

- *Places*: the Holy Land, Rome, Fatima, Lourdes, the National Shrine, and other places of pilgrimage; chapels and retreat centers.
- *Prayers*: short prayers recited throughout the day; grace before and after meals.
- *Sacred Time*: holy days; feasts of saints; special days of prayer, fasting, and abstinence (for example, Fridays in Lent).

Conclusion

The sacraments are celebrations of God's presence and love. Recall that the church itself is a sacrament. To appreciate the seven individual sacraments fully, you should remind yourself that as a member of the church, you too are a sign of God's love.

Faith, of course, is a necessary ingredient for appreciating the sacraments. Faith is needed to see God working through ordinary realities like water, bread, and wine.

The sacraments also convey God's life to you. The sacraments bring, for example, new life, special strengths of the Holy Spirit, communion with God and others in the church, forgiveness, healing, and special ways to live out your baptismal vocation of service.

Sacraments are not magic; rather, they demand your participation. Because Jesus is really present in the sacraments, this participation takes the form of a celebration. *You are a sacrament!* Only in your joyful service of others and your sharing of sacramental values will anyone else ever know.

focus questions

1. Define sacrament.
2. How is the church a sacrament?
3. How are Jesus and the sacraments "efficacious symbols"?
4. In what way are sacraments "visible signs of invisible grace"?
5. Explain one official church teaching about the sacraments.

6. Explain the meaning of "sacramental character."

7. Identify *RCIA*. List its four major periods.

8. What does it mean "to baptize"? What is the formula for baptism?

9. Summarize the effects of baptism.

10. List and explain the meaning of two of the baptismal symbols.

11. What are the three principal effects of confirmation?

12. What is the meaning of the term *eucharist*?

13. Briefly explain these titles and descriptions of eucharist: *sacred meal, holy sacrifice, Blessed Sacrament,* and *holy communion*.

14. What is the meaning of the term *Mass*?

15. How is Christ "really present" in the Eucharist?

16. Define the term *liturgy*.

17. Outline the key parts of the eucharistic liturgy.

18. Why is Sunday the foundation of the liturgical year?

19. What was Jesus' response to suffering?

20. List the four key elements in the sacrament of reconciliation.

21. What is the advantage of frequently celebrating the sacrament of reconciliation?

22. Define the terms *extreme unction* and *viaticum*.

23. What are the two essential signs of the sacrament of the anointing of the sick?

24. Explain one effect of the sacrament of the anointing of the sick.

25. What is the meaning of the term *vocation*?

26. Explain how marriage is a "covenant" relationship.

27. What scriptural basis is there for the church's prohibition against divorce and remarriage?

28. What is an *annulment*?

29. What are the three levels of the sacrament of holy orders?

30. Define and list an example of a sacramental.

▪ *exercise* ▪

Use any form of art medium to create a symbol for one of the sacraments. Explain its meaning to your classmates. Display it in the classroom.

▪

Prayer Reflection

First, seek a quiet space and a quiet moment. Put yourself in the Lord's presence. Thank God for all the good things that have come your way during the previous day. Offer to God all of your pain and hurt.

Now review your day in more detail. Think back to the times you failed to act as brother or sister to friends, family members, classmates, and others you met. Think of your actions and words that hurt others. Examine any missed opportunities you had to love and to serve.

After this examination of conscience, you might wish to recite the following traditional "Act of Contrition," expressing to God your sorrow for your sins. Say the prayer slowly, reflecting on the meaning of each word.

Act of Contrition

O my God, I am sorry for my sins with all my heart. In choosing to do wrong and failing to do good, I have sinned against you whom I should love above all things. I firmly intend, with your help, to do penance, to sin no more, and to avoid whatever leads me to sin. Our Savior Jesus Christ suffered and died for us. In his name, my God, have mercy. Amen.

▪ *reflection* ▪

What area of your life needs the most work **right now**?

▪ *resolution* ▪

Think of someone you have hurt and resolve to make amends with him or her this coming week.

▪

▪ *vocabulary* ▪

Look up the meaning of the following words in the dictionary. Transcribe the definitions into your journal:

**consecrate
efficacious**

chapter 9

Prayer and
Pray-ers

> "Ask, and it will be given to you; search, and you will find; knock, and the door will be opened to you. Everyone who asks receives; everyone who searches, finds; everyone who knocks will have the door opened."
>
> —Matthew 7:7–8

In This Chapter

You will look at:

■ prayer basics, including various forms and expressions

■ the meaning of the Lord's Prayer

■ Jesus and Mary as model prayers

■ getting started in prayer

Once, a little boy was trying to lift a heavy box but he simply could not budge it. His father happened to pass by and stopped to watch his son's futile efforts. The boy exerted all his energy but still he made no progress. Finally, the father said to his son: "Are you doing everything possible to lift your load?"

In frustration, the boy yelled, "Yes, I am."

"I don't think so," the father replied calmly. "You haven't asked me to help you."

This simple story can serve as a reminder that your journey to God requires you to ask for God's help along the way. Prayer is essential to Christian life. Through prayer, you can experience God's presence. Prayer can help you to recognize ways that God stands ready to help you.

This chapter examines prayer—its meaning, modes, and ways that you can personally express yourself to God. Also, you will focus on Jesus and Mary as model pray-ers and as helpers for you as you proceed along your own spiritual journey.

Prayer and You

How do you feel about prayer? Rank in order from 1–8 (most helpful to least helpful) the following definitions, descriptions, or statements that express different feelings about prayer.

_____ 1. "One prays best who does not know that he or she is praying" (St. Anthony of Padua).

231

——— 2. "In prayer it is better to have a heart without words, than words without a heart" (John Bunyan).

——— 3. "The biggest problem in prayer is how to 'let go and let God'" (John Chapman).

——— 4. "Prayer is conversation with God" (St. Clement of Alexandria).

——— 5. "You need not cry very loud; he is nearer to us than we think" (Brother Lawrence).

——— 6. "Prayer enlarges the heart until it is capable of containing God's gift of himself" (Mother Teresa).

——— 7. "All that should be sought for in the exercise of prayer is conformity of our will and the divine will, in which consists the highest perfection" (St. Teresa of Avila).

——— 8. "Prayer means launching out of the heart towards God; it means lifting up one's eyes, quite simply, to heaven, a cry of grateful love, from the crest of joy or the trough of despair" (St. Thérèse of Lisieux).

There are many times, places, and ways to pray. Make a check by any of the following which match your own experience:

——— asking God's forgiveness when you sin

——— reading the Bible

——— going to Mass

——— meditating in a chapel

——— doing a good deed and offering it up to God

——— saying "thanks"

——— discussing religion with a friend

——— praying for another

——— reflecting on how God is working in your life

——— reflecting on God in nature

——— asking God for help

——— other: ———————

▪ *journal* ▪

Choose two of the following suggestions to write about in your journal. Share one of your entries with the class.

1. What is your favorite way to pray? Why?

2. Write of a time when prayer helped you. Be specific.

3. Compose your own definition of prayer.

4. Interview three people of various ages. Ask them about how and when they pray. Ask them how prayer has helped them in their daily lives. Record your findings.

What Is Prayer?

As the exercise suggests, there are many suitable ways to pray. But, what of a general definition of prayer? One definition is that prayer is "the lifting of one's mind and heart to God." Another popular way to describe prayer is "loving conversation with God." In other words, in prayer you enter into a dialogue with God. You both *listen* to the Spirit who speaks to you as well as *speak* your own heartfelt thoughts and words of:

> *Adoration,*
> *Contrition,*
> *Thanksgiving, and*
> *Supplication.*

The acronym ACTS spells out the various kinds of prayer conversations. All prayer involves divine and human action. Conversational prayer includes an *active* dimension of taking your concerns, worries, petitions and the like to God. It also involves a *passive* dimension when you pause and allow God to speak to you.

Thomas Merton defined prayer as "the consciousness of one's union with God, an awareness of one's inner self." This definition is appropriate in light of Jesus' revelation that "You are my friends...I shall no longer call you servants" (Jn 15:14, 15). When you pray, you become aware of yourself as a friend of Abba, the God who deeply loves you.

Regardless of how prayer is defined, you should remember that prayer means always being ready to turn to God. In prayer you recall that God is always present, always willing to speak to you and show you how much you are loved.

St. Teresa of Avila imaged prayer as a conscious turning to the invisible friend who is always near. Prayer indeed can deepen your friendship with God and strengthen you for the ongoing journey to God. As food is to the body, prayer is to the spirit of Jesus' friends.

Prayer types.   The Catholic tradition has a rich variety of different types of prayer. For example, prayers can be public or private, formal or spontaneous, vocal or silent. Here is some more information on each type:

Public.   The liturgy is the prime example of the church's public prayer. As church, members of Christ's body come together openly to praise and adore God, seek forgiveness, ask for help, and offer thanks in the name of the Lord Jesus. Think about how each of these actions takes place at Mass.

Private.   Jesus instructed his disciples to pray in private, to "go to your private room, shut yourself in, and so pray to your Father in that secret place, and your Father who sees all that is done in secret will reward you" (Mt 6:6). The content of the private prayer should embrace the concerns of others: for example, family members and friends, fellow Christians, government leaders, the needy, and even personal enemies.

Formal.   Formal prayer means using prayers already composed in a certain form. When you recite the Lord's Prayer or the Hail Mary or read the psalms aloud, for example, you are engaging in formal, vocal prayer. The psalms especially are a rich source of prayer for both Jews and Christians alike. Both personal and communal, the psalms express and proclaim God's saving works in a variety of prayer forms including hymns of praise, thanksgiving, and meditation. The psalms are an example of formal prayer that expresses the gamut of human emotion and aspirations.

Spontaneous.   Spontaneous prayers are prayers made in your own words; they follow no set formula. Young children often are taught to pray spontaneously; for example, "Thank you, God, for the gift of sun and sky." You may have prayed spontaneously when you offered a petition at a communal prayer service.

Vocal v. silent prayer.   Vocal prayers—those spoken aloud—can follow a set formula or be spontaneous. The eucharist and other sacraments are public, vocal prayers of the church. Many Catholics also recite the Liturgy of the Hours, the official daily prayer of the church that is recited during certain times of the day and night. Formal prayers like the Apostles' Creed, Morning Offering, and the Memorare are other examples of formal prayers many people pray regularly. Vocal prayer does not have to take place in private. Reciting the Rosary in a group, participating in special devotions like the Stations of the Cross or Forty Hours, or singing a religious song with a youth group are examples of vocal prayers that can help foster unity among those who pray aloud together.

One technique for silent prayer is to reflect on the words of familiar formal prayers that are often spoken aloud, like the Lord's Prayer. Usually, formal prayers become so familiar that the words are simply recited without giving any thought to their meaning. A way to counteract this is to pause, call on the Lord to be present, think about the reason you are praying, and then slowly reflect on the individual words and phrases.

Forms of prayer. The Catechism of the Catholic Church lists the following prayer forms:

1. **Blessing and adoration.**   When you bless God you respond to God's gifts. Blessing means "to declare holy." You can only bless God—the source of all blessings—because God first blesses you. Adoration means "to pay great love, devotion, and respect." When you adore God, you recognize that God is the creator and you are the created. Prayer of adoration means loving God for God's own sake, simply because God **is** goodness and worthy of all love.

2. **Petition.**   Prayers of petition are prayers of supplication or "prayers of asking." The opening scripture passage of this chapter (Matthew 7:7–8) tells of your ability to fulfill your needs through prayer. This translates into being able to confidently approach God for all your needs: help on a test, health for a sick grandmother, loyal friends, a good career, love and understanding.

■ *research* ■

Prepare a short report on the history and method of the Stations of the Cross, the annual parish eucharistic devotion, or the Liturgy of the Hours. Share your report with the class.

Jesus also instructs his disciples to pray for the coming of God's reign and the gift of the Holy Spirit who provides the strength to lead a good Christian life.

3. **Intercession.**   Intercessory prayers are petitions on behalf of others. When you pray for others, you imitate the prayer of Jesus at the Last Supper (see Jn 17). Jesus also promised to continue to intercede for all people until the end of time.

4. **Thanksgiving.**   Prayers to express gratitude to God for God's many gifts—creation, your family and friends, your health and talents—are most appropriate. A spirit of gratitude is a pretty minimal expectation. God deserves your thanks; without God, you would not even exist.

5. **Praise.**   "To praise" means "to laud the glory of." Prayers of praise sing to and glorify God simply because God is God—gracious, loving, saving. True prayers of praise show no self-interest. They take joy in God alone: "Praise the Lord! Alleluia!"

The Perfect Prayer

The eucharist exemplifies all forms of prayer. In the eucharist, the faithful bless, adore, praise, and thank God. Recall that the word "eucharist" means "thanksgiving."

Prayer expressions.   Besides vocal prayer, two other ways that prayer is expressed are meditation and mental prayer. Through words mentally or vocally expressed, a person's prayer is revealed.

Meditation is "to think deeply and continuously." When meditation is used to describe a form of prayer, it involves "tuning into God" using thoughts, imaginations, emotions, and desires. One goal of meditation is to see how God is revealed in everyday life. Another is to know God better so that God might be better loved and served.

There are many spiritual masters that have taught meditation in the Catholic tradition. St. Teresa of Avila and St. Ignatius of Loyola are two examples. One suggestion for beginning to meditate is to focus on one reading, item, or thought. A scripture passage, liturgical text of the day or season, spiritual writing of a saint, an icon, or current world event are worthy starting points for meditation.

Mental prayer is prayer centered on God. It may be in the form of a friendly conversation with Jesus or a deep reflection on the mysteries of his life. Mental prayer often leads to *contemplation*, the silent, wordless prayer of simply being in the presence of the all-loving God. St. John Vianney described contemplative prayer by telling of the peasant who used to sit daily before the tabernacle in church. "What do you do here all day?" the peasant was asked. "I look at the Lord, he looks at me," the peasant answered.

In contemplative prayer, a person attempts to empty his or her mind of thoughts and images and simply allow God to be present. In contemplative prayer, a person simply enjoys God's company in much the same way that two lovers sit on a seashore speechless, enjoying a beautiful sunset and each other. To be able to pray contemplatively is a gift both to God and from God.

Meditating on Scripture

Here is a format and directions for meditation on a scripture passage:

1. Find a quiet place to pray, a place where you will not be disturbed.

2. Quiet your body. Let the cares of the day disappear. Breathe slowly. Relax your body so your mind can focus on the meditation. Sit with your spine straight, hands on your lap, with your eyes closed.

3. Now, direct your attention to some object of meditation. For this exercise, try meditating on one of the following parables of Jesus:

   Laborers in the Vineyard (Mt 20:1–6)
   Merciless Official (Mt 18:21–35)
   Rich Man and Lazarus (Lk 16:19–31)
   Good Samaritan (Lk 10:25–37)
   Good Shepherd (Jn 10:1–21)
   Prodigal Son (Lk 15:11–32)
   Treasure and the Pearl (Mt 13:44–46)

   a. Put yourself imaginatively into the story. Ask yourself: "What is going on here? What is Jesus saying? What do the words mean? What is Jesus like? How does he look? What does he reveal about God? How does this story affect others? What does this story say to me? How am *I* a character in the story?"

   b. Determine the theme of the passage (for example, God's love for the sinner). Try to see all the implications of this theme for your life right now.

   c. Pause periodically to talk intimately to Jesus. Let him speak to you through the reading.

d. Share with God your deepest thoughts and feelings. Turn over to God your cares and needs. Praise God's goodness. Ask God to forgive your sins and failings. If distractions come your way, return to the scripture passage. Take your time and enjoy these moments with God.

4. Thank God for your time of prayer. Think of one way to translate what you gained in meditation to an action in your everyday life.

The Lord's Prayer

The Lord's Prayer, or "Our Father," is the preeminent Christian prayer. Tertullian, a church father of the late second century, called the Lord's Prayer "the summary of the whole gospel." From the earliest centuries until today, the church has prayed the Lord's Prayer in its liturgical celebrations, especially the eucharist. The Lord's Prayer is central to a Christian's daily prayer and it merits further investigation of its specific petitions.

The Lord's Prayer appears in the gospels of both Luke and Matthew. In Luke's version, the apostles approach Jesus who is praying quietly. They ask him to teach them how to pray. Jesus then gives them the prayer beginning with the words "Father, may your name be held holy, your kingdom come" (see Lk 11:2). The uniqueness of the prayer is that Jesus has instructed his disciples to call God, "Abba," or "Daddy." This marked the disciples in a new and special way, since those in the Jewish tradition rarely even uttered the name of Yahweh. Luke's version of the Lord's Prayer, possibly the older of the two, has only five petitions.

Matthew's version of the Lord's Prayer has seven petitions. It is the one that has been adopted by the church and is recited at Mass. Matthew's gospel records Jesus teaching the Lord's Prayer as part of the Sermon on the Mount (see Mt 5–7). He teaches the Our Father as a short but profound example of prayer which asks for total reliance on God.

The Lord's Prayer was so revered by the early church that Christians were not permitted to learn it until after their baptisms. You have undoubtedly recited the words of the Lord's Prayer countless times. Nevertheless, it is important

■ *journal* ■

Read Luke 11:2–4 and Matthew 6:9–13. Note similarities and differences between these two versions of the Lord's Prayer.

to occasionally pause to analyze the meaning of the words you pray. Consider the following examination of the various phrases and petitions:

Our Father. Jesus' invitation to call God *Abba* implies two very important truths. First, Jesus' Father is the Father of all. This makes people brothers and sisters of the Son, Jesus, as well as children of the Father. Like little children, all people should trust Abba to care for their needs.

Also, not only are people brothers and sisters of Jesus, but each person is intimately related to one another. By addressing God as "Our Father," Christians pledge to commit themselves to understand, love, and respond to **everyone** who comes into their lives.

Who art in heaven. The biblical expression "in heaven" does not refer to a specific place but rather to God's way of being. Christians affirm that through Jesus, God lives in the hearts of the just. This expression is a profession that the people of God are in union with Christ in heaven. At the same time, Christians anticipate the full realization of their heavenly reward.

▪ *discuss* ▪

1. How do you image God as Father? Jesus as brother?
2. Tell how you can improve one relationship with someone you have not been able to get along with as brother or sister.

Hallowed be thy name. A person's name calls forth his or her uniqueness. In the ancient world, a person's name typically **was** the person. Jesus wanted *Simon bar Jonah* to be the leader of the apostles, so he renamed him *Peter* which means "rock"; Peter was to be the solid foundation on which Christ would build his community. Today, personal names carry meaning, too: for example, David means "beloved," Jennifer means "gentle spirit," and Christopher means "Christ bearer."

When you pray for the "hallowing" of God's name, you are praying that everyone on earth will regard God as holy

Doxology

The conclusion, or doxology, to the Lord's prayer that is recited at Mass—"For thine is the kingdom, the power and the glory forever and ever, Amen"—comes from the *Didache*, a first-century catechetical manual. This doxology reiterates in praise and thanksgiving the first three petitions to the heavenly Father: the glorification of God's name, the coming of the kingdom, and the power of God's saving will.

(as God is holy in heaven). God is the source of all holiness, of all that is good, of all love. You can help to make God's name holy when you believe in God's love and act on your belief by taking on the identity of Jesus Christ.

■ *discuss* ■

1. How does your name represent who you are?
2. What have you done recently to take on the identity of Jesus Christ?

Thy kingdom come; they will be done on earth as it is in heaven. With the coming of Jesus Christ, God's rule—firmly established in heaven—has broken into the world. Peace, justice, truth, community, and mutual love reign in heaven. Jesus has inaugurated this reign on earth through his own ministry. For example, he preached the gospel to the poor, brought liberty to captives, wholeness to the broken, and healing and salvation to everyone.

Though God's kingdom will not be fully established until the end of time, Christians are called to live, experience, and work for the kingdom right now. This means simply to respond to the needs of "the least" of society, including the hungry, thirsty, stranger, sick, and imprisoned.

■ *discuss* ■

Tell one way that you are actively engaged in doing one of the corporal works of mercy. (These can be found on page 110.)

Give us this day our daily bread. Bread represents life. It also suggests a meal and the companionship which comes with a meal. When Christians pray for "our daily bread," they are petitioning for life's basic requirements: things needed for physical life (food, shelter, and clothing), psychological life (friendship, love, and companionship), and spiritual life (the eucharistic Jesus).

The petition also includes the needs of all people. The Lord's Prayer challenges Christians to share with others, especially the less fortunate. The parable of the last judgment (see Mt 25:31–46) and the parable of Lazarus and the rich man (see Lk 16:19–31) teach the sharing of one's material goods with the poor.

The word "daily" in the original Aramaic Jesus spoke may also have meant something similar to "for tomorrow, today." Praying for "our daily bread" also means praying

■ *discuss* ■

1. What does receiving the eucharist mean to you?
2. What are your most pressing physical, psychological, and spiritual needs?

for the fullness of God's material and spiritual blessings which will only come in heaven.

And forgive us our trespasses as we forgive those who trespass against us. This petition lists two difficult tasks: to ask for forgiveness and to be forgiving yourself. By asking God for forgiveness, you are acknowledging your sinfulness and your need for God's saving love. Your confession speaks of your dependence on God's mercy.

Jesus connects the mercy of God to a person's love and forgiveness of others. For example, the first letter of John states that "Anyone who says, 'I love God' and hates his brother, is a liar" (1 Jn 4:20). Also, the parable of the unforgiving debtor tells of a king who forgave the debt of his servant and then expected the servant to do the same in his own relationships (see Mt 18:23–35). Your forgiveness of those who have hurt you is a powerful sign of love that encourages others to respond in the same way. This petition of the Lord's Prayer is a call to action: to forgive as we have been forgiven.

And lead us not into temptation. Saint Paul writes that "God will not let you be put to the test beyond your strength" (see 1 Cor 10:13). Therefore, this petition does not likely speak of daily temptations which can be overcome easily with God's help, but rather the final testing that is to come at the end of time (see Mt 24:21–22).

Nevertheless, this petition does have implications for your life today. It asks you to pray for the strength to overcome any difficulties that might lead you away from a Christian life, including the temptations of consumerism, power, greed, jealousy and the like.

But deliver us from evil. Literally, this petition means a deliverance from Satan, "the evil one." The sin of Satan was self-reliance, choosing self over God. Consider the many ways that general society ignores God today. Praying for a deliverance from the evil one means praying to remember that God is active in your life, a part of every decision that you make, and all that you choose to do.

■ *discuss* ■

What is one relationship of yours that needs repair? How can forgiveness help to heal this hurt?

■ *discuss* ■

Give evidence from your own life that supports St. Paul's words that God "will not let you be put to the test beyond your strength."

▪ *discuss* ▪

List some of the most common temptations which people your age face in trying to live a Christian life. Rank the list from most severe to least severe. Compare your list with a classmate's. Share a plan to help you avoid the temptations when they arise.

▪ *project* ▪

Illustrate each of the petitions of the Lord's Prayer using any form of art medium. For example, you may create a video with background music or a notebook collage using magazine photos or current newspaper headlines. Share your work with the class.

▪ *journal* ▪

Analyze the petitions or phrases of another formal Christian prayer, for example, the Hail Mary. Include questions for personal growth.

Jesus and Mary: Models of Prayer

Jesus and his mother Mary are examples to Christians of model pray-ers. Each showed how a consistent prayer life was a necessity for determining God's will and for making decisions based on God's will for their own lives.

In fact, the prayer lives of Jesus and Mary are very much inter-related. It was Mary's prayer and resounding trust that allowed her to accept God's will to become the mother of Jesus, the mother of God. Jesus, like all Jewish children, first learned how to pray at home, from Mary and his foster father, Joseph.

The church continues to look to Jesus and Mary as models and teachers of prayer. By examining their prayer lives and the examples that are preserved in the gospels, you can gain great insight on how to have a fruitful prayer life of your own.

How Jesus prayed.   There is scriptural evidence that Jesus prayed at all the significant times in his life on earth. Also, as a member of a family of faithful Jews, it is likely that he first learned traditional Jewish prayers as a child, both at home and at the synagogue. Jesus often quoted the Hebrew scriptures—especially the psalms—while praying.

Jesus prayed before making important life decisions. For example, he prayed in the desert for forty days before beginning his public ministry (see Lk 4:1–13). He prayed the entire night before choosing his apostles (see Lk 6:12–16). In the most important decision he had to make, the one of whether or not to accept death on the cross, he prayed for the courage to be able to submit to God's will:

> "Father," he said, "if you are willing, take this cup away from me. Nevertheless, let your will be done, not mine" (Lk 22:42).

Jesus also prayed in different ways. He *praised* God for revealing the divine will to those who humbled themselves like children (see Lk 10:21). When he raised Lazarus from the dead, he expressed *thankfulness* in prayer. He said: "Father, I thank you for hearing my prayer" (Jn 11:41). He also *petitioned* God; for example, he prayed that Peter might not have to undergo temptation by Satan (see Mk 14:38). At the Last Supper, Jesus offered a prayer of *intercession* for the needs of all people (see Jn 17).

Even at the moment of his death, Jesus prayed: "Father, into your hands I commit my spirit" (Lk 23:46). These were words of final, self-abandonment to the will of God.

How Mary prayed. Mary exhibited two qualities necessary for a good prayer life: faith and humility. Faith, the virtue of trusting on the word of another, was at the heart of Mary's life. Not fully understanding why or how, Mary accepted the invitation to become God's mother. At the annunciation, she said to the angel: "You see before you the Lord's servant, let it happen to me as you have said" (Lk 1:38). Mary was also humble. She knew that all that was happening to her took place through the power of God: "The almighty has done great things for me," she said (Lk 1:49).

Though Mary is not quoted often in the scriptures, there is other evidence that she was a woman of prayer. After finding out that she was pregnant, she went to see her cousin Elizabeth and sang of God's greatness. These words in Luke

1:46–55 are known as the *Magnificat*. She also went with her family to Jerusalem for key feasts (see Lk 2:41–50). After Jesus' ascension to heaven, Mary remained with the early Christian community in prayer:

> With one heart all these joined constantly in prayer, together with some women, including Mary the mother of Jesus, and with his brothers (Acts 1:14).

Mary's style of praying can best be described as meditation and contemplation. She meditated on the incomparable action of God in her life when the shepherds appeared at the nativity to glorify the birth of God's Son:

> As for Mary, she treasured all these things and pondered them in her heart (Lk 2:19).

At the infant Jesus' presentation at the Temple, Simeon revealed to Mary that he had seen in Jesus the salvation that God had readied for the world. Mary "wondered at the things that were being said" about Jesus (Lk 2:33). When she found her lost twelve-year-old son teaching the doctors of the Jewish faith in the Temple, Jesus told her she should have expected to find him in "my Father's house." When they returned home to Nazareth, the gospel records that Mary "stored up all these things in her heart" (Lk 2:51).

These examples point to Mary as the model of contemplative prayer. In contemplation, she basked in the warmth of God's love, delighted in God's presence.

Honoring Mary.   Mary is a model of prayer for all Christians because she points the way to her son, Jesus. Catholics have also always believed that Mary is worthy of honor herself. This belief is based on the idea that when the church honors Mary, it honors her son. Catholic beliefs about Mary find their roots in faith in Jesus Christ.

Simply put, Catholics give special devotion to Mary because she is the mother of God and the mother of the church. Praying to and honoring Mary can lead you to love her and to imitate her many virtues, especially her total commitment to live God's will.

Mary's main role in salvation is to draw people closer to her son. Notice how in any famous artwork featuring Mary

■ *journal* ■

The *Magnificat* ("to proclaim greatness") captures well the fruit of all prayer: a desire to give your whole being to God. Mary lived such a life in the power of the Holy Spirit. The Magnificat also expresses the hopes of the poor who look to the fulfillment of God's promise of salvation.

Read Mary's Magnificat in Luke 1:46–55. Make note of verses that would give hope to the poor. Explain why you chose the verses you did.

and Jesus—the Pieta, for example—the focus of the painting or statue is on Jesus, not Mary. Mary leads people to Jesus, shows them how to live in response to Jesus, and intercedes on their behalf.

Special devotion to Mary is different from the worship which is due the Blessed Trinity alone. True devotion to Mary *honors* her; only God may be worshipped. By honoring Mary, the church actually is simultaneously praising God for the goodness of so perfectly blessing a human being.

The Rosary

A special devotion to Mary is the Rosary, a blend of vocal prayers and meditation.

The vocal prayers include decades of Hail Marys marked by beads strung together in groups of ten. Larger beads before each decade signify saying a Lord's Prayer and Glory Be. Introductory prayers to the Rosary include the Apostles' Creed, the Lord's Prayer, three Hail Marys and a Glory Be. As these vocal prayers are recited, certain events, or mysteries, from the life of Jesus and Mary are meditated on.

The complete Rosary contains 15 decades marking the joyful, sorrowful, and glorious mysteries of the lives of Jesus and Mary.

The repetition of the Hail Marys helps you to keep your mind from distractions as you meditate on the mysteries. Next to the Lord's Prayer, the Hail Mary is the most popular of all prayers among Catholics. The first part of the Hail Mary has its roots in the New Testament. It combines the greeting of the angel (Lk 1:28) and the greeting of Elizabeth, Mary's cousin (Lk 1:42). The second part requests Mary's intercession for all people:

> Hail Mary, full of grace, the Lord is with you;
>> blessed are you among women and blessed is the
>> fruit of your womb, Jesus.
>
> Holy Mary, mother of God, pray for us sinners now
>> and at the hour of our death. Amen.

The mysteries of the Rosary are divided as follows:

Joyful Mysteries	Sorrowful Mysteries	Glorious Mysteries
1. The annunciation	1. The agony in the garden	1. The resurrection
2. The visitation of Mary to Elizabeth	2. The scourging at the pillar	2. The ascension
3. The birth of Jesus	3. The crowning with thorns	3. The descent of the Holy Spirit on the apostles
4. The presentation of Jesus in the Temple	4. The carrying of the cross	4. The assumption of Mary into heaven
5. The finding of Jesus in the Temple	5. The crucifixion	5. The crowning of Mary, Queen of Heaven

Beliefs About Mary

Over the centuries, the church has formalized many of its beliefs about Mary. Some of the most important of these beliefs are summarized below:

Mother of God

In reflecting on the identity of Jesus, the early church, under the inspiration of the Holy Spirit, taught that Jesus is *one* divine person who has a human nature and a divine nature. Further, the church taught that Jesus was divine from the very first moment of his conception. Thus, the Council of Ephesus (A.D. 431) declared Mary to be *theotokos*, that is, "bearer of God." By being the mother of Jesus, Mary is truly the mother of God. It is most appropriate for Christians to address Mary with the lofty title: mother of God.

Mother of the Church

On the cross, Jesus addressed the apostle John as he stood next to Mary: "This is your mother" (Jn 19:27). This statement is the basis for Mary's role as mother of the church. The scripture text goes on, "And from that hour the disciple took her into his home" (Jn 19:27). Mary's home is the church.

Immaculate Conception

Mary was conceived without original sin. Full of grace, Mary was always free of any alienation from God caused by original sin. Because of Mary's special role in God's saving plan, God graced her this way in anticipation of her son's death and resurrection.

Ever Virgin

Mary conceived Jesus without a human father, and the church has traditionally taught that she was a virgin "before, in, and after" the birth of Jesus. The doctrine of Mary's virginity stresses that God's Son has truly become human. More significantly, it highlights the profound truth that God takes the absolute initiative in the incarnation: God is the unique Father of Jesus Christ.

Assumption of Mary into Heaven

In 1950 Pope Pius XII officially proclaimed the doctrine of the Assumption: "The Immaculate Mother of God, the ever Virgin Mary, having completed the course of her earthly life, was assumed body and soul into heavenly glory." Mary is the first to share in Christ's resurrection; Christians look forward to their own resurrection in the Lord.

■ *journal* ■

Note insights you gained from meditating on particular mysteries from the lives of Jesus and Mary after praying the Rosary.

■ *research* ■

1. Find information and report on one of these popular Marian devotions:
   - the Angelus
   - Marian novena
   - litany of the Blessed Mother
   - First Saturday devotion

2. Prepare a short report on one of the following Marian apparitions:

   Guadalupe   Lourdes   Fatima

■ *journal* ■

Read the following parables on prayer from the gospel of Luke: the friend at midnight (Lk 11:5–8), the persistent widow (Lk 18:1–8), and the pharisee and tax collector (Lk 18:9–14). What does each parable have to do with prayer? Explain the main points that Jesus is making.

Teachers of prayer.   The models of prayer life left by Mary and Jesus translate into several concrete actions. The first action of the successful pray-er is to acquire a spirit of conversation and reconciliation with those around you. This means you should *pray with forgiving hearts:*

> "And when you stand in prayer, forgive whatever you have against anybody, so that your Father in heaven may forgive your failings too" (Mk 11:25).

Also, Jesus teaches that you should make your prayers to God in secret (see Mt 6:5–6). You should also pray with *childlike simplicity* and with *faith.* Jesus said that God will always listen to your petitions and will give you what is good:

> "If you then, evil as you are, know how to give your children what is good, how much more will the heavenly Father give the Holy Spirit to those who ask him!" (Lk 11:13).

> "And if you have faith, everything you ask for in prayer, you will receive" (Mt 21:22).

Persistence is another quality of a good prayer life. Persistence is a sign of faith in Jesus' words:

> "Ask, and it will be given to you; search, and you will find it; knock, and the door will be opened to you" (Lk 11:19).

Another direction Jesus left concerning prayer was to *pray with others.* The value of praying in communion is explained as follows:

> "In truth I tell you once again, if two of you on earth agree to ask anything at all, it will be granted to you by my Father in heaven. For where two or three meet in my name, I am there among them" (Mt 18:19–20).

These directions, coupled with the very examples of the lives of Jesus and Mary, provide the model as well as the incentive to approach the loving God. Jesus and Mary show the way to confidently pray the words of the Lord's Prayer,

"Thy kingdom come, thy will be done"—the primary goal of all Christian prayer.

Getting Started in Prayer

You have read various definitions of prayer, explored forms of prayer, and examined ways that prayer is expressed, be it vocally, mentally, or through meditation. Finally, you witnessed the examples of Jesus and Mary, model pray-ers. Now that you **know** more about prayer, how will you be able to improve your prayer life?

God gives you the gift of wanting to pray, but you have to do your part and accept the gift. This requires discipline, humility, trust in God's presence, and perseverance. Here are some basics to help you develop a better, fuller prayer life:

Place/Time. You can pray anywhere, but it is good to find a special place where you can slow down, relax, and focus your attention. The outdoors, a chapel, a corner of your room with a Bible and sacred images (icons) are all appropriate places for prayer.

You can also pray at any time, but it is a good idea to develop a regular routine and to pray at the same times each day. The biggest excuse most people give for not praying is that they cannot find the time. However, anyone can find ten or fifteen minutes each day to spend with God in prayer, providing they discipline themselves by finding a prayer time and staying with it. Prayer is a habit. You can learn to pray better by praying often.

Relaxation. Prayer demands your undivided attention. If you are tired, distracted, or edgy, you will not be able to pray well. Assuming various body positions can keep you alert and can also help you to relax. Sitting in a chair with your back in a straight line, lying on the floor, kneeling, or sitting in the lotus position are all helpful prayer positions.

Just as a person would methodically warm up before doing strenuous exercise, you should also spend some time calming your body so that your mind and spirit are free to communicate with God. Rhythmic breathing, listening intently to the sounds around you, noticing the tensions in your body and consciously allowing them to fade away are some of the ways that you can prepare for prayer.

Proper Attitude.   Prayer requires openness and devotion to God. It is always good to begin your prayer by recalling God's ongoing presence and friendship in your life, and the many gifts God has bestowed on you.

Distractions.   A typical problem most people face when praying is distractions. A wandering mind, reliving an incident from the day just past, an overactive imagination, attending to external noises—all of these can distract you when you pray. What can you do about distractions? It is usually not a good idea to be anxious about the distractions or to try to fight them head on.

Instead, try gazing at an icon, crucifix, or lit candle to help refocus your prayer. You might also recite a particular prayer-word or phrase like "Jesus help me" or "loving Abba." Or, ask the Holy Spirit to help you to be free of distractions. These practices can help "distract you from the distractions." Remember, God values your attempts to pray, even if distractions do bombard you or your prayer seems dry and empty. Simply wanting to pray is itself a prayer.

Conclusion

Preparing to go off to college, a young man asked his mother how she defined success, as he wanted to please her when he went away.

His mom wisely replied, "Make one person happy each day." And she quickly added, "Even if that person is you!"

Happiness on the Christian journey is to experience the incredible love God has for you. You do this when you "stop, look, and listen" to the many ways Jesus is alive in the world and in your own personal life. If you take the time to pray on a daily basis, you will indeed notice the many ways that God is active in your life. And if you do this, you will be a happier, more peaceful person. A **real** success.

■ *focus questions* ■

1. Define prayer. Explain the key elements in your definition.
2. List the active and passive dimensions of conversational prayer.
3. Briefly explain three different types of prayer.
4. What is the Liturgy of the Hours?
5. List and briefly explain five forms of prayer.
6. Distinguish between meditation and mental prayer (contemplation).
7. In which gospels does the Lord's Prayer appear? Which version is the earlier? Which version does the church recite at Mass?
8. Briefly discuss the meaning of each petition of the Lord's Prayer.
9. Give several examples of how Jesus modelled prayer.
10. Briefly discuss three of Jesus' specific teachings about *how* to pray.
11. List some examples of how Mary modelled prayer.
12. In what way does Mary model faith and humility?
13. Why does the church honor Mary?
14. What is the purpose of the "mysteries" of the Rosary?
15. What is a good time and place *for you* to pray? Explain why.
16. How do you handle distractions in prayer?

■ *exercise* ■

Read Psalms 4, 5, 11, and 23 from the Book of Psalms. Make note of how God's saving work is described in each.

■ *vocabulary* ■

Look up the meaning of the following words in the dictionary. Transcribe the definitions into your journal:

aspiration   gamut   icon

■

Prayer Reflection

The *Angelus* commemorates the incarnation. Catholics traditionally recite it in the morning, at noon, and in the evening. It recalls the angel Gabriel's announcement to Mary that God had chosen her to be the mother of the Lord. It also includes Mary's humble acceptance. Three Hail Marys and a special prayer are also part of the Angelus.

The Angelus

The angel of the Lord declared unto Mary.
R: And she conceived by the Holy Spirit.

Hail Mary...

Behold the handmaid of the Lord
R: May it be done unto me according to your word.

Hail Mary...

And the word was made flesh.
R: And dwelled among us.

Hail Mary...

Pray for us, O holy mother of God.
R: That we may be made worthy of the promises
   of Christ.

Let us pray: We beseech you, O Lord, to pour out your grace into our hearts. By the message of an angel we have learned of the incarnation of Christ, your Son; lead us, by his passion and cross, to the glory of the resurrection. Through the same Christ our Lord. Amen.

▪ *reflection* ▪

Consider the prominence Christ has in your life.

▪ *resolution* ▪

Recite the Angelus at lunchtime for the next two weeks.

chapter 10

Living the
Catholic Faith:
Open & Ecumenical

"You are light for the world. Your light must shine in people's sight, so that, seeing your good works, they may give the praise to your Father in heaven."

—Matthew 5:14, 16

A group of teenagers got off the bus and stumbled into a younger boy, blind and obviously poor, selling bags of oranges on the street corner.

One of the teens deliberately kicked a bag of oranges, spilling them all over the street. Everyone laughed heartily as they continued on to the video store. But one boy in the group began to feel sorry for what his friend did. He quietly left the group at the store and went back to the blind boy. He helped gather up the salvageable oranges. He also gave the boy a ten dollar bill.

"I'm sorry for what my friend did," he said. "I hope you're going to be OK."

As he began to walk away, the blind boy said, "Thank you." He then added in a quiet voice, "Are you Jesus?"

The compassionate teenager stopped in his tracks. He repeated the question to himself: "Am I Jesus?" And thought about an answer to the question for the rest of the day.

Are *you* Jesus? The vocation of every Catholic is to bring Jesus to the world. You do this when you love and serve others. As you complete this particular study of the Catholic faith, the Lord is asking you: "Are you mine? Will you help me in my work of spreading the good news?"

■

Believing and Living the Catholic Faith

Use the following points and the accompanying scale to help you assess your commitment to the Catholic faith and teachings. How do these points help you to define what it means to be Catholic?

255

1—I am strongly committed to this point; my actions support my words.

2—I am committed to this point.

3—I am lukewarm to this point but I would like to increase my commitment.

4—This point has no relevance to my life.

_____ 1. I believe in a God who is like a loving parent; the "Abba" that Jesus described.

_____ 2. I acknowledge that Jesus Christ is Lord. I believe that the passion, death, resurrection, and glorification of Jesus have won eternal life for me.

_____ 3. I believe the Holy Spirit is alive in the world. This Spirit has endowed me with the gifts of a Christian life, enabling me to respond to the Lord Jesus.

_____ 4. I believe in the one, holy, catholic, and apostolic church.

_____ 5. I pray regularly.

_____ 6. I accept the scriptures as God's word. I try to read them, pray them, and seek guidance from them.

_____ 7. I acknowledge my sinfulness by celebrating the sacrament of reconciliation.

_____ 8. I live a sacramental life, especially by participating in the Sunday celebration of the eucharist.

_____ 9. I model my life on Jesus Christ by loving God above everything and loving my neighbor as myself.

_____ 10. I consult the teaching of the church before making moral decisions.

_____ 11. I respect church leaders and all other proper authority.

_____ 12. I do something specific to serve the needs of others, especially the poor, rejected, and lonely.

_____ 13. I share my Christian faith with others.

_____ 14. I honor Mary and the saints.

_____ 15. I respect and defend human life.

Add two other items to this list that describe your Catholic commitment:

_____ 16. _____

_____

_____ 17. _____

_____

▪ *journal* ▪

What does it mean *to you* to be a Christian? to be a Catholic?

▬▬▬▬▬▬▬▬▬▬ ▪ ▬▬▬▬▬▬▬▬▬▬

Catholicism: A Recap of Belief, Practice, Mission

As you know, "being Catholic" has many different definitions and forms. People who attend Mass twice a year on Christmas and Easter, those who bring their children to church for baptism and never return, and even those who haven't had any contact with the church since they graduated from a Catholic high school may all call themselves "Catholic."

Certainly the catholic definition of being "open to all" would be welcoming to people of this kind and many others. But, as you have likely gathered from this course and years of study and practice, being Catholic is something you can hardly pay lip service to. Being Catholic is a demanding vocation centered in the call to "give up everything, pick up your cross, and follow Jesus Christ" (see Mk 8:34). Being a Catholic is first of all being a baptized, committed disciple of Jesus Christ. The following key points help to translate what that means to a Catholic identity:

A Catholic is a Christian. This definition is paramount; as Christians, Catholics profess their belief in Jesus Christ, the Son of God. This is a belief that unites Catholics with Christians from many religious denominations. In addition, being a Catholic Christian means acknowledging Jesus by:

- **proclaiming** his word, the good news of salvation.
- **commemorating** the paschal mystery of redemption through the celebration of the sacraments, especially the eucharist.
- **witnessing** through good deeds to the truth of the gospel.
- **serving** the needs of others.
- **promoting** peace and justice, thus working with Jesus to help his reign grow on earth as it is in heaven.

Catholics are sacramental people. Theologian Fr. Richard McBrien describes the *principle of sacramentality* as seeing God's presence in all things—people, events, objects, places. This principle holds that God's majesty, grandeur, and love can be appreciated through the visible world. In this scheme, the great sacrament of meeting God is Jesus Christ. Catholics believe that it is in the church and the seven ritual sacraments that Jesus is most perfectly encountered.

The seven sacraments are special signs of Christ's grace. Although several other Christian communities accept seven sacraments (for example, the Orthodox and Anglican churches), many Protestant denominations recognize only baptism and eucharist.

The eucharist is the focus of the sacraments, and indeed the entire life of the church. For Catholics, the eucharist is the summit of Christian worship. It both creates and celebrates Christian community. McBrien also describes a *principle of communion* in which God meets people and people meet God through their participation in the life of the church, especially at eucharist. The eucharist is central to Catholic life because it states so strongly the importance of community. The eucharist is a foretaste of the heavenly banquet. It proclaims for Catholics a "holy communion" with Christ and the community of people who make up the church.

The church continues to bring Christ and his grace to humanity, principally through the sacraments. For example, the blessed oil of confirmation strengthens the recipients to live a Christian life. The love of a husband and wife in the sacrament of marriage is both a sign and means of grace for the couple. The simple words of absolution in the sacrament of reconciliation actually pronounce Jesus' forgiveness to the repentant sinner.

Catholics recognize the pope. Catholics regard the pope as the "vicar of Christ" and the successor of St. Peter. The bishop of Rome has the key position of authority in the church. Although some Christian denominations understand and respect the need for a strong teaching authority like the papacy, Catholics uniquely regard the pope as Christ's representative on earth, the final arbiter in matters of faith and morals.

Catholics honor Mary. Traditionally, Catholics have honored Mary in a special way. Marian devotion is a key feature of Catholic life. Devotions like the rosary and celebrations of holy days in Mary's honor help to distinguish Catholicism from other Christian churches. For example, of the six holy days celebrated in the United States, three celebrate a Marian feast: the Solemnity of Mary, Mother of God (January 1), the Assumption of Mary into heaven (August 15), and the Immaculate Conception (December 8).

The Church Is Open to All

One of the four marks of the church described in the creed is that it is *catholic*, meaning "universal" or "open to all." The church is able to express this fullness because of Jesus' presence. Jesus bestows on the church the fullness of the means of salvation—the complete creed, full sacramental life, and an ordained ministry traceable to the apostles. Second, the church is catholic because it exists to bring *all* people to Christ—in all places and in all times. To achieve this mission, the church has always been radically open to the spirit and practice of truth.

This openness to truth has been expressed throughout history. For example, the church employs a variety of theological approaches to understanding the gospel and it endorses a wide array of spiritualities. Catholic openness to the world and its people has resulted in massive, organized efforts to help others. The church has sponsored and supported missionary, educational, and health care systems worldwide. Another element of the church's truth-seeking has been its love for the arts. Through history, the church has inspired and encouraged artists and musicians, encouraged a love of literature, and helped to lay the foundations for modern science.

Today, the Catholic openness to truth and to all people continues to be evident. Two of the most prominent ways the church lives out is mandate to be universal and embracing are in the issues of *openness to life* and *ecumenism*. To support and defend all life shows a commitment to the entire human community. *Ecumenism* means "worldwide." To participate in the "ecumenical movement" is to support efforts to extend the welcoming arms of the body of Christ to all people.

The following sections examine these two issues in more detail.

Openness to life. Jesus' statement: "I have come so that they may have life and have it to the full" (Jn 10:10) is at the core of church teaching on "openness to life." Because of Jesus' life, death, and resurrection, human life has great meaning. Jesus valued human life so much that he gave his own life to redeem it.

Throughout history there have been many abuses to human life. Poverty, wars, and other social injustices have plagued societies. With the developments of science and technology in the twentieth century, even more visible and deadly crimes against human life have been perpetrated.

Typically, those who are weakest and are least able to speak for themselves have been most abused. At one end of the life spectrum, the unborn are greatly threatened. Latest estimates place the number of abortions in the United States at 1.6 million per year. In some larger cities there are more than twice as many abortions as there are live births. At the other end, the elderly and sick are at risk. Tolerance of euthanasia, or "mercy killings" has increased. Left unchecked, this phenomena is likely to lead to a call

■ *journal* ■

Define "openness to life." What is your understanding of the church's position on life issues? How do you feel about that position? Why?

for the selected killing of others who may be vulnerable: the poor, the physically or mentally handicapped, the terminally ill. You might ask yourself who, in reality, is safe in a society whose mind set approves of the selective killing of anyone?

The church speaks out for the openness and defense of life from conception to death. Cardinal Joseph Bernardin of Chicago described this as a "seamless garment" connecting all of the life issues together from beginning to end. Looking at life as a seamless garment means taking on the outlook of God who views all of creation as it is happening now.

Understood in this perspective, it is the task of Catholics to be open to **all** human life. For example, from the first century until today, the church has firmly condemned abortion, that is, the deliberate killing of unborn human life through medical procedures. Pro-life Christians strongly disagree with the contemporary pro-abortionist position (also called pro-choice) that claims that humans have an *absolute* right to their own bodies. Today, pro-abortionists rarely express doubts about the basic humanity of the unborn baby. Nevertheless, pro-abortionists continue to hold that a woman has a right—for whatever reason—to terminate life in the womb.

Being "pro-life" is not a political label; rather it is a requirement of being a Christian. It is expressed not only through opposition to abortion, but also through opposing things like poverty, war, and euthanasia. According to the documents of Vatican II:

> For God, the Lord of life, has conferred on all the surpassing ministry of safeguarding life—a ministry which must be fulfilled in a manner which is worthy of all. Therefore from the moment of its conception life must be guarded with the greatest care, while abortion and infanticide are unspeakable crimes (*Pastoral Constitution on the Church in the Modern World*, No. 51).

What are some ways that you can participate in this ministry? Consider the following actions. Add some more of your own to the list:

- Respect your own life. Eat the right foods. Get proper rest. Exercise. Avoid harmful substances.
- Respect the dignity of others. Treat all people fairly.

- Remove prejudicial feelings from your life.
- Drive carefully.
- Share your resources with the poor.
- Learn pro-life responses to pro-abortion arguments.
- Support the unborn by writing letters to legislators, government officials, and the media, or by participating in pro-life rallies.
- Support health care initiatives for poor women and children.
- Respect your own sexuality and that of others.
- Visit the sick and elderly. Help to care for their physical and spiritual needs.
- Pray.

Before I formed you in the womb I knew you;

before you came to birth I consecrated you.

—Jeremiah 1:5

▪ *discuss* ▪

Which statement do you **most** closely associate with the phrase "openness to life"? Explain your choice.

- Human life begins at conception.
- All pregnant women deserve adequate prenatal care.
- Everyone has the right to adequate food, clothing, and shelter.
- Disabled people deserve the rights to equal education, housing, and job opportunities.
- Euthanasia is an affront to the dignity of human beings.

Church Teaching on Euthanasia

Euthanasia literally means "happy or good death." There are two basic types of euthanasia:

1. *Direct (active or positive) euthanasia* is the directly willed inducement of death for merciful reasons. (This is the type of euthanasia people usually have in mind when they talk about euthanasia.) Regardless of the means used or one's intentions, direct euthanasia results in the death of a sick, handicapped, or dying person. It is morally unacceptable and forbidden by the church.

2. *Indirect (passive or negative) euthanasia* is allowing oneself or another to die; for example, when the person is terminally ill, where there is no obligation to continue life-support systems, and where there is no reasonable hope for recovery. Speaking of *indirect* euthanasia confuses the issue because most people mean *active or direct* euthanasia when debating this issue.

The following points summarize the Catholic teaching on the issue of euthanasia:

- **Life is sacred.** Regardless of a person's physical, mental, or emotional state, each human life is sacred in itself.

- **All ordinary means must be used to preserve life.** Individuals and society must do all that is reasonably necessary to preserve and safeguard God's gift of human life. However, there is *no obligation* to continue medical procedures that are unnecessarily dangerous, burdensome, *extraordinary*, and out-of-line with the hoped for results.

- **The direct killing of another is wrong.** Thus, *active euthanasia is immoral.* Any action or failure to act, which in itself or by its intention, brings about death to end suffering is a form of murder. The Catholic church strongly condemns all *direct* and *intentional* acts which have as their purpose the taking of human life.

- **A person has the right to meet a natural death in peace.** Morality does not oblige society to use extraordinary means to maintain life at any cost. Christian faith holds that death is not the end of human existence. Rather, death is a birth into a new, glorious life with the risen Lord. Christians also believe that out of the evil of suffering can come good when it is joined to the redemptive suffering of Christ.

Euthanasia presents many challenging moral questions that have no easy answers. For example, medical science has the ability to maintain life in many cases for quite some time, and what is an "extraordinary means" today will be an "ordinary means" tomorrow. This raises other morally complex questions. The one guiding principle in all these

issues is the sacredness of human life. This principle forbids anyone from actively performing any action that directly results in the death of a fellow human being.

■ *research* ■

Locate and read a church document that explains the church's teaching on one of the following issues. Write a report of your findings. Share the information with the class.

1. Does a dying AIDS patient have to participate in experimental treatments to prolong his life? Why or why not?
2. Are kidney transplants ordinary or extraordinary means?
3. What facts should you know before withdrawing life-support systems from a comatose patient?
4. How does suicide dishonor God?
5. What is the Catholic position on "living wills"?

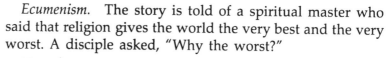

Ecumenism.   The story is told of a spiritual master who said that religion gives the world the very best and the very worst. A disciple asked, "Why the worst?"

The Master replied, "Because people mostly pick up enough religion to hate but not enough to love" (from *More One-Minute Nonsense,* by Anthony DeMello S.J.).

Today, the church has committed itself to an *ecumenical* outlook. In Greek, *ecumenism* means "worldwide." The ecumenical movement refers to two primary efforts:

1. The attempt among world religions to understand one another better and to overcome needless opposition.
2. The efforts of Christian denominations to work for greater unity among themselves and to better understand and improve relations with the other major world religions.

What does the Catholic church teach about ecumenism? The church teaches that the fullness of the truth and grace of Jesus Christ exists in the Roman Catholic church. Because of this, the church is to be unified in the profession of the same apostolic faith, in the common celebration of divine worship, especially the seven sacraments, and in apostolic succession through holy orders. The Second Vatican Council documents state:

> For it is through Christ's Catholic Church alone, which is the all-embracing means of salvation, that the fullness of the means of salvation can be obtained. It was to the apostolic college alone, of which Peter is the head, that we believe our Lord entrusted all the blessings of the new covenant, in order to establish on earth the one Body of Christ into which all those should be fully incorporated who already belong in any way to God's people (*Decree on Ecumenism*, No. 3).

These teachings are not limiting, however. The church is quick to acknowledge that the Holy Spirit works in all people of good will to help build God's kingdom. For example, many means of sanctification and truth exist outside the visible boundaries of the Catholic church. These include the Bible, the life of grace, the theological virtues of faith, hope, and love, and the gifts of the Holy Spirit. Other churches and ecclesial communities participate in the work of salvation by sharing in the fullness of truth and grace which Christ gave to the Catholic church.

Christ endowed his church with unity from the time he established it. But unity is a gift that must be preserved through work and prayer. Catholics do this in several ways: by faithfully living the gospel, by witnessing their faith as a means to draw others to Jesus and the church, and by acknowledging the spiritual gifts which Jesus has endowed on all Christians in the various denominations. In addition, there are several ways that you, personally, can participate in the ecumenical movement. These include:

Prayer. You can pray **for** Christian unity, asking the Spirit to guide ecumenical efforts, and **with** Christian brothers and sisters from other churches. Prayer is transforming and leads to holiness of life.

Study. You have a duty to know your own faith well and to share its truths with others. This is a lifelong quest.

Knowledge of other Christian denominations and religions can also be very helpful for mutual understanding.

Communication.   Since Vatican II, theologians from all faiths have engaged in dialogue in order to gain a better grasp of various doctrines and beliefs in order to arrive at common professions of faith. The Council instructs Catholics to share dialogue with other Christians charitably, and with understanding.

Collaboration.   You are called to work together with all Christians on service and social action projects. Joint efforts of Christian charity is a productive way to bring Christians together.

Ecumenical Roots

The Christian Ecumenical Movement began among Protestant denominations in Edinburgh, Scotland, in 1910. In 1948 the World Council of Churches was founded. The Catholic church did not officially participate in non-Catholic ecumenical efforts until the Second Vatican Council (1962–1965). The goal of Christian ecumenism is a common Christian commitment to live the gospel and be open to the unifying action of the Holy Spirit.

Church Teaching on Other Religions

Understanding what the church teaches about other Christian denominations and major world religions can help you understand more about their commonalities and differences as well as current efforts at unification.

Eastern Orthodox.   The Eastern Orthodox church celebrates seven sacraments and has a valid hierarchy and priesthood. The basic difference is that the Orthodox church claims jurisdiction of the pope does not extend over the whole church. Major efforts toward reunion have been made in the years since the Second Vatican Council. Pope Paul VI said "that it lacks little to attain the fullness that would permit a common celebration of the Lord's eucharist" (*Discourse*, December 14, 1975).

Protestants. The Catholic church has much in common with most Protestant churches, including: faith in God the Father, Jesus Christ, and the Holy Spirit; acceptance of the Bible as the living word of God; a life of prayer and grace; the gifts of faith, hope, and charity, and other gifts of the Holy Spirit; baptism; commemoration of the Lord's Supper; work done in service for the kingdom and hope for the day of its glory; and a common moral code.

The church teaches that all Catholics should honor Protestants who are saved by faith and baptism. They "are accepted as brothers and sisters by the children of the Catholic Church" (*Decree on Ecumenism*, No. 3).

Jews. All Christians owe the Jewish faith special reverence and respect. The Christian religion finds its spiritual roots in Judaism. Jesus himself was a pious Jew who loved his religion. St. Paul wrote of Jews:

> It was they who were adopted as children, the glory was theirs and the covenants; to them were given the Law and the worship of God and the promises. To them belong the fathers and out of them, so far as physical descent is concerned, came Christ who is above all (Rom 9:4–5).

Jews have not ceased to be God's Chosen People. God's gifts are irrevocable:

> The Jews still remain most dear to God because of their fathers, for he does not repent of the gifts he makes nor of the calls he issues (cf. Rom 11:28–29) (*Declaration on the Relationship of the Church to Non-Christian Religions*, No. 4).

The Jewish people witness to God and revere the books of the Hebrew scriptures (what Christians call the Old Testament). Furthermore, they live by the same moral code handed down to Moses, the Ten Commandments.

The church speaks out strongly against *anti-Semitism*, prejudice directed against Jews. The church reminds us that any persecution against the Jews—and any form of discrimination because of race, color, condition of life, or religion—is contrary to the will of Christ and a direct violation of his call to love.

Islam.   The church also esteems the Moslems who worship the one God. Moslems do not acknowledge the divinity of Jesus Christ, but they do revere him as a great prophet, and they honor Jesus' mother Mary. With Christians they await judgment day and resurrection, prize the moral life, and worship God through prayer, almsgiving, and fasting.

Vatican II recognized that the history of Christians and Moslems has seen conflicts and hostilities, but the church now calls for cooperation. The Council has urged Moslems and Christians to work in common for social justice, moral values, and the causes of peace and freedom.

Other Religions.   The church recognizes that in God's own mysterious way, God extends salvation to all people everywhere. Thus, the church,

> rejects nothing which is true and holy in these religions. She looks with sincere respect upon those ways of conduct and life, those rules and teachings which, though differing in many particulars from what she holds and sets forth, nevertheless often reflect a ray of that Truth which enlightens all (*Declaration on the Relationship of the Church to Non-Christian Religions*, No. 2).

Even those with no professed faith deserve full respect as persons. God extends grace to them. If they strive to live good and loving lives, they are responding to the gift of salvation. Whatever is good or true found among these people is a preparation for the gospel.

> Those also can attain to everlasting salvation who through no fault of their own do not know the gospel of Christ or his Church, yet sincerely seek God and, moved by grace, strive by their deeds to do his will as it is known to them through the dictates of conscience (*Dogmatic Constitution on the Church*, No. 16).

▪ *research* ▪

Do one of the following:

1. Report on what a major Eastern religion believes about the concept of God or divinity and its major ethical teachings.

2. Report on an initiation rite of a primitive religion.

3. Report on the causes of the Orthodox schism of 1054.

4. Report on the causes of the Protestant Reformation.

5. Compare Catholic beliefs in five areas to the teachings of **one** of the following Protestant churches: Lutheran, Presbyterian, Methodist, Baptist, Episcopalian (Anglican), or Pentecostal.

6. Research key beliefs of the Mormons, the Jehovah Witnesses, and the Christian Scientists. What do these groups believe about Jesus Christ?

The Missionary Church

The risen Jesus said:

> "All authority in heaven and on earth has been given to me. Go, therefore, make disciples of all nations; baptize them in the name of the Father and of the Son and of the Holy Spirit, and teach them to observe the commands I gave you. And look, I am with you always; yes, to the end of time" (Mt 28:18–20).

The diversity and pluralism among the world's people and religions make Jesus' command especially difficult. How do you tell others that your way is the "real thing"? The church does not shrink from the challenge because of the enormity of the task. By its very founding and nature, the church is missionary. The church persists in making the good news of Jesus Christ known to all. Jesus is truth. From truth comes freedom and salvation.

In all ages to the present, people have searched for meaning for their lives. Everyone who has ever lived has looked for answers to the deep questions: "Who am I? Where did I come from? Does my life have meaning? What will happen to me after I die?" Too many stray down false paths.

Catholics believe that in Jesus all of life's questions are answered. In Jesus, people find full and deep meaning to their lives. In Jesus, all truth is revealed.

Once, a mother sat in the waiting lounge of a doctor's office waiting for her nine-year-old son who was in a counseling session to deal with his ongoing depression.

The mother shared her anxieties and worries with another woman seated nearby. The second woman listened intently. When the mother had finished, the woman said, "What you need is Jesus. The gift Jesus offers is peace."

The mother looked at the woman. "I have read about Jesus and I do understand one thing about Christianity: a Christian is expected to suffer just as their leader did. I do not choose a life of suffering."

The woman was surprised by the mother's response, but inspired. She quoted the words of Jesus:

> "Come to me, all you who labor and are overburdened, and I will give you rest. Shoulder my yoke and learn from me, for I am gentle and humble in heart, *and you will find rest for your souls.* Yes, my yoke is easy and my burden light" (Mt 11:28–30).

The two women sat in silence until the mother's young son returned. "Thank you," said the mother. "Believe it or not, I really **heard** what you said."

The Catholic church has missionaries in every nation. Once a year, you may hear a missionary preach at your parish and appeal for your prayers and financial aid. Is this all you are called to do?

Individual Catholics, too, must continually seek conversion as a means of preparing themselves to share Christ's gospel with others through words and actions. Your very life is to be a missionary effort.

Conclusion

As you finish this part of your Christian journey, and ready yourself for the next, make this prayer of Mother Teresa of Calcutta your prayer too:

> Make us worthy Lord,
> to serve our fellow human beings throughout the
>   world who live and die in poverty and hunger.
> Give them through our hands this day their daily
>   bread.
> And by our understanding love,
> give peace and joy.
> Amen.

▪ *focus questions* ▪

1. Name one belief and one practice that Catholics share with all Christians.
2. Briefly explain the *principle of communion*.
3. Explain a traditional way that Catholics are distinguished from other Christians.
4. What does it mean to say that the Catholic church is universal or "open to all"?
5. What is one statement associated with "openness to life"?
6. What is the meaning of the "seamless garment" in connection with life issues?
7. Why are the unborn, sick, and elderly more vulnerable than ever today?
8. What are some ways you can adopt a "pro-life" attitude?
9. Distinguish between direct and indirect euthanasia.
10. Why is direct euthanasia wrong?
11. Must a person use "extraordinary" means to preserve human life? What are extraordinary means?
12. Define *ecumenism*.
13. What are two things the Catholic church teaches about ecumenism?
14. How can you help to foster ecumenical understanding?
15. What is the Catholic attitude toward other Christian faiths?
16. Why should Christians show special reverence and respect to Jews?
17. What do Christians have in common with the Islam faith?
18. How can God's salvation extend even to people with no religion?
19. Why is the church missionary?
20. How are you called to be a missionary?

▪ *exercises* ▪

1. Write a brief essay explaining what it means for you to be a Catholic.

Look up the meaning of the following words in the dictionary. Transcribe the definitions into your journal:

anti-Semitism   schism

2. Talk to a non-Catholic friend. Discuss his or her religion. Report on some common beliefs you have with this person.

3. Find information on one of the church's missionary organizations. Report on the method of their missionary efforts.

———————————— ▪ ————————————

Prayer Reflection

The source of unity and peace in Christ's church and in our world is the Holy Spirit. Recite the following traditional prayer to the Holy Spirit.

Come, Holy Spirit

Come, Holy Spirit, fill the hearts of your faithful
    and kindle in them the fire of your love.
Send forth your Spirit, O Lord,
    and renew the face of the earth.

O God,
on the first Pentecost
you instructed the hearts of those who believed in you
by the light of the Holy Spirit:
under the inspiration of the same Spirit,
    give us a taste for what is right and true
and a continuing sense of his joy-bringing presence
        and power,
through Jesus Christ our Lord.

Amen.

▪ *reflection* ▪

Where in your life do you need the fire of the Spirit's love the most?

▪ *resolution* ▪

Express your gratitude to a friend or family member for his or her presence in your life.

———————————— ▪ ————————————

Glossary of Selected Terms

Abba—A term of endearment from the Aramaic language meaning "daddy." Jesus used this word to teach that God is a loving Father.

Abortion—The deliberate killing of unborn human life by means of medical or surgical procedures. Direct abortion is seriously wrong because it is an unjustified attack on innocent human life.

Absolution—The statement by which a priest, speaking as the official minister of Christ's church, declares forgiveness of sins to a repentant sinner in the sacrament of reconciliation. The formula of absolution reads: "I absolve you from your sins; in the name of the Father, and of the Son, and of the Holy Spirit. Amen."

Adultery—Sexual relations between a married person and another who is not one's marriage partner. Adultery is a serious breakdown in the covenant love between a husband and wife.

Annulment—An official church declaration that what appeared to be a Christian marriage never existed in the first place.

Anointing of the sick—A sacrament of healing in which the Lord extends his loving, healing touch through the Christian community to those who are seriously ill or dying.

Apostle—One who is sent by Jesus to continue his work.

Asceticism—The religious practice of works of self-discipline like fasting, prayer, and almsgiving which are motivated by the love of Jesus Christ and contribute to growth in holiness.

Assumption—The official church dogma that the body of the Blessed Mother was taken directly to heaven when her life on earth ended.

Baptism—The first sacrament of initiation that makes a person a child of God and an heir to God's promises of eternal salvation.

Beatific vision—Seeing God "face-to-face" in heaven; the final union with God in eternity.

Bible—The inspired word of God; the written record of revelation.

Bishop—A successor to the apostles who governs the local church in a given territory and governs the worldwide church in union with the pope.

Blasphemy—An insult or contempt of God or to holy persons and things.

Canon (of the Bible)—The official list of the inspired books of the Bible. Catholics list forty-six Old Testament books and twenty-seven New Testament books in the canon.

Canon law—The code of church laws that governs the life of the Catholic community.

Canon of the Mass—The eucharistic prayer which includes the words of consecration. It is the central prayer of the liturgy of the eucharist. There are several canons in today's eucharistic rite.

Canonization—The process whereby the pope ultimately declares that a martyr and/or a person who lived a heroic Christian life of virtue is now in heaven and worthy of honor and imitation by Christians and Catholics.

Capital sins—Moral vices that give rise to many other failures to love. They are: pride, avarice, lust, anger, gluttony, envy, and sloth.

Cardinal virtues—The four hinge virtues from which moral living springs. They are: *prudence*, or moral common sense concerning the best way to live morally; *justice*, or giving each person his or her due by right; *fortitude*, or courage to persist in living a Christian life; and *temperance*, or moderation in controlling our desires for physical pleasures.

Catechesis—The process of religious instruction and formation in the major elements of the Christian faith.

Catechumen—A person who is studying the main elements of the Christian faith in preparation to receive the sacraments of initiation.

Catholic—A Greek word that means "universal." The term *Catholic church* refers to the Christian community that is open to all people everywhere and in all ages and that preaches the fullness of God's revelation in Jesus Christ.

Celibacy—The state of being unmarried that priests and other religious choose in order to dedicate their lives totally to the Lord and the People of God. Celibate men and women, as well as single and married people, must practice *chastity*.

Charism—A gift of the Holy Spirit that enables the recipient to do good works in the building up of Christ's body. Examples include wisdom, prophecy, zeal in witnessing to Christ, discernment of spirits, and exemplary loving service of others.

Charity—Love of God above all things and love of neighbor as oneself; the greatest of the three theological virtues.

Chastity— The virtue that enables us to act morally in sexual matters according to our station in life.

Christ—Greek translation of the Hebrew word *messiah*; a significant title of Jesus meaning "the anointed one."

Church—For Christians, the community of God's people who profess faith in the risen Lord Jesus and live lives of loving service under the guidance of the Holy Spirit.

Collegiality—The bishops in union with the pope as their head sharing teaching and pastoral authority over the worldwide church.

Common good—Those spiritual, material, and social conditions needed for a person to achieve full human dignity.

Communion of saints—The entire community of Christians—those on earth, in purgatory, and in heaven.

Confirmation—A sacrament of initiation that seals the recipient with the Holy Spirit and bestows gifts that enable the confirmed Christian to live courageously for Jesus Christ.

Conscience—The practical judgment that helps a person decide the goodness or sinfulness of an action or attitude. It is the subjective norm of morality which we must form properly and then follow.

Contrition—Heartfelt sorrow and aversion for sins committed along with the intention of sinning no more.

Corporal works of mercy—Charitable works Jesus taught (see Mt 25: 35–46) as ways to respond to him through others. They include: feeding the hungry, giving drink to the thirsty, clothing the naked, visiting the imprisoned, sheltering the homeless, visiting the sick, and burying the dead.

Covenant—The open-ended contract of love God made with the Israelites and with all people everywhere in the person of Jesus Christ.

Creed—A formal statement of faith. Catholics recite the Nicene Creed at Mass each Sunday. The Apostles' Creed is another famous summary of Christian faith.

Deacon—An ordained minister who assists a bishop or priest.

Disciple—A follower of Jesus. Christians are disciples who try to model their lives on Jesus.

Divorce—The legal dissolution of a marriage. Based on the teaching of Jesus, the church cannot dissolve valid Christian marriages which are lifelong covenants of love. Nor can the church remarry a divorced person who has previously entered a valid Christian marriage while the other spouse is still living.

Dogma—A church doctrine (teaching) issued with the highest authority and solemnity; a core teaching of the church.

Ecumenical council—A worldwide, official assembly of the bishops under the direction of the pope. There have been twenty-one ecumenical councils, the last being the Second Vatican Council (1962–1965).

Ecumenism—The movement that seeks Christian unity and eventually the unity of all peoples throughout the world.

Encyclical—A papal letter written on some important issue and circulated throughout the worldwide church. Encyclicals are often addressed not only to Catholics but also to all Christians and people of good will throughout the world.

Eschatology—Teaching about the last things—death, judgment, heaven, hell, purgatory, the *parousia*, and the resurrection of the body.

Eucharist—A sacrament of initiation that makes one a full member of Christ's body. The word is derived from the Greek word for "thanksgiving." Other names for this sacrament are the Mass and the Lord's Supper. The eucharist is the summit of Christian worship which celebrates and creates Christian unity.

Euthanasia—Active euthanasia, also called mercy killing, refers to acts in which direct, intentional means are used to bring about the death of a person, or reasonable, ordinary means are not used to keep a person alive. Euthanasia is a violation of the fifth commandment and is condemed by the church.

Evangelist—A person who proclaims the good news of Jesus Christ. "The four evangelists" refers to the authors of the four gospels: Matthew, Mark, Luke, and John.

Evangelization—The proclamation of the gospel of Jesus Christ, the process of ongoing conversion that all Christians are called to as witnesses of the gospel.

Excommunication—The formal declaration that a person is expelled from the Catholic church and thus unable to participate in the eucharist.

Extreme unction—The "last anointing," the common name for the sacrament of the anointing of the sick until relatively recent times.

Faith—One of the three theological virtues. Faith refers to (1) personal knowledge of God; (2) assent of the mind to truths God has revealed, made with the help of his grace and on the authority and trustworthiness of his revealing them; (3) the truths themselves (the content of faith); and (4) the lived witness of a Christian life (living faith).

Fathers of the church—An honorary title given to outstanding early Christian theologians whose teaching has had lasting significance for the church.

Fruits of the Holy Spirit—Love, joy, peace, patience, kindness, goodness, trustfulness, gentleness, and self-control (see Gal 5:22–23).

Gifts of the Holy Spirit—God-given abilities that help us live a Christian life with God's help. Jesus promised these gifts and bestows them through the Holy Spirit, especially in the sacrament of confirmation. The seven gifts are wisdom, understanding, knowledge, right judgment (counsel), courage (fortitude), reverence (piety), and wonder and awe (fear of the Lord).

Gospel—Literally, "good news." Gospel refers to (1) the good news preached by Jesus; (2) the good news of salvation won for us in the person of Jesus Christ (he is the good news proclaimed by the church); (3) the four written records of the good news—the gospels of Matthew, Mark, Luke, and John.

Grace—The free gift of God's life and friendship.

Heresy—A false teaching that denies an essential (dogmatic) teaching of the church.

Hierarchy—The sacred leadership in the church; the body of ordained ministers in the church: pope, bishops, priests, and deacons.

Holy orders—A sacrament of vocation whereby Christ, through the church, ordains men to serve as deacons, priests, or bishops.

Hope—One of the three theological virtues which enables us to trust firmly in God's salvation and to believe that God will bless us with the necessary gifts to attain it.

Idolatry—Worship of anyone or anything other than the true, living God. To put anything before God is a violation of the first commandment.

Immaculate conception—The church dogma that teaches that the Blessed Mother was free from sin from the very first moment of her human existence. [This dogma is sometimes confused with the doctrine of the *virginal conception* which holds that Jesus was conceived of the Virgin Mary by the power of the Holy Spirit without the cooperation of a human father.]

Immanence—A trait of God which refers to God's intimate union with and total presence to his creation.

Incarnation—A key theological term for the dogma of the Son of God becoming man in Jesus Christ, born of the Virgin Mary. (The term literally means "taking on human flesh.")

Infallibility—The gift (or charism) given to the church by Christ whereby it is protected from error in matters of faith and morals. It can be exercised by a pope or by an ecumenical council teaching in union with him.

Inspiration (of the Bible)—The guidance of the Holy Spirit that enabled the biblical writers to record what God wanted revealed.

Just-war doctrine—Derived from the natural law and Christian revelation, this teaching carefully sets out the conditions necessary for participation in a war.

Kerygma—The core or essential message of the gospel. An excellent example of the kerygma is found in Acts 2:14–36.

Law—A reasonable norm of conduct given by proper authority for the common good. In the Hebrew scriptures the Law is summarized in the Ten Commandments. Jesus taught the law of love of God and neighbor.

Liturgical year—The reliving through liturgical celebration of the key mysteries of the Christian faith according to a set schedule on an annual calendar beginning with the first Sunday of Advent.

Liturgy—The official public worship of the church. The seven sacraments, especially the eucharist, are the primary forms of liturgical celebrations.

Magisterium—The official teaching authority of the church. The Lord bestowed the right and power to teach in his name on the apostles and their successors, that is, the bishops and the pope as their leader.

Marks of the church—Traditional signs of the church of Christ: one, holy, catholic, and apostolic.

Matrimony—A sacrament of vocation in which Christ binds a man and woman into a permanent covenant of love and life and bestows his graces on them to help them live as a community.

Metanoia—A Greek term that means repentance or conversion. It means a change of mind or heart, a turning from sin, and following Jesus and the way of the cross.

Monotheism—Belief in and worship of one God. Judaism, Christianity, and Islam are monotheistic religions.

Morality—The science of responsible Christian living based on human reason and divine revelation.

Mortal sin—Personal sin that involves serious matter, sufficient reflection, and full consent of the will. It results in total rejection of God and alienation from God.

Mystery—A reality filled with God's invisible presence. The term is often applied to the church and to the sacraments.

Natural law—God's plan written into the way he made things. Human intelligence and reflection can aid us in discovering the natural law and living a life in harmony with it.

Original sin—The state or condition of sin into which all generations of people are born since the first human beings turned away from God.

Papal primacy—The pope's authority over the whole church.

Parable—A short story told by Jesus with a striking, memorable comparison that teaches a religious message.

Parousia—The second coming of Christ, which will usher in the full establishment of God's reign on earth as it is in heaven.

Paschal mystery—God's love and salvation revealed to us through the life, passion, death, resurrection and glorification of Jesus Christ. The sacraments celebrate the paschal mystery and enable us to live it in our own lives.

Pentateuch—The first five books of the Old Testament which contain the Torah or Law of the Chosen People. These books are Genesis, Exodus, Leviticus, Numbers, and Deuteronomy.

Personal sin— A personal failure to love God above everything and our neighbor as ourselves.

Prayer—Talking with and listening to God. Joining one's thoughts and love to God in adoration and blessing, petition, intercession, thanksgiving, and praise.

Priest—A mediator between God and people. All baptized Christians share in Jesus' priestly ministry. The Catholic church celebrates the sacrament of Holy Orders which ordains certain men to the office of priesthood which ministers in a special way to God's people.

Principle of discrimination—Requires the combatants in a war to make a distinction between aggressors and innocent people.

Principle of proportionality—Requires that the damage inflicted and costs incurred by a war (or a particular action in a war) be proportionate to the good expected.

Prophet—One "who speaks for God" or one "who speaks before others." All Christians are called to be prophets, that is, to testify in word and action that God's kingdom is in our midst.

Real presence—The sacramental presence of Jesus Christ in the eucharist.

Reconciliation—A sacrament of healing, also known as penance or confession, through which Christ extends his forgiveness to sinners.

Reign of God—The reign of God (also called kingdom of God) proclaimed by Jesus and begun in his life, death, and resurrection. It refers to the process of God's reconciling and renewing all things through his Son, to the fact of his will being done on earth as it is in heaven. The process has begun with Jesus' earthly ministry and will be perfectly completed at the end of time.

Repentance—From the Greek word *metanoia*, it means change of mind or change of heart. A key aspect of following Jesus is to turn from our sins and embrace the way of the cross.

Resurrection—God's gift of eternal life given to humans who will receive a glorified body in union with Jesus Christ at the end of time. Through Jesus' death and resurrection all people have been saved.

Revelation—God's free self-communication to us through creation, historical event, prophets, and most fully in Jesus Christ.

Rights—Claims that individuals can make on other people and on society in order to live in dignity. For every right there is a corresponding duty.

Ritual—Traditional religious actions that celebrate the mystery of our redemption and serve to worship God.

Sacrament—A visible sign of an invisible grace. An efficacious symbol. Traditionally *sacrament* is defined as an outward sign instituted by Christ to confer grace. The seven sacraments are baptism, confirmation, eucharist, reconciliation, anointing of the sick, matrimony, and holy orders.

Sacramental character—A lasting effect which the sacraments of baptism, confirmation, and holy orders bestow on their recipients. Baptism marks us as a child of God; confirmation seals us as a witness for Jesus Christ; holy orders permanently designates a man as a deacon, priest, or bishop—a special minister for God's people. As a result, these sacraments may be conferred only once.

Sacramentals—Sacred signs that resemble the sacraments and prepare a person to receive them.

Salvation—The process of healing whereby God's forgiveness, grace, and loving attention are extended to us through Jesus Christ in the Holy Spirit. Salvation brings about union with God and our fellow humans through the work of our brother, Lord, and savior—Jesus Christ.

Salvation history—The story of God's saving action in human history.

Schism—A break in Christian unity that takes place when a group of Christians separates itself from the body of Christ. This happens historically when the group breaks its union with the pope, for example, when the Eastern Orthodox church broke with the Roman Catholic church in 1054.

Social justice doctrine—The principle of church teaching that deals with the obligations of individuals and groups to apply the gospel to the systems, structures, and institutions of society.

Spiritual works of mercy—Good actions that apply gospel love to those in need. They include counseling the doubtful, instructing the ignorant, admonishing sinners, comforting the afflicted, forgiving injuries, bearing wrongs patiently, and praying for the living and the dead.

Synoptic gospels—The gospels of Matthew, Mark, and Luke. When we read them together we note certain similarities in content and style.

Subsidiarity—The principle of church social teaching that holds that a higher unit of society should not do what a lower unit can do as well or better.

Synod—An official church assembly at one of these levels: diocesan, provincial, regional, national, or international.

Tabernacle—The holy receptacle in which the blessed sacrament is reserved.

Theological virtues—Three key virtues bestowed on us at baptism which relate us to God: *faith*, or belief in and personal knowledge of God; *hope*, or trust in God's salvation and God's bestowal of the graces needed to attain it; and *charity*, or love of God, love of neighbor, and love of self.

Torah—The Law handed down to the Israelites which they were to live in response to God's covenant with them. A good summary of the Torah is found in the Ten Commandments.

Tradition—The process of handing on the faith as well as that which has been handed on; can be found in the scriptures, church doctrine, writings of the church fathers, the liturgy of the church, and the living and lived faith of the church through the centuries.

Transcendence—A trait of God that refers to God's total otherness and being infinitely beyond and independent of creation.

Transubstantiation—The official Catholic church teaching that the substance of the bread and wine is changed into the substance of the body and blood of Jesus Christ at the consecration of the Mass.

Trinity—The Christian dogma that holds that there are three persons in one God: Father, Son, and Holy Spirit. *Immanent Trinity* refers to the inner life of the Trinity, the relations of the three divine persons one to another. *Salvific Trinity* refers to the active work of the triune God in salvation history; the Father as Creator, the Son as Redeemer, the Holy Spirit as Sanctifier.

Venial sin—Personal sin that weakens but does not kill our relationship with God.

Vice—A bad habit or disposition (like lust) that turns us from good to embrace evil.

Virgin birth—The doctrine that holds that Jesus was conceived through the virgin Mary by the power of the Holy Spirit without the cooperation of a human father.

Virtue—A power to accomplish moral good; a good habit that enables us to live moral lives; the ability to live the Christian life joyfully and courageously.

Vocation—A call from God to live the Christian life in a particular way. Vocations can be to the married life, to the single life, to the religious life, or as an ordained deacon, priest, or bishop.

Worship—Prayerful acknowledgement of God's goodness and greatness.

Yahweh—The sacred Hebrew name for God—YHWH—which means "I am who am" or "I cause to happen." Because the name was too holy to say aloud, the word *Lord* (*Adonai* in the Hebrew) was substituted whenever the sacred texts were read aloud.

Index